INSPIRE / PLAN / DISCOVER / EXPERIENCE

MADRID

D0879546

MADRID

CONTENTS

DISCOVER 6

EXPERIENCE 58

NEED TO KNOW 202

Left: Ornate exteriors in the Plaza Mayor
Previous page: Magnificent Catedral de la Almudena
Front cover: Impressive Edificio Metrópolis at
the corner of Calle Alcalá and the Gran Vía

DISCOVER

Calle de Alcalá on a bright day

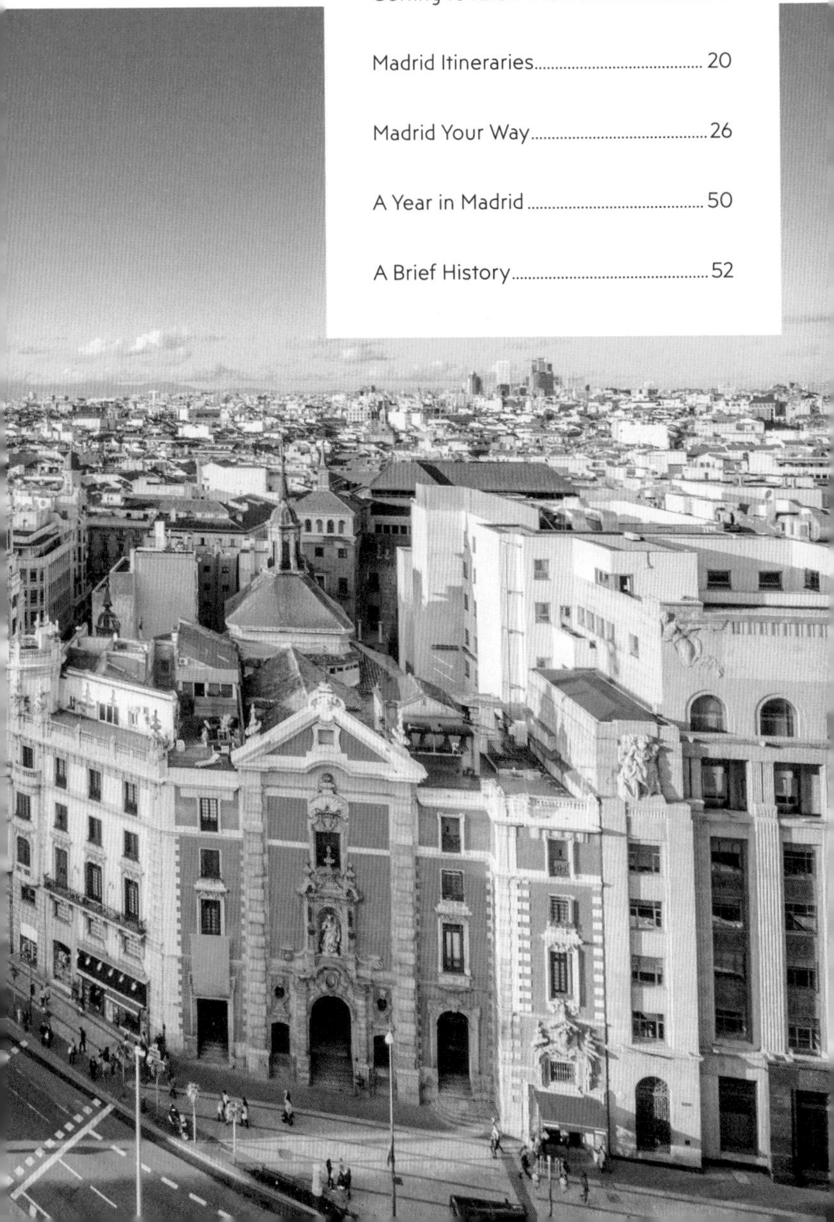

WELCOME TO
MADRID

World-class museums brimming with Goya's visions, pavements that tell the story of a rich literary heritage and Europe's most varied nightlife in a city that refuses to sleep - Madrid is the cultural epicentre of Spain. Whatever your dream trip entails, this DK Eyewitness travel guide is the perfect companion.

1 Mercado de San Miguel, a popular covered market.

2 A musician busking in the cool capital.

3 The beautiful 17th-century Plaza Mayor.

4 Relaxing at the Parque del Retiro as the sun sets.

At the very heart of Spain, Madrid embodies the best of the country. From the lavish elegance of the Palacio Real to the manicured gardens of the Parque del Retiro, the city's landmarks are a testament to its colourful history. Inspiration is everywhere: Spain's greatest painters live on in a trio of glittering galleries that make up the Golden Triangle of Art, while the haunts of legendary writers occupy the aptly named Barrio de Las Letras. Beyond the city centre, day trips to the legendary medieval city of Toledo or fairy-tale Segovia are equally rewarding.

The city also has a deserved reputation for European cool. Food is a way of life here, with gastro markets and showpiece squares paving the way for the sociable dining and alfresco living that Madrileños thrive on. Whether you tuck into anchovies at a *taberna* or nibble tiny courses at an avant-garde restaurant, Madrid's renowned food scene will keep you well fed. And, with more bars than any other city in Europe, you won't need to travel far to find the city's vibrant nightlife. Order dinner at 10pm, head to a club at midnight and finish the night with hot chocolate and *churros* at dawn.

Compact enough to easily travel around, Madrid can still overwhelm with the volume of unmissable sights on offer. We've broken the city down into easily navigable chapters, with detailed itineraries, expert local knowledge and colourful, comprehensive maps to help you plan the perfect visit. Whether you're staying for a weekend or longer, this DK Eyewitness travel guide will ensure that you see the very best the city has to offer. Enjoy the book, and enjoy Madrid.

REASONS TO LOVE
MADRID

Its nightlife is legendary. Its art is world-class. It's a gourmet's delight. Ask any proud *Madrileño* and you'll hear a different reason why they love their city. Here, we pick some of our favourites.

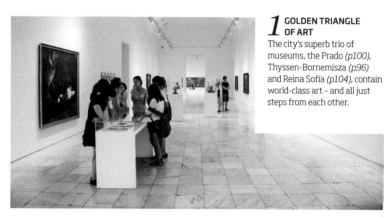

1 GOLDEN TRIANGLE OF ART

The city's superb trio of museums, the Prado *(p100)*, Thyssen-Bornemisza *(p96)* and Reina Sofía *(p104)*, contain world-class art – and all just steps from each other.

2 NIGHTLIFE

Madrid wakes up when other cities go to sleep. Clubs don't come alive until 2am – the beginning of the *madrugada* – the hours before dawn when the party goes into full swing.

3 PLAZA MAYOR

The gathering place of Madrid since the early 17th century, Plaza Mayor *(p68)* is the heart of the sunny city. Grab a seat at an umbrella-topped café table and survey the scene.

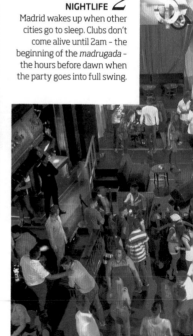

HISTORY-FILLED TABERNAS 4

Lined with scenic tiles, *tabernas* (taverns) have always been an integral part of Madrid. Savouring simple food and drink in these cosy refuges is a time-honoured tradition.

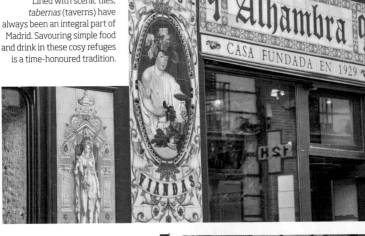

GASTRO MARKETS 5

Many of Madrid's historic public food markets have been reborn as eating, drinking and socializing destinations. Every stall is a gastronomic adventure in Spanish flavours.

SOCIAL BAR SCENE 6

In Madrid, the neighbourhood bar functions like a community living room. Despite the vermouth or sherry in front of you, the alcohol is incidental: you're there to talk and laugh.

FAIRY-TALE SEGOVIA 7

An easy train ride outside the city, take a day to explore ancient Segovia *(p178)* with its soaring Roman aqueduct and its fairy-tale turreted Alcázar on a rocky clifftop.

SIGNATURE SPANISH SPECTACLES 8

Passion burns bright in the Spanish capital. Move to the insistent rhythms of flamenco at a small club, or laugh at the musical comedy of Spain's unique light opera, *zarzuela*.

9 SUNDAY AT EL RASTRO

Madrid's enormous open-air flea market *(p86)* is a scene worthy of Fellini, with a heaving mass of *Madrileños* jostling for deals on everything from scarves to saucepans.

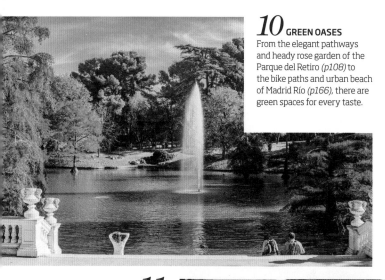

10 GREEN OASES

From the elegant pathways and heady rose garden of the Parque del Retiro *(p108)* to the bike paths and urban beach of Madrid Río *(p166)*, there are green spaces for every taste.

CHOCOLATE HEAVEN 11

Satisfy your chocolate cravings around the clock with a plate of sugar-sprinkled *churros* (doughnut sticks) dipped into thick hot chocolate – an iconic form of street food in Madrid.

TRAPPINGS OF ROYALTY 12

The magnificence of the Palacio Real *(p64)* only hints at the royal flavour of Madrid, where a series of kings built great museums and lent their cachet to the city's football team.

EXPLORE
MADRID

This guide divides Madrid into three colour-coded sightseeing areas, as shown on this map. Find out more about each area on the following pages. For sights beyond the city centre see p156, and for day trips out of Madrid see p172.

CHAMBERÍ

GAZTAMBIDE

ARAPILES

TRAFALGA

UNIVERSIDAD

ARGÜELLES

Palacio
de Liria

Cuartel del
Conde Duque

Museo de
Historia de Madrid

Parque
del Oeste

MALASAÑA

Templo
de Debod

Museo
Cerralbo

Parque
de la
Montaña

Plaza de
España

Estación del Norte
(Príncipe Pío)

Palacio del
Senado

Jardines del
Palacio Real

Monasterio de la
Encarnación

CENTRO

Monasterio de las
Descalzas Reales

Palacio
Real

Teatro
Real

Real Academia
de Belles Artes
de San Fernando

WEST MADRID
p60

Campo del
Moro

Catedral
de la
Almudena

AUSTRIAS

Casa de
Correos

SOL

Parque de
Atenas

Mercado de
San Miguel

Palacio de
Santa Cruz

Te
Es

Manzanares

Jardines de
Las Vistillas

Colegiata
de San Isidro

San Francisco
el Grande

Mercado de
la Cebada

LAVAPIÉS

Parque de
la Cornisa

La
Corrala

IMPERIAL

EMBAJADORES

Atlantic
Ocean

FRANCE

EL VISO

Bilbao

SPAIN

Barcelona

RÍOS ROSAS

Madrid

Balearic
Islands

PORTUGAL

Valencia

Seville

Murcua

Málaga

ALGERIA

MOROCCO

SPAIN

Museo
Lázaro
Galdiano

Museo
Sorolla

CASTELLANA

Museo de
Arte Público

LISTA

Fundación
Juan March

**MALASAÑA, CHUECA
AND SALAMANCA**
p130

SALAMANCA

AR

Mercado
de la Paz

luseo del
omanticismo

JUSTICIA

Museo
de Cera

*Jardines del
Descubrimiento*

Palacio del
Marqués de Linares

Museo
Arqueológico
Nacional

CHUECA

RECOLETOS

Palacio de
Linares

Palacio de
Comunicaciones

Puerta de
Alcalá

IBIZA

Banco de
España

Círculo de
Bellas Artes

Museo Nacional
de Artes Decorativas

Congreso de
os Diputados

Museo
Naval

Thyssen
Bornemisza
Museum

Estanque

teneo
Madrid

EAST MADRID
p92

*Parque
del Retiro*

eal Academia
de la Historia

CORTES

Museo
Nacional
del Prado

Palacio de
Fernán
Núñez

*Real Jardín
Botánico*

CaixaForum

*Viveros
Municipales*

Ministerio de
Agricultura

Real Observatorio
Astronómico de Madrid

Museo Reina Sofía
(MNCARS)

Museo
Nacional de
Antropología

Estación
de Atocha

Real Fábrica
de Tapices

0 metres   400

0 yards   400

N

GETTING TO KNOW
MADRID

A patchwork of architecturally and culturally distinct neighbourhoods, Spain's capital has a number of great Habsburg and Bourbon monuments at its core, along with three great art museums. Compared to many cities, most of the main attractions are fairly close to each other, giving it an intimate feel.

WEST MADRID

PAGE 60

Perched on the ridgeline between Puerta del Sol and the Río Manzanares, West Madrid oozes historic majesty. From the grandeur of the Palacio Real to the music box elegance of the Teatro Real, this area exemplifies the harmony of royal power wielded with artistic taste. The spiritual heart of the city – as well as the country – West Madrid embodies alfresco living. Here, *Madrileños* spend afternoons mingling on the Plaza Mayor or seeking a bargain at El Rastro flea market on a Sunday. A flood of cosmopolitan hotels makes this a lively, as well as convenient, base but West Madrid still retains its authentic charm.

Best for
Elegant squares, city strolls and history

Home to
Palacio Real, Plaza Mayor, San Francisco el Grande

Experience
Sipping a café con leche on the grand Plaza de Oriente, overlooked by the palace

EAST MADRID

For lovers of high culture, the east of the city is without question the bustling arts district. The city's Golden Triangle of Art – a trio of world-class museums – lies along the Paseo del Prado. On one side of this axis is the aptly named Barrio de Las Letras ("Literary Neighbourhood"), where an artistic atmosphere prevails. Here, you can walk in the footsteps of literary giants and take advantage of the lively bar scene. On the other side of the Paseo del Prado is the city's most impressive green lung – the Parque del Retiro – the perfect place to take a break from urban life.

Best for
World-class art and leafy strolls

Home to
Museo Nacional Thyssen-Bornemisza, Museo del Prado, Museo Nacional Centro de Arte Reina Sofía, Parque del Retiro

Experience
Posing for a photo in front of CaixaForum's vertical garden wall

MALASAÑA, CHUECA AND SALAMANCA

The area on the north side of central Madrid marries sophisticated Salamanca to earthier Chueca and Malasaña. Exquisite boutiques stand shoulder to shoulder on Salamanca's orderly grid of streets – Madrid's premier shopping district. Rainbow flags fly in Chueca – Madrid's principal LGBTQ+ area – while Malasaña derives much of its hipster ambiance from the nearby university community. As the home of *la movida*, this is the place to come after dark.

Best for
Lively nightlife and vintage shopping

Home to
Museo Arqueológico Nacional, Museo Lázaro Galdiano

Experience
Upscale shopping in Salamanca's trendy boutiques

$\rightarrow$

BEYOND THE CENTRE

So compact is Madrid (and so well served by public transport) that few places require much effort to get to, even those beyond the city centre. Old and new Madrid come together in the attractions here, where you can revel in the local sporting spirit and cheer on Real Madrid at the monumental Estadio Santiago Bernabéu, or head to the unique Egyptian Templo de Debod to soak up ancient mythology. The east side opens into verdant parklands and the buzzing area around one of Spain's most striking architectural landmarks, Las Ventas. Go south and west towards the river into Lavapiés and Embajadores for artsy neighbourhoods and cutting-edge contemporary art.

Best for
Quirky museums, football and green spaces

Home to
Templo de Debod

Experience
Watching the sky burn red as the sun sinks over the mountains from the Templo de Debod

DAYS OUT FROM MADRID

There's nowhere better to soak up the history of Spain than at its heart, and Madrid's location makes it perfectly situated for day trips, with high-speed rail putting some of the country's most intriguing cities within a half hour's travel. Enter a fairy-tale in Segovia, northwest of Madrid, bracketed by the soaring arches of its Roman Aqueduct at one end and its turreted Alcázar at the other. Southwest of the city is medieval Toledo, Spain's first capital, with a multicultural heritage in the form of churches, synagogues and Moorish fortresses. The area of central Spain, just outside of Madrid, is also home to some of the country's most beautiful and unspoiled landscapes.

Best for
Fairy-tale castles, charming historic towns and mountain hikes

Home to
El Escorial, Segovia, Toledo, Cuenca

Experience
Tucking into a dish of the legendary cochinillo *(roast suckling pig) in Segovia*

←

1 The bustling Plaza Mayor.

2 Admiring Caravaggio's *St Catherine of Alexandria* in the Museo Nacional Thyssen-Bornemisza.

3 A flamenco show at Villa Rosa in Huertas.

4 Dipping a *churro* in sauce.

Madrid is a treasure trove of things to see and do, and its compact size means that much exploring can be done on foot. These itineraries will inspire you to make the most of your visit.

24 HOURS
in Madrid

Morning

Nothing sets you up for a weekend in Madrid like a breakfast of fried *churros* dipped in hot chocolate, and nowhere has been serving them as long as the Chocolatería San Ginés (p77). Check out the photos of its famous patrons on the walls. From here, it's a short walk to the grand, arcaded Plaza Mayor (p68). Built by the Habsburgs in the 17th century, it's still the hub for many of the city's celebrations. Exit down the elegant flight of steps under the Arco de los Cuchilleros and turn immediately right for the cool Mercado de San Miguel (p76), a handsome century-old iron and steel market building, which has been converted into a gourmet food court. Admire the glistening vegetables and perfectly sliced fish, and try to resist your rumbling tummy. Exiting at the far end, you'll be close to the Plaza Conde Miranda, a graceful, quiet square where you can buy biscuits via a revolving panel in the wall of the Convento de las Carboneras (p76) – the perfect souvenir to take back home. Stroll back through the Plaza Conde Barajas to find the legendary Botín (p77), the world's oldest restaurant and a great spot to savour a dish of suckling pig, roasted in an oak-wood oven.

Afternoon

Choosing between the trio of museums in Madrid's Golden Triangle of Art is tough but, containing masterpieces from almost every movement from Flemish masters to Russian constructivism, the Museo Nacional Thyssen-Bornemisza (p96) is the ultimate all-rounder. Here, you'll see works by El Greco and Edward Hopper, Salvador Dalí and Canaletto, Picasso and Gauguin. It's a vast collection, so leave some time to recuperate with an ice-cold *caña* (beer) in the nearby Plaza de Santa Ana (p82). This square is at the heart of the Huertas neighbourhood, famous for its literary past but blessed with a present that moves to the soulful rhythm of flamenco. Take a tour of the shops and taverns connected with this most Spanish of arts, before taking in an authentic performance that will finish just in time for dinner (www.theflamencoguide.com).

Evening

Huertas heaves with superb bistros these days, but one of the best is the tiny and friendly TriCiclo (p111). Chow down on meaty prawns and delicate *amuse-bouches* before indulging in a nightcap in one of the nearby bars. For something a little out of the ordinary, head back past the Museo Nacional Thyssen-Bornemisza to the fine NH Suecia hotel, a side entrance of which will take you downstairs through some bathrooms to Hemingway – an Art Deco speakeasy open until the early hours (Calle Marqués de Casa Riera 4; 910 51 35 92).

←

[1] A sculpted cypress tree in the popular Parque del Retiro.

[2] The stunning fresco above the staircase at the Palacio Real.

[3] Alexander Calder's *Carmen* sculpture at the Museo Reina Sofía.

[4] An evening at Museo Chicote.

3 DAYS
in Madrid

Day 1

Morning The best place to start in Spain's buzzing capital is at one of the world's greatest art museums, the Prado (p100). It's a good idea to book ahead to skip the mammoth queues, but once you're in, concentrate on the leading Spanish painters and don't miss Diego Velázquez's Las Meninas and Goya's Dos de Mayo.

Afternoon Embark on a scenic stroll north for lunch at the elegant Café Gijón (p147), best known as a watering hole for poets and novelists. Parque del Retiro (p108), a popular green lung, is a lovely place to relax post-meal, but if you're in the mood for more culture, seek out the contemporary art exhibits in the park's Palacio de Cristal. Don't leave without snapping a picture of the structure.

Evening Do as the Madrileños do and dine late at chef Ramón Freixa's eponymous restaurant in Hotel Único (p146). His 20-course tasting menu is guaranteed to become the fine-dining meal by which you measure all others.

Day 2

Morning Get stuck into a regal day with a visit to the jewel-box opera house Teatro Real (p84), commissioned by Queen Isabel II. Stagecraft buffs can opt for a guided tour to peek inside the dressing rooms and even step onto the stage itself. Exit stage left on the Plaza de Oriente (p74) and snag an outdoor table at its café for an early lunch and some socializing.

Afternoon Don't rush your visit to the illustrious Palacio Real (p64). Seek out the Royal Armoury first, where you'll find an elaborate suit of armour that once belonged to Carlos I. The crown jewel, though, is the painted ceiling above the central staircase. From here, take the metro to Moncloa and meander through the gardens of the Parque del Oeste (p159), climbing the hill to the Templo de Debod (p158) for a spectacular sunset.

Evening For a meal fit for royalty, dine at Restaurante Sandó (restaurantesando.es/en), the Madrid outpost of famed San Sebastián chefs Elena and Juan Marí Arzak, known for their contemporary interpretations of Basque cuisine.

Day 3

Morning Begin the day by contemplating Picasso's iconic Guernica at the Museo Reina Sofía (p104). Get some fresh air in the Sabatini Building's patio, where you can still continue your fill of art by admiring Alexander Calder's Carmen sculpture. A bocadillo de calamares (calamari sandwich) at the adjacent El Brilliante (barelbrillante.es) makes for a great snack before jumping on the metro to Banco de España.

Afternoon Cast your eyes upwards at the historic buildings as you stroll along Gran Vía (p81). The stretch has plenty of shops, but head to Chueca for hip window-shopping. Give your feet a rest and grab a bite to eat at the upstairs stalls of the Mercado de San Antón (p29), one of Madrid's newest gastro markets.

Evening Sip a cocktail in the retro ambiance of Museo Chicote (p81) before heading to a Chueca club that suits your musical taste to dance until dawn.

→

1 The Puerta del Sol.

2 Admiring the paintings at the Real Academia de Bellas Artes de San Fernando.

3 Ceramics at the Museo Sorolla.

4 Segovia's fairy-tale castle, the Alcázar.

5 DAYS
in and around Madrid

Day 1

Start your day perusing the stalls of books along Calle de Claudio Moyana, picking up a novel to dip into while having lunch at a café on Plaza de Platería de Martínez. Continue your literary day with a house tour at the Casa-Museo de Lope de Vega (*p114*) before strolling around the Barrio de Las Letras (*p40*) neighbourhood, which has been home to many iconic Spanish authors. Make a reservation for the late flamenco show at Cardamomo (*www.cardamomo.com*), and cap your night with dinner in its fine restaurant.

Day 2

Tuck into a pastry at La Mallorquina (*www.pastelerialamallorquina.es*) in Puerta del Sol before immersing yourself in the fine collections at the Real Academia de Bellas Artes de San Fernando (*p80*) – including Goya's final palette. Make a stop at the Círculo de Bellas Artes' (*p116*) café for lunch, which doubles as an architectural haven with its impressive chandeliers. Once satiated, cross to the Palacio de Comunicaciones (*p113*) and take in the best view of Madrid from its rooftop. End your day with a meal of tapas washed down with sherry at Casa María in the Plaza Mayor (*p68*).

Day 3

Venture out of the city with a half-hour train ride south to the medieval marvel that is Toledo (*p184*). Spend the morning wide-eyed in front of the mystic visions of El Greco in the Museo de Santa Cruz (*p186*). After lunch at a Plaza de Zocodover café of your choice, stroll down Calle Comercio to see Spain's largest cathedral (*p188*). Once back in Madrid, unwind on the Plaza Mayor, watching street performers and buskers on the square.

Day 4

Roman, Visigoth and Moorish Spain comes alive at the Museo Arqueológico Nacional (*p134*): the place to start your day. Don't miss the Visigothic crown jewels – a 1,400-year-old triumph of the goldsmith's art. For a change of artistic pace, walk through the Museo de Arte Público (*p146*) to marvel at modern sculptures. Enjoy lunch in Salamanca before spending the afternoon immersed in the Museo Sorolla (*p147*), once the home and studio of one of Spain's most celebrated painters. Complete your art-filled day at Taberna del Alabardero (*Calle de Felipe V 6*) with tapas and cocktails.

Day 5

Dynamic Segovia (*p178*), a Roman capital, lies just a half hour away from Madrid by train. Your first stop should be the grand Roman Aqueduct, still an impressive engineering feat 2,000 years later. Order roast suckling pig at Restaurante José María (*restaurantejosemaria.com*) for lunch before heading to Segovia's number-one attraction: the fairy-tale castle, the Alcázar. The towers are its most famous feature, but the Hall of the Kings is a must for history buffs. Head back to Madrid for a night at Taberna Antonio Sanchez (*Calle del Mesón de Paredes 13*).

Mi Casa Es Tu Casa

Inhabit the lives of Madrid's greatest artists and art collectors by visiting their homes. The Museo Sorolla (*p147*) captures the family life of 20th-century painter Joaquín Sorolla, where you can imagine him playing with his children in the Andalucían-style garden before locking himself in his studio to paint. The Museo Cerralbo (*p87*) invites you into the 19th-century lifestyle of a family of collectors who hosted grand parties and dances here.

$\rightarrow$

Joaquín Sorolla's paintings on the walls of his former home in the Museo Sorolla

MADRID FOR
ART LOVERS

Madrid became a visual arts leader in the 19th century, and some of the best art created around Spain now resides in its Golden Triangle of top museums. Augmenting those astonishing permanent collections, a series of art centres help create one of the liveliest urban art scenes in Europe.

Hit the Streets

From graffiti to sculptures, Madrid is packed with amazing public art. If you're in Salamanca, check out the Museo de Arte Público (*p146*), a free outdoor museum of contemporary abstract sculpture. In Lavapiés, you'll find striking murals covering the walls of La Tabacalera (*p165*), thanks to a 2014 initiative set up by the Madrid Street Art Project for the Spanish Ministry of Culture. Take a tour with Cool Tour Spain (*cooltourspain.com*) to really immerse yourself in the city's street art.

↑ Murals painted by Animalitoland and others at La Tabacalera

Madrid's Masterpieces

With three of the world's finest museums clustered together in Madrid's "Golden Triangle of Art", it's no surprise that the city houses some of the greatest paintings in art history. Transport yourself back to Madrid's "Golden Age" by seeking out *Las Meninas* by Diego Velázquez in the Prado *(p103)*, or get your fill of Impressionism with Degas' *Swaying Dancer* at the Thyssen-Bornemisza *(p98)*. If you only have time for one masterpiece, tick Picasso's anti-war painting *Guernica*, one of the most influential paintings of the 20th century, off your bucket list at the Reina Sofía *(p106)*.

← Picasso's famous *Guernica* hanging in the Reina Sofía

TOP
5
OFF-THE-BEATEN-TRACK GALLERIES

La Tabacalera
Housed inside a former tobacco factory, this gallery is known for its cool murals *(p165)*.

Matadero Madrid
This former slaughter-house is alive with working artists *(p170)*.

La Neomudéjar
Video art festivals set the avant-garde tone here *(p125)*.

Conde Duque
Located in 18th-century barracks, cultural events here include artist residencies *(p152)*.

La Casa Encendida
This centre specializes in cutting-edge programmes *(p167)*.

INSIDER TIP
Contemplate Contemporary

Madrid hosts ARCO, the International Contemporary Arts Fair *(ifema. es/arco-madrid)*, every February, which sees artists and collectors from around the world come together.

Cool Art Centres

Escape the crowds that gather at Madrid's permanent collections by seeking out the city's lively social art scene. Temporary exhibitions of contemporary art and photography abound at the hip CaixaForum *(p120)* and CentroCentro *(p113)*, but art connoisseurs should head to the Fundación Juan March *(p145)* for thought-provoking exhibits that probe the social and educational uses of art.

→ The modern CaixaForum, in a much-photographed former power station

Sup Like a Spaniard

Madrileños swear by *churro* with hot chocolate, so head Chocolatería San Ginés *(p77)* for a sugary snack. If you're after something hearty, fin an eatery that serves *cocid* (offal-filled stew) or a *tortill de patatas* (potato omelett but don't leave the city without sampling a calamar sandwich. Though landlocke Madrid is noted for its seafoc sent daily from the ports.

←

A *bocadillo de calamares*, or calamari sandwich, a popular afternoon snack

MADRID FOR
FOODIES

Taste the best of Spain in Madrid: fresh fish and vegetables, cured meats and cheeses and striking wines pour in from the whole country. Convivial *tabernas* still serve tasty traditional dishes, while a new generation of chefs are turning Madrid into one of the most exciting places in Europe to dine.

Cook Up a Storm

From the sizzling seafood of the north to the sherry-soaked dishes of Andalucía, Madrid is brimming with Spain's regional specialities, and you can take those flavours back home with you. Go from market to table at Cooking Point *(cookingpoint.es)* culinary school, where the paella class includes a shopping excursion to the neighbourhood market. Cook Madrid *(cookmadrid.com)* also runs fun classes.

> ### HUNGRY MADRID
>
> It could be assumed that the first business establishment in Madrid was a *taberna* (tavern). Today, only about 100 classic *tabernas* remain in the city. Each is unique, but you can expect a carved wooden bar with a zinc counter, marble table tops and colourful ceramic tiles lining the walls.

Preparing a traditional ↑
Spanish dish in a sociable
setting with Cooking Point

astro Food Markets

any of Madrid's traditional food markets have olved into sleek destinations where dining, inking and socializing trump simple food shopping. a result, they stay open late, and are a great way immerse yourself in Madrid's late-night, sociable ning culture. Join *Madrileños* at the Mercado de n Antón *(mercadosananton.com)* in the heart of ueca or the Mercado de San Miguel *(p76)* to tuck o gleaming, jewel-like fruit and vegetables, huge gs of *jamón serrano* hanging from butchers' stalls d tempting tapas washed down with vermouth.

1725

The year the world's oldest restaurant, Botín *(p77)*, was established in Madrid.

↑ Colourful produce on display at the Mercado de San Antón in Chueca

Tasty Tours

Sample your way through Madrid with a tour from Devour Madrid *(madridfoodtour.com)* and meet chefs, restaurant owners and vendors at places where locals love to dine. To immerse yourself even further, walk in the footsteps of a lifelong *Madrileño* as he reveals his top eating spots on Secret Food Tours *(secretfoodtours.com)*.

←
Beautifully decorated snacks to sample on Secret Food Tours

New Wave Wonders

Madrid's economic boom has spawned a wave of restaurants that redefine the city's dining scene. Head to the casual digs of DSTAgE *(dstageconcept.com)* to try the innovative Spanish-Mexican-Japanese fusion, or the Korean-Spanish mix at LUKE *(lukerestaurante.com)*. Culinary adventures await the discerning diner at the butcher-shop minimalism of Sala de Despiece *(saladedespiece.com)*, which serves raw fish and meat.

→
A tasty tapas dish impeccably crafted at LUKE

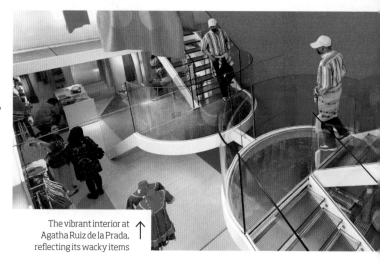

The vibrant interior at Agatha Ruiz de la Prada, reflecting its wacky items

MADRID FOR
SHOPPERS

Every regional Spanish style ends up in Madrid, making the city the perfect place to shop for everything from flirtatious fans to equestrian-inspired leather goods. Peruse high-end boutiques, bargain at Europe's largest flea market or seek out small shops for handicrafts with true Spanish style.

Vintage Shopping

Malasaña is undoubtedly Madrid's hippest neighbourhood, with rents low enough to allow for one-of-a-kind shops. Stroll down Calle de Velarde for the best concentration of quaint stores selling vintage clothing, then branch out to discover the studios of up-and-coming designers and speciality shops for ceramics and housewares. Calle de Augusto Figueroa in Chueca is a shoe-lover's heaven with discounts on Spain's top brands.

↑ Wandering past a vintage clothing store, Chopper Monster, in Malasaña

High Fashion

With its "Golden Mile" of designer stores, Salamanca is where you'll find international luxury brands as well as pieces by top Spanish designers. The chic district brims with stylish locals, and you don't need to look far to overhaul your own wardrobe. Pick up classic Madrid-made leather bags at Loewe *(Calle Serrano 34)* or give quirky patterns a try at Agatha Ruiz de la Prada *(Calle Serrano 27)*. Queen Letizia favours the feminine fashions of Felipe Varela *(Calle José Ortega y Gasset 30)*, so head here for some truly regal ensembles.

INSIDER TIP
Club Colours

While the city is full of many souvenir shops selling Real Madrid merchandise to take home, the best place to buy authentic official items is the Real Madrid store by Puerta del Sol *(shop.realmadrid.com)*.

Handmade Souvenirs

Spain's rich and varied popular art makes it relatively easy to pick up an original piece of handicraft in the capital. Traditional handmade fans make for a wonderful gift, and Casa de Diego *(casade diego.info)* sells them in bucketloads, along with shawls and other essentials of Spanish couture. At Antigua Casa Talavera *(antigua casatalavera.com)* you'll find a broad range of artistic ceramics from every region of the country, while Taller Puntera *(puntera.com)* specializes in top-quality hand-tooled leather goods - look out for the artists at work here, too.

←

Fans decorated with beautiful flower designs at Casa de Diego

To Market, To Market

Weekends in Madrid are reserved for meandering through its fantastic maze of markets. Sunday is bargaining day at the iconic El Rastro *(p86)* flea market in La Latina, packed with everything from castoffs to vintage collectibles and cheap clothing. For more fashionable finery, the Mercado de Motores *(mercadodemotores.es)*, held the second weekend of the month in the Museo del Ferrocarril *(p165)*, showcases 200 independent designers and artists. Grab some food from one of the many vendors and shop for retro items and unique furniture while live music fills the area.

→

A variety of goods on sale at El Rastro, the largest flea market in Europe

Inclusive Districts

The street films of Pedro Almodóvar *(p42)* established Chueca as the city's premier gaybourhood in the 1980s, creating the image that it was a good area to meet like-minded people. Today, the district throbs with bars and dance clubs by night, run with an LGBTQ+ culture in mind, while young and hip shoppers prowl its welcoming boutiques and shoe stores by day, passing rainbow flags hanging from shop windows and balconies. For a great introduction to Chueca, join a walking tour of the area to learn about local history and sights *(visitchueca.com/en/guided-tours)*. Energy and vitality are not only a defining feature of everyday life here, though: while the whole city is open and inclusive, hipster Lavapiés, La Latina and Malasaña are especially buzzing.

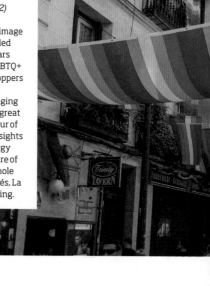

→

An abundance of rainbow flags strung through the streets of Chueca

MADRID FOR
LGBTQ+
CULTURE

The *la movida* movement led to a sea change in attitudes in the capital, with LGBTQ+ culture becoming more mainstream in the 1990s, building to today's open city. Madrid flourishes as one of Europe's top destinations for LGBTQ+ travellers, with legendary nightlife and one of the biggest Pride events.

Life is a Cabaret

After midnight on most nights of the week, the drag, stripper and cabaret clubs of Chueca offer glammed-out and tongue-in-cheek entertainment in a party atmosphere. A Noite *(Calle Hortaleza 43)*, LL Bar *(Calle Pelayo 11)* and Black & White *(Calle Libertad 34)* are celebrated for their drag culture. You can also get your groove on in two separate dance rooms at Black & White.

←

Drag performance at Chueca pioneer Black & White

TOP 3 · CHUECA DANCE CLUBS

Fluid Scape
⌂ Calle Gravina 13
🕐 Midnight-5:30am Wed-Sat
🌐 escapefluidochueca.es
Lesbian dance legend that especially hots up at the weekends.

DLRO Live
⌂ Calle Pelayo 59
🕐 Midnight-6am Thu-Sat
🌐 deliriochueca.com
Diva disco lives forever at this club, where you can expect fantastic live performances as well as cabaret.

Bearbie
⌂ Plaza de Pedro Zerolo 2
📞 620 81 25 37
🕐 Midnight-6am Fri-Sun
A fun weekend disco for bears and admirers.

Socializing in a bustling club in Chueca

Club Life

There's an LGBTQ+ bar or club for every taste in Chueca, but some legendary spots, like lesbian hangout Club 33 *(Calle Cabeza 33)*, are located in edgy Lavapiés. Some clubs change identity almost nightly: Disco bar COOL *(Calle Isabel la Católica 6)* becomes dance mecca Baila Carino on Saturdays, while Boite *(Calle Tetuan 27)* becomes Ultrapop on Fridays.

Come Together

The city hosted World Pride in 2017, and it's no surprise that Madrid Pride, or MADO, festivities are the largest in Europe, with 10 days of cultural, social and sporting activities. More than one million people attend in late June and early July, and the festival sees the whole city come together. Don't miss the infamous Carrera de Tacones in Chueca, where participants in the road race wear 9cm+ stiletto heels. In early November, LesGaiCineMad *(LesGaiCineMad.com)* shines the spotlight on LGBTQ+ Spanish-language films with a week of screenings that are a must for movie fans.

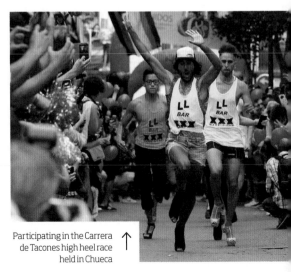

Participating in the Carrera de Tacones high heel race held in Chueca ↑

Follow in the Footsteps

For a great orientation to the city, several companies offer tip-based "free" guided walking tours. Free Tour *(freetour.com/ madrid)* has several variations to choose from, whether you're looking to explore the historic essentials or grab some tapas. Ogo Tours *(ogotours.com)* promises to make you feel like a *Madrileño*, with locals sharing their favourite spots and the best of the city.

→

Walking along Calle Mayor in Madrid, compact enough to explore on foot

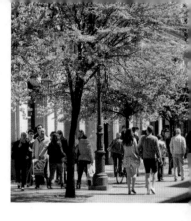

MADRID
ON A
SHOESTRING

Madrid is one of Western Europe's least expensive capitals, and its vibrant street life and inexpensive drinks make it a frugal traveller's dream. Add in free museum admissions at certain hours and bargain walking tours, and you should have enough left over for a splurge.

Art on the Cheap

Madrid's world-class art museums may all charge admission, but you can save a bundle by timing your visits for the generous free hours. It's best to check the websites of the individual attractions before you plan your trip, but the mix includes free entry to the Museo Nacional Thyssen-Bornemisza on Mondays, and to the Prado between 6pm and 8pm Monday to Saturday. If you're not prepared to share the space with a mass of other culture catchers at these free times, though, opt for a Paseo del Arte pass *(p211)* to the "Golden Triangle" to save 20 per cent off admissions and skip the queues. It's also worth checking the schedule for free temporary art exhibitions at the Fundación Juan March *(p145)* culture centre, which even offers 300 free seats to every concert.

Admiring a temporary exhibit at the Museo Reina Sofía, part of Madrid's "Golden Triangle" ↑

Fantastic Festivals

With a host of vibrant festivals that permit dancing in the streets, enjoyment in the capital needn't cost a penny. In mid-May, join *Madrileños* to honour the patron saint San Isidro with religious processions, concerts and a parade with giant carnival figures. During the first two weeks in August, enjoy street music as San Cayetano (El Rastro), San Lorenzo (Lavapiés) and La Paloma (La Latina) take over three neighbourhoods.

↑ San Cayetano and San Isidro *(inset)* are two of Madrid's top festivals

TOP 4 FREE SIGHTS

Museo de Historia de Madrid
This museum offers an excellent introduction to the city and its locals *(p149)*.

Ermita de San Antonio de la Florida
Goya rests beneath a fresco he painted in 1798 *(p171)*.

Palacio de Cristal
A stunning glass palace situated in the Parque del Retiro that mounts art exhibitions *(p108)*.

Jardínes de Sabatini
Beautiful Neo-Classical terraced gardens adjacent to the Palacio Real *(p64)*.

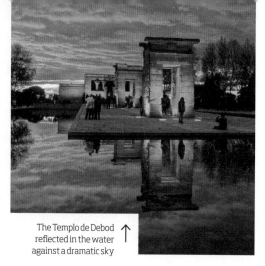

Sunset Splendour

While the most sweeping sunset views are from the city's rooftops, you'll get the best photographs along the western edge of the old city where you can place other objects in the frame. The Templo de Debod (p158) makes a stunning image on an early evening – stand on the east end of the pool to pick up sky reflections in the water. For an aerial view, ride the Teleférico to Casa de Campo (p158), before walking back along Madrid Río (p166) to catch the last light behind the Puente de Toledo.

The Templo de Debod reflected in the water against a dramatic sky ↑

MADRID FOR
PHOTOGRAPHERS

From monumental buildings and colourful byways to bustling street life and electrifying performances, Madrid is a photographer's dream. There are iconic shots around every corner, so keep your camera at the ready to snap the perfect picture of this beautiful city.

TOP 3 ROOFTOPS FOR PANORAMIC SHOTS

Radio ME Rooftop Bar
⌂ Plaza de Santa Ana 14
ⓦ radiomemadrid.com
Striking sunset views over a Cubist jumble of tiled roofs.

La Terraza de Óscar
⌂ Plaza Vázquez de Mella 12
ⓦ room-matehotels.com/en/oscar/terrace
Sweeping overviews of Chueca in one direction, Gran Vía in the other.

Azotea del Círculo de Bellas Artes
⌂ Calle de Alcalá 42
ⓦ circulobellasartes.com
360-degree perspective of buildings like the Metrópolis as well as the Cibeles fountain.

City Lights

The backdrop of an inky night sky makes Madrid's city lights a sequence of dream-like images. Dramatically lit, the Cibeles (p111) and Neptuno (p116) fountains are more majestic at night. You can't shoot fast enough to freeze the spray, but the fluid motion is more suggestive anyway. For a truly atmospheric shot, capture the famous Edificio Metrópolis (p118) from the CentroCentro Terrace Bar (p116).

Divine Doors

Five triumphal *puertas* (doors or gates) have graced the city of Madrid for centuries: Puerta de Alcalá (between Parque Retiro and Plaza de Cibeles), Puerta de Toledo (La Latina), Puerta de San Vicente (Príncipe Pío), Puerta de Hierro (El Pardo) and La Puerta de Felipe IV (Parque Retiro). Get creative when photographing these historic monuments by using the arches to frame what lies in the space beyond.

→

The stunning Puerta de Alcalá at dusk

¡Ole!

Some of your most dramatic - and typically Spanish - photos will be of flamenco. Anticipation is everything, as every performance has still points where the musicians and dancers almost seem to be posing. Be quick and decisive, but avoid using the flash. You'll get better photos at a bar performance than in a flamenco nightclub because you can get closer to the performers.

←

Capturing the dancer's passion mid-performance at a flamenco show in the Spanish capital

Tile-tastic

Traditional ceramic tiles are ubiquitous in Madrid, and seeking out the most quirky designs is an afternoon well spent. Head to Villa Rosa, a *tablao* on Plaza de Santa Ana *(p82)*, to snap a wide shot of its images of renowned Spanish buildings before closing in for the perfect Instagram detail shot. The colourful Farmacia Juanse *(Calle de San Andres 5)* in Malasaña should be next on your list, with tiles promoting remedies for the likes of toothaches and rheumatism.

→

A beautiful tile design fronting the Farmacia Juanse in Malasaña

↑ Water spraying from the Fuente de Cibeles, illuminated at night

Lovely Landscapes

Whether you're looking to cycle in a sumptuous setting or picnic beside plants, Madrid has it covered. The newest major park, Madrid Río *(p166)* creates long vistas of green pathways along the banks of the Río Manzanares – perfect for running. Just beyond the centre, the French and Italian gardens at the Parque de El Capricho *(p199)* are perfect for picnics.

← Roller blading through the innovative and reclaimed Madrid Río

MADRID FOR
GREEN SPACES

More than 300 days of sunshine annually make Madrid Europe's sunniest capital, and the city remains lush and green in every season. From neighbourhood green patches to rolling parks in the centre, these refreshing natural areas are the perfect excuse to chat, picnic and escape the hectic pace of city life.

TOP 4 PARK PLAYGROUNDS

Zona de Recreo, Parque del Retiro
A great spot to reward kids after seeing the sights *(p108)*.

Salón de Pinos, Madrid Río
10 children's play areas equipped with balance logs, rope hammocks and other games *(p166)*.

Plaza de Santa Ana
This square has a small enclosed playground where kids can play while parents dine *(p82)*.

Plaza del Dos de Mayo
An enclosed sandy *"area infantil"* is stocked with slides and swings *(p148)*.

Showcase Parks

The city's loveliest green spaces are, unsurprisingly, its biggest and most popular parks. Laid out to provide respite from urban bustle, the Campo del Moro *(p74)* is the perfect spot to stroll through, with its deep shade of woodlands. Meanwhile, the Parque del Retiro *(p108)* – literally meaning " a nice place to retreat to" – is the top place for locals to gather and relax.

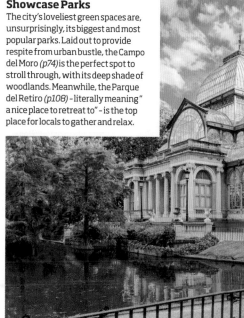

Quirky Gardens

Not every green space in Madrid is a rolling landscape; there are also unique and artistic constructions to delight in. Designed by Patrick Blanc in 2008, the vertical garden at the CaixaForum *(p120)* forms a four-story living wall of greenery to counter the intense sun – and the perfect backdrop for a selfie. Inside Atocha Station *(p124)*, follow winding paths through the indoor jungle of its tropical garden and take a breather on benches shaded by breadfruit trees and coconut palms.

→

Relaxing in the lush, impressive garden in Estación de Atocha

Hidden Gems

Charming gardens lurk just steps off the beaten tourist path. Nestled within the Museo del Romanticismo *(p149)* is a tranquil garden café with lush vegetation. If you're seeking Madrid in bloom, the quiet showpiece rose garden La Rosaleda tucked away in the Parque del Retiro perfumes the air in May and June.

←

The pretty La Rosaleda in the Parque del Retiro

Beyond City Limits

A vast wilderness lies on Madrid's doorstep, providing endless possibilities for hiking, climbing and camping. Stretching across central Spain, the Sierra de Guadarrama and Sierra de Gredos hillsides and valleys – barely an hour's drive outside the city – are covered with pine forests, glacial lakes and lush wild pastureland.

↑ Early morning fog enveloping Sierra de Gredos

↑ The Palacio de Cristal at the Parque del Retiro, the city's green lung

Barrio de Las Letras

The historic home of Madrid Golden Age authors, the "Writers' Quarter" remains the literary heart of the city it was here that Cervantes produced part of *Don Quixote* after all. Take a free tour of the area to immerse yourself in its history and look out for classical authors enshrined in busts and statues and pavements lined with quotes

←

Statue of Spanish poet Federico García Lorca on the Plaza de Santa Ana

MADRID FOR
BOOKWORMS

Ever since Spanish writers began to make their mark in Madrid in the 17th century, the city has been a magnet for famous scribes. Bibliophiles will rejoice in Madrid, where literary quotations are embedded in its pavements and the places that inspired some of your favourite authors are still standing.

Book Nooks

The stalls lining Calle de Claudio Moyano are Madrid's answer to the *bouquinistes* found in Paris. Selling new and second-hand books, it's the perfect place to spend a lazy Sunday morning browsing. Anglophone and bilingual readers will find their own kind at the readings and signings held at Desperate Literature *(p84)*, while Berkana *(libreriaberkana.com)*, Spain's leading LGBTQ+ bookshop, offers a broader view of romance novels.

→

English and Spanish books lining the shelves at Desperate Literature

> **HIDDEN GEM**
> **You're All Write**
>
> Why not document your travels to Madrid with a writing class? Ask for an invitation to the Madrid Writers' Club *(madridwritersclub. com)* so that you can attend one of their many workshops.

Writers' Pads

Literary genius Lope de Vega lived his last 25 years in a modest house on the aptly named Barrio de Las Letras. Inside the fancifully restored Casa-Museo de Lope de Vega *(p114)*, you can see his writing studio, and, in the garden, smell the citrusy orange trees that permeate his works. Ironically, the museum is just a stone's throw from the tomb of Lope de Vega's arch-rival, Cervantes, on Calle Lope de Vega 18. Fans of Cervantes, meanwhile, can visit his childhood home at Calle Mayor 48, where the Museo Casa Natal de Cervantes *(p198)* mounts exhibitions.

↑ Statues of Don Quixote and Sancho by the Museo Casa Natal de Cervantes

Literary Festivals

Madrid is the place to be to celebrate all things literature. Early June sees Spain's biggest literary festival – the Feria del Libro Madrid *(ferialibromadrid.com)* – enticing readers with the latest literary offerings in the Parque del Retiro. If you're heading to Segovia in September, check out the prestigious Hay Festival *(hayfestival.com)*, with four days of readings, signings, lectures and discussions.

←
Hay Festival attendees checking out new works of literature in Segovia

Keep up with Don Ernesto

The novels of the 20th-century American writer Ernest Hemingway, known as "Don Ernesto", helped the world fall in love with Spain, and his antics in Madrid after long nights of sipping gin at the Hotel Ritz *(p110)* made him a local favourite. Hitting all of his most frequented sites in the city is a game of stamina. Drink to his memory with a cocktail at Museo Chicote *(p81)* and follow in his footsteps through the Plaza Mayor *(p68)* and down the steps of Arco de Cuchilleros before heading to Botín *(p77)* for a roast suckling pig dinner.

→
Visitors gathering outside Botín, where Hemingway frequently dined

Film-ivals

Madrid is sufficiently movie obsessed that it supports a slew of festivals throughout the year. If you're visiting in June, head to Madrid's central cinemas to watch the FilMadrid Festival *(filmadrid.com)*. Entries come from around the globe, but the vast majority of films are Spanish-language. For a more global look at the film landscape, you can attend the Madrid International Film Festival *(madridinternationalfilmfestival.com)* in August, which helps indie film-makers establish distribution. To witness red-carpet glamour, arrive in time for the Festival de Cine de Madrid *(festivalcinemadrid.es)* in October. The premier showcase of emerging Spanish film, it screens up to 150 films featuring new actors and directors, and you can catch the films at cinemas and even watch the awards ceremony on television.

Settling in to watch a documentary at Madrid International Film Festival ↑

MADRID FOR
FILM LOVERS

Spaniards love arthouse movies and Hollywood blockbusters in equal measure, and cinematic culture in Madrid reflects the full range of tastes of its locals. Cinephiles can delight in a host of cinemas and, if you time it right, see the best of Spanish-language cinema at four major film festivals.

PEDRO ALMODÓVAR

Pedro Almodóvar is one of the most highly acclaimed film-makers of modern times. Born in La Mancha in 1949, he became part of Spain's *la movida* movement *(p138)*. *Women on the Edge of a Nervous Breakdown* (1988) brought him fame but *All About My Mother* (1999) is known to be his masterpiece.

Location, Location, Location

Madrid is the setting for many of Almodóvar's films, and you can follow his vision by drinking in the Taberna de Ángel Sierra *(tabernadeangelsierra.es)* like the women in *The Flower of My Secret* (1995) or taking a selfie on the Segovia Viaduct used in *I'm So Excited!* (2013). Aside from Almodóvar's works, you can also channel Jason Bourne by strolling through Atocha Station *(p124)* as in *The Bourne Ultimatum* (2007).

Arthouse Cinemas

Madrid brims with cool cinemas showing a range of locally produced Spanish films and international hits. If you're a film purist, you'll adore Cine Doré Filmoteca Española *(culturaydeporte. gob.es)*, which only screens films in their original languages with Spanish subtitles. Even better, films at this Art Deco landmark are bargain-priced. Beyond its busy screening schedule, Sala Berlanga *(salaberlanga. com)*, named for Spanish director Luis García Berlanga, also hosts a wide range of film-related events, such as art exhibitions. You can also catch non-fiction film all year at Matadero Madrid.

 The attractive façade of Cine Doré Filmoteca Española

SHOP

Ocho y Medio Libros de Cine

The only thing better than a bookshop with a coffee bar is a bookshop/ coffee shop for film buffs. Sip a *café con leche* as you peruse the impressive stock held here, including biographies, original screenplays, scripts, magazines, and even signed posters at this cine-lover's haven named for Federico Fellini's famous movie, *8½* (1963).

🏠 **Calle Martín de los Heros 11**
📞 **915 59 06 28**

 Watching a film with friends and food at Matadero Madrid

Sultry Summer Screenings

On scorching summer nights, pop-up screens show old classics and new releases in the great outdoors. Madrid claims Spain's largest drive-in cinema – the Autocine Madrid RACE *(autocines madrid.es)* on the north end of the city – but you can still enjoy movies under the stars without a car at several central spots. The popular La Casa Encendida *(p167)* transforms its rooftop into La Terraza Magnética for evening screenings, and Matadero Madrid *(p170)* also moves its series of non-fiction and documentary films outdoors.

↑ Alba perched on the Segovia Viaduct, in La Latina, in *I'm So Excited!*

Fantastic Festivals

Guaranteed warm weather proves the perfect complement to Madrid's summer music festivals that start late and continue into the early hours. International bands playing rock, indie and electronica will keep you partying all night at Mad Cool *(madcoolfestival.es)* in mid-July, but if you're after something more quintessentially Spanish, head to Tomavistas *(tomavistasfestival. com)* in May to listen to Spanish musicians.

↑ Partying at Mad Cool festival, arguably one of Europe's best

MADRID
AFTER DARK

When the sun sets, Madrid rises. *Madrileños* live much of their lives in bars, socializing over drinks and small plates of food before getting serious about dinner around 10pm, then heading out for entertainment at midnight. You can be sure to party into the *madrugada*, the hours just before dawn.

Clubbing Central

With the action only hotting up around midnight, Madrid's club scene requires stamina. Revellers will be spoiled for choice with venues to dance in until dawn. Kapital *(grupo-kapital.com)* keeps Madrid grooving with seven levels blasting the likes of retro disco and electronica, but save your energy for Madrid's once best-kept secret: Medias Puri *(mediaspuri.com)*. What looks like a men's clothing store actually houses three dance floors that promise a pop extravaganza.

←

A group of dancers performing at Madrid's Medias Puri

Live!

You'll rarely experience silence in Madrid: it has one of Europe's most exciting live music scenes, with endless venues to suit every taste. La Riviera *(salariviera.com)* has a monster stage and vast dance floor to rock out on, but if you yearn for dimly lit underground jazz bars, spend a mellow night at Café Central *(cafecentralmadrid. com)*. The cosy Blackbird Rock Bar *(Calle Huertas 22)* is the top venue for those seeking a bluesy edge, and you can even show off your own talents at the monthly jam sessions.

↑ Skye Edwards performing with Morcheeba at La Riviera

Go Flamenco

Although flamenco is native to Andalucía, it thrives in Madrid. Most flamenco *tablaos*, or supper clubs, operate with a cast of house artists; some of the best dance at Cardamomo *(cardamomo.com)*. If you can't get the rhythms and swirling movement out of your head, check out the late-night performers at flamenco bars. Experience *duende* (the spirit of flamenco) at Teatro Flamenco Madrid *(teatroflamencomadrid.com)*, but make sure you reserve ahead.

← A flamenco dancer mid-twirl at Cardamomo

Alfresco After Hours

Spaniards live outside when they can and Madrid is brimming with opportunities for socializing on the streets and living like a local after the sun goes down. The white plastic chairs seemingly abandoned on sidewalks become instant after-dark discussion salons, but if you're itching to get moving to keep yourself awake, the pre-dinner *paseo*, or evening stroll, remains popular, especially for couples.

↑ Crowds of locals and tourists dining and drinking alfresco on a busy street in Madrid

▷ Operatic Opulence
The company of the Teatro Real *(p84)* produces most of Madrid's world-class opera, but even if you visit out of season in August, you can take a behind-the-scenes tour of the beautifully restored building and its stage. Some contemporary opera shifts to smaller but no less beautiful venues such as the Teatro Español.

◁ Classical Music Masters
With three major symphony orchestras and top conductors, you can catch a concert in almost every season. Start with the Orquesta Nacional de España and its singing counterpart, the Coro Nacional de España, which perform at the two concert halls at Auditorio Nacional de Música *(auditorionacional.mcu.es)*.

MADRID FOR
TRADITIONAL
ENTERTAINMENT

Spaniards have a tendency to describe a performance as an *espectáculo*, and that's on the mark when it comes to the city's performing arts and major sporting events. A night at the opera or in a bar watching a football match in the capital will be an unforgettable Spanish experience.

▷ Timeless Theatrics
From the classics of Lope de Vega to the expressionistic dramas of García Lorca, Madrid is the theatrical capital of the Spanish-speaking world. The Compañía Nacional de Teatro Clásico stages works by Spanish dramatists, mainly in the Teatro de la Comedia *(teatroclasico.mcu.es)*, but don't leave without catching a play at the Teatro Español *(p116)*.

▽ Flamenco Fever

Many of the best exponents of flamenco are based in Madrid. Aside from visiting *tablaos* to see the dance performed *(p45)*, mark your calendar for June to attend the Suma Flamenca *(madrid.org/sumaflamenca)* festival - one of the most comprehensive gatherings of artists.

▷ Zesty Zarzuela

No visit to the Spanish capital is complete without spending a night at the *zarzuela (p119)*. Madrid's own strain of comic operetta originated in the 17th century and still keeps audiences in stitches with its broad humour, regardless of whether you miss the local references or struggle to keep up with the narrative. The best productions are staged at the popular Teatro de la Zarzuela *(teatrodela zarzuela.mcu.es)*.

◁ Football Frenzy

Madrid has one of the great athletic rivalries in sports, and *Madrileños* are either fans of Real Madrid or of Atlético Madrid - both powerhouse teams. Real Madrid's Santiago Bernabéu stadium *(p167)* is one of the great theatres of the game, but tickets tend to be scarce and expensive. Watching a stadium game isn't the only way to immerse yourself in the sporting spirit, though: catching a live match at a local bar is a great way to delight in and share the locals' passions.

Bold Bourbon

Master architects Ventura Rodríguez and Juan de Villanueva changed the face of Madrid in the 18th century with their Neo-Classical designs. Look no further than the airy order of the Plaza Mayor *(p68)* and the magisterial formal rooms in the Palacio Real *(p64)* for the best examples. And a visit to the Golden Triangle *(p10)* is not just about the art: take some time to admire their harmonious Neo-Classical buildings.

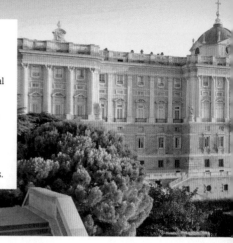

→

Madrid's enormous, lavish Palacio Real, built to impress

MADRID FOR
ARCHITECTURE ENTHUSIASTS

As you stroll through Madrid, you'll be astonished by its architectural riches Whether it's the Neo-Classical elegance of the Palacio Real or the ornate Neo-Mudéjar tilework gracing Las Ventas, Madrid is a showcase of great design from every era that reflects the ever-changing styles of the city.

Handsome Habsburg

When Felipe II made Madrid the capital of Spain in 1561, he began building in the fashionable Baroque style. A rewarding day trip from the capital, El Escorial *(p174)* is by far the most stunning and dramatic example, with artistic masterpieces by the likes of Velázquez and Titian softening the largely unadorned monastery and palace. In central Madrid, head to the Monasterio de las Descalzas Reales *(p80)* to delight in the carved staircases and frescoed stairwells of the convent's Baroque interior.

→

Art lining the long cloister at El Escorial's monastery

Reach for the Sky

In 1946, a government plan to build a business district, Azca *(p164)*, north of the then-new government offices launched an insurgence of notable Modernist skyscrapers a generation later. Peer upwards from the pavement as you walk north on Paseo de la Castellana *(p138)*, strolling from Minoru Yamasaki's 2007 Torre Picasso, a sleek example of New Formalism, to the 1996 KIO Towers that straddle the Plaza de Castilla. At the north end of the Paseo, César Pelli's 2009 Torre Cristal cuts the sky like a sword.

MODERNISME IN MADRID

You don't have to visit Barcelona to see that city's signature Modernisme architecture, the Catalan cousin of French Art Nouveau. In the early 20th century, financier Javier González Longoria commissioned a Modernista family home in Malasaña, now known as the Palacio Langoria *(p143)*, which today serves as the headquarters of the Sociedad General de Autores y Editores. The imposing building with corner turret is embellished with the style's signature flowing organic forms and elegant iron grillwork. An iron and glass dome crowns the structure.

The KIO Towers, the first leaning skyscrapers in the world ↑

↑ The patterned red brickwork of the Casa Árabe

Moorish Fantasies

Characterized by its horseshoe arches and elaborate stucco work, Madrid's Neo-Mudéjar structures transport you to the Islamic world. To travel across the continents, opt for an audioguide tour to ogle the interior of the tile-bedecked Las Ventas bullring *(p162)* and walk alongside the fine brickwork of the Casa Árabe *(en.casaarabe.es)*. Away from the bustling centre you'll find Matadero Madrid *(p170)*, a former slaughterhouse that exemplifies Neo-Mudéjar symmetry with its horseshoe arches, geometric tiles and contrasting red and tan brickwork.

A YEAR IN
MADRID

JANUARY

△ **Cabalgata de los Reyes** *(5 Jan)*. Three Kings parade involving an evening procession from the Parque del Retiro, with floats, animals and even celebrities.

San Antón *(17 Jan)*. Animals are blessed at the Iglesia de San Antón for the feast of St Anthony.

FEBRUARY

△ **ARCOmadrid** *(end Feb)*. This week-long contemporary art fair sees collectors and artists from around the globe come together.

Carnival *(week of Shrove Tuesday)*. Parties and parades around the city, with the main celebration beginning in the Plaza Mayor.

MAY

Labour Day *(1 May)*. Countrywide public holiday, with a rally held in the Puerta del Sol.

Dos de Mayo *(2 May)*. Exhibitions are held in Malasaña to commemorate the day the people of Madrid rose up against Napoleon's troops.

△ **San Isidro** *(15 May)*. Public holiday and the feast of the city's patron saint, featuring fiestas.

JUNE

Corpus Christi *(late May/early Jun)*. Religious holiday honouring the Eucharist with processions in Madrid and Toledo.

Fiesta de San Antonio de la Florida *(13 Jun)*. *Señoritas* throw pins in a baptismal font, dip their hands in and ask St Anthony for a boyfriend.

△ **Madrid Pride** *(end Jun)*. Wild parties in and around Chueca and a huge parade through the city.

SEPTEMBER

△ **Apertura Madrid Gallery Weekend** *(mid-Sep)*. Galleries and museums across the capital launch their new exhibitions with free entry.

Procesión Fluvial *(2nd Sat)*. A river procession in Fuentidueña de Tajo, with illuminated barges.

Romería Panorámica *(2nd Sun)*. The Virgen de Gracia is carried on a decorated cart from San Lorenzo de Escorial to a picnic in La Herrería.

OCTOBER

△ **International Book Fair: Liber** *(1st week)*. A biennial event that brings together international publishers and holds cultural activities.

Virgen de Pilar *(12 Oct)*. Various district fiestas are held, such as that in the Plaza Dalí in Salamanca.

MARCH

Cristo de Medinaceli *(first Fri)*. Thousands come to the Iglesia de Medinaceli to make three wishes before the image of Christ.

△ **Teatralia** *(1–24 Mar)*. A three-week festival of theatre, puppet shows, dance and music for young people.

APRIL

△ **Semana Santa** *(Mar/Apr)*. Evening processions are held in Toledo and across Madrid on Holy Thursday and Good Friday.

El Día de Cervantes *(23 Apr)*. On the anniversary of Cervantes' death, Alcalá de Henares and other towns throughout Spain celebrate Book Day with book fairs and literary discussions.

JULY

△ **Mad Cool** *(mid-Jul)*. A huge three-day indie music festival with big headliners hits a Madrid suburb.

Veranos de la Villa *(Jul–Aug)*. A performing arts festival offering a varied programme of open-air evening events, including cinema, opera and *zarzuela*, across the city.

AUGUST

△ **Castizo Fiestas** *(6–15 Aug)*. Traditional *castizo* fiestas in La Latina and Lavapiés, including San Cayetano, San Lorenzo and La Virgen de la Paloma, which run back-to-back.

NOVEMBER

Todos los Santos *(1 Nov)*. On All Saints' Day, flowers are taken to the graves of relatives, and street stalls sell roasted chestnuts and sweet potato.

Romería de San Eugenio *(14 Nov)*. A *castizo* procession in Rascafría to honour the local saint.

△ **Festival de Otoño** *(2nd half Nov–mid-Dec)*. An annual theatre, ballet and opera festival that now spans several months.

DECEMBER

△ **Christmas Fair** *(mid-Dec–5 Jan)*. A twinkling, lively Christmas market, held in the popular Plaza Mayor.

Nochevieja *(31 Dec)*. Crowds in the Puerta del Sol eat a grape for each chime of midnight on New Year's Eve.

VILLA DE MADRID CORTE DELOS REYES CATOLICOS DE ESPA
Hacia 1635

A BRIEF
HISTORY

Madrid is a young city by Spanish standards, born 21 centuries after the Phoenicians founded Cádiz and six centuries after the Romans constructed Itálica near Seville. From humble rural beginnings as a defensive outpost of Toledo, rose the Spanish capital; now a global city and one of Europe's biggest.

Muslim Beginnings

Although archaeological evidence suggests that early humans came to the area in prehistoric times, the story of Madrid truly begins in the 9th century AD. Moors from North Africa, who had stormed Spain's southern shores in the 8th century, swiftly penetrated north, conquering most of the Iberian Peninsula. They reached what is now Madrid in 852, establishing an *alcázar* on the site where the Palacio Real stands today. A community arose around this fortress, named "Mayrit"; this name later became "Magerit", eventually evolving into "Madrid".

1 A 17th-century map of Madrid.

2 The *alcázar* built by the Moors to protect Toledo, just outside of the city.

3 The siege of Toledo in 1085.

4 Spain's Catholic Monarchs, as they were known.

Timeline of events

711
Moors invade the Iberian Peninsula, beginning the era of al-Andalus (Muslim Spain).

852
Moors found Mayrit, which will later be named Madrid.

1202
Madrid is granted town status.

1085
Madrid is captured by the kingdom of Castile.

1469
Fernando of Aragón and Isabel of Castile marry, kick-starting Spain's political union.

Christian Conquest

At the turn of the first millenium, Muslim Spain, known as al-Andalus, occupied the majority of the peninsula, with Christian kingdoms in the north. These kingdoms pushed south, taking lands back from the Moors in the *reconquista* (reconquest). By the mid-11th century, Castile had arisen as the biggest Christian kingdom. In 1085, Alfonso VI took Mayrit from Muslim control. Assimilated into Castile, monks moved into the area, establishing monasteries and churches for the new Christian population.

The Catholic Monarchs

On Enrique IV of Trastámara's death in 1474, a dynastic struggle ensued between those supporting his daughter Juana's claim to the throne, or his half-sister Isabel's. Madrid's nobility backed Juana, but Isabel and her husband Fernando of Aragón ended up conquering Madrid with the help of town supporters. The Catholic Monarchs united Castile and Aragón, creating the precursor to the modern Spanish state. They visited Madrid often, but most of the momentous events of their reign, such as sponsoring Columbus's voyage to the Americas, took place elsewhere.

AL-ANDALUS

Al-Andalus, also referred to as Muslim Spain, Islamic Iberia, or Muslim Iberia, was the name given to the Iberian Peninsula when it was under Moorish control in the Middle Ages. The Moors left a huge mark on the architecture of southern Spain, but since they were expelled from Madrid relatively quickly, their historic presence is felt less there.

1474
Supporters of Queen Isabel besiege Madrid.

1478
Start of Spanish Inquisition.

1492
Granada falls to Christian forces, completing the *reconquista*; Columbus reaches the Americas.

1520
Madrid joins *Comunero* rebellion of Castillian towns against Carlos I.

A City is Born

Since Castile's foundation, its rulers had travelled constantly around the realm, taking their entire court with them. Fed up with this nomadic form of government, the Habsburg ruler Felipe II established the centrally located Madrid as the capital in 1561. People from all over the peninsula flocked here, and what followed became known as the Siglo de Oro (Golden Age), which saw money pour in from the Americas, an artistic boom with influential writers drawn to the city, and the construction of the Plaza Mayor, the epitome of Habsburg Madrid.

The War of the Spanish Succession

When Carlos II died without an heir in 1700, the Spanish crown found itself without a natural claimant. France favoured the Bourbon prince Philippe of Anjou. Alarmed at the implications of a French-Spanish alliance, England, Austria and Holland supported the Habsburg Archduke Charles of Austria. This dispute led to the 14-year-long War of the Spanish Succession. Madrid backed the Bourbon cause, which eventually emerged victorious: Philippe was crowned as Felipe V.

↑ Titian's portrait of King Felipe II of Spain, painted around 1554

Timeline of events

1561
Felipe II establishes capital of Spain in Madrid.

1588
The Spanish Armada fails to make landfall in England.

1601
Felipe III moves Spanish capital to Valladolid.

1606
Madrid permanently reinstated as capital.

1700
Carlos II dies without an heir; War of the Spanish Succession begins.

The Bourbons

With the help of French advisers, Felipe V aimed to make Madrid look as French as possible. When the *alcázar* burned down in 1734, he ordered the construction of a royal palace modelled on Versailles. While Spain began to grow, the archaic financial systems resulted in treasury deficits and in 1739 the country was effectively insolvent. Carlos IV came to the throne in 1788, ushering in the decline of the monarchy thanks in part to his lack of proper authority; the real power sat with his wife María Luisa of Parma, and chief minister Manuel Godoy.

Napoleon and the French Occupation

Godoy struck a deal with Napoleon's France, allowing French troops to cross Spain to conquer Portugal. In the end, however, the French occupied Spain itself. Riots broke out, and the king was forced to abdicate in favour of his son, Fernando VII, who ruled in name only. Spanish resentment increased when Napoleon installed his brother on the throne as José I. In 1810, the British and Portuguese armies came to Spain's aid, starting a campaign to drive the French from the Iberian Peninsula.

⚀ Anton van den Wyngaerde's drawing of Madrid in 1562, after it was made the capital.

⚁ A battle that took place in 1711 during the War of the Spanish Succession.

⚂ Carlos IV and his family, painted by Goya.

⚃ Goya's *The Third of May 1808* depicting the riots in Madrid.

1701
Felipe V arrives in Madrid as first Bourbon king.

1734
Fire destroys Madrid's Moorish *alcázar*.

1788
Carlos III dies, succeeded by Carlos IV.

1808
French soldiers occupy Spain; riots in Madrid; Napoleon's brother installed as king.

1813
French forces defeated within Spain.

The Ensanche and First Republic

Following the French defeat and Napoleon's abdication, Fernando VII was restored to the throne and ruled Spain as an absolute monarch. His death in 1833 triggered a succession of *coups d'état* and uprisings, including a civil war over his successor. In 1868, Isabel II, whose cause had prevailed in the civil war, was ousted. Five years later, the First Republic was ushered in, but this lasted only 11 months before the restoration of the monarchy under Isabel II's son Alfonso XII. Against this backdrop, Madrid enjoyed a period of prosperity and unstoppable growth known as the Ensanche.

The Spanish Civil War

Spain's political landscape remained a warzone, culminating in General Miguel Primo de Rivera installing himself as dictator in 1923. His disastrous economic policy saw the country bankrupted, and he stepped down in 1930, triggering elections which returned a Republican majority demanding that the king abdicate. This Second Republic was opposed by the Nationalists, and Spain was plunged once more into Civil War.

1. Queen Isabel II's coronation in 1843.

2. A Civil War battle in Spain in 1937.

3. Juan Carlos with his wife and children.

4. Real Madrid players celebrating victory.

33

The number of Spanish governments between 1902 and 1923.

Timeline of events

1814
Fernando VII restored as king of Spain.

1873
First Spanish Republic lasts 11 months.

1874
Bourbon monarchy restored under Alfonso XII.

1931
Second Republic established; Alfonso XIII goes into exile.

1936
Civil War begins between Republicans and Nationalists.

Madrid was one of the Republican government's last strongholds, initially resisting the Nationalists, but it fell to their forces in 1939. Franco later declared victory and established a military dictatorship, which solidified his control of Spain, shepherding in an age of isolation and oppression. Franco died in 1975 and his named successor, Juan Carlos (Alfonso XIII's grandson), ascended the throne, restoring Spain's Bourbon monarchy. He orchestrated Spain's first post-Franco democratic elections in 1977, ushering in a smooth transition to democracy.

Madrid Today

Today, the Community of Madrid, which encompasses the city, the surrounding metropolitan area and beyond, is one of Spain's 17 autonomous communities, with its own regional president. This presidency has been held by the conservative Partido Popular (People's Party) since 1995; the city's council is headed by a mayor. One of the largest cities in Europe, Madrid as a leading cultural centre, played host to the international LGBTQ+ festival WorldPride in 2017; not to mention it is home to two world-class football teams: Atlético Madrid and Real Madrid.

↑ Celebrating WorldPride in 2017 in the welcoming sunny city

1939
Madrid falls to Franco's forces; Civil War ends as Franco becomes dictator.

1975
Franco dies; Juan Carlos I becomes king.

2002
Real Madrid makes soccer history winning its ninth European Cup.

2014
Felipe VI is crowned king of Spain.

2019
Pedro Rollán Ojeda elected president of the People's Party.

EXPERIENCE

Watching the sun setting over Madrid

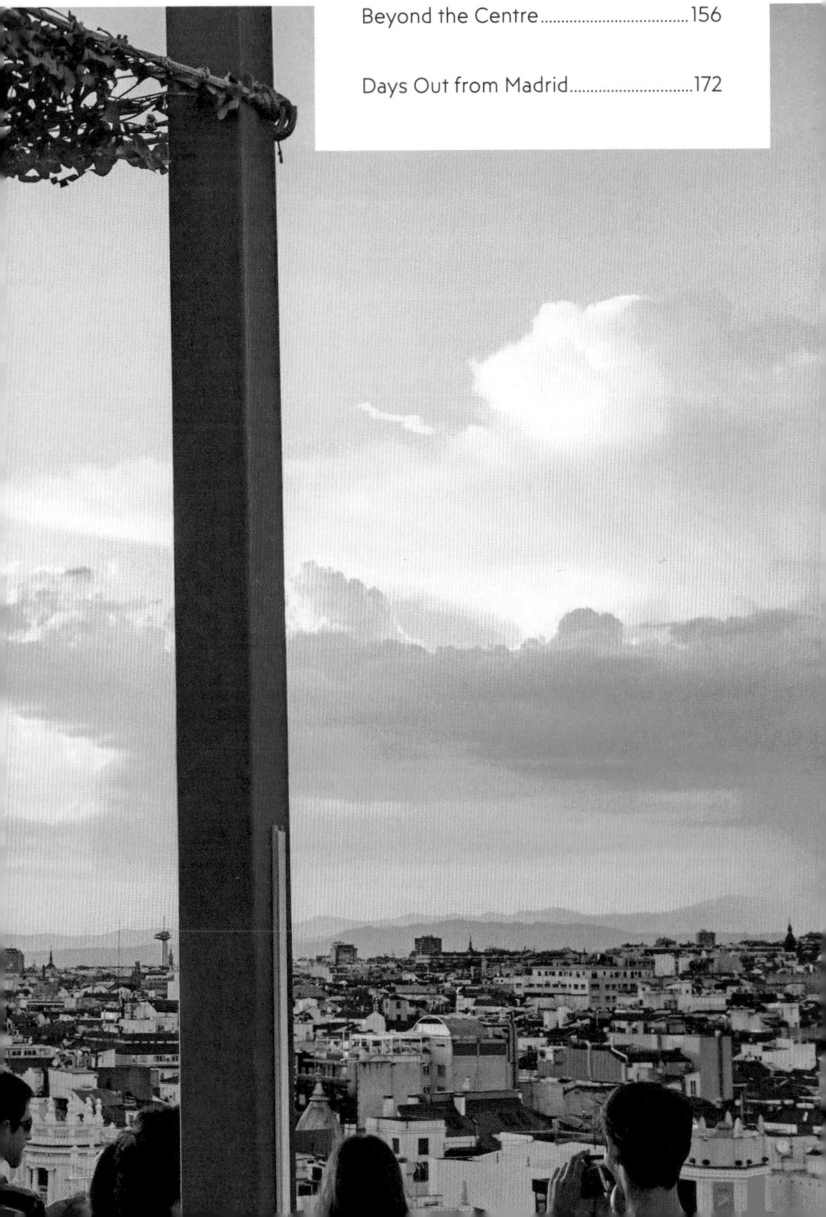

WEST MADRID

When Felipe II chose Madrid as his capital in 1561, it was a small Castilian town of little real significance. In the following years, it was to grow into the nerve centre of a mighty empire.

According to tradition, it was the Moorish chieftain Muhammad ben Abd al Rahman who established a fortress above the Río Manzanares. Magerit, as it was called in Arabic, fell to Alfonso VI of Castile between 1083 and 1086. Narrow streets with houses and medieval churches began to grow up on the higher ground behind the old Arab *alcázar* (fortress). When this burned down in 1734, it became the site of the present Bourbon palace, the Palacio Real.

The population had scarcely reached 20,000 when Madrid was chosen as capital, but by the end of the 16th century the population trebled. The 16th-century city is known as the "Madrid de los Austrias", after the reigning Habsburg dynasty. During this period royal monasteries were endowed and churches and private palaces were built. In the 17th century, the Plaza Mayor was added and the Puerta del Sol, the "Gate of the Sun", became the spiritual and geographical heart not only of Madrid but of all of Spain.

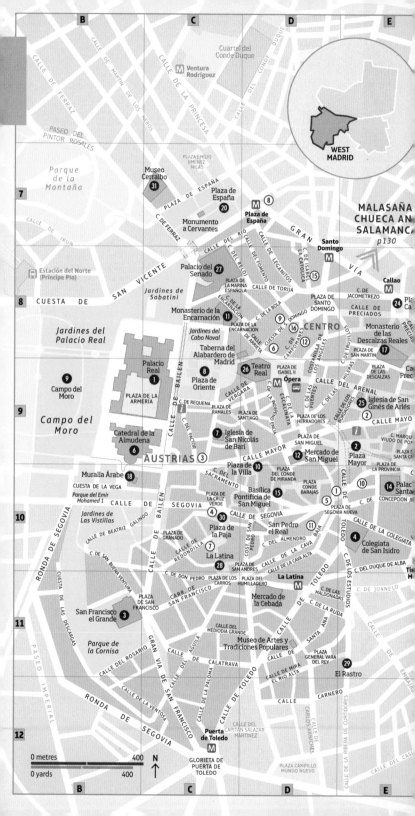

WEST MADRID

Must Sees
1 Palacio Real
2 Plaza Mayor
3 San Francisco el Grande

Experience More
4 Colegiata de San Isidro
5 Puerta del Sol
6 Catedral de la Almudena
7 Iglesia de San Nicolás de Bari
8 Plaza de Oriente
9 Campo del Moro
10 Plaza de la Villa
11 Monasterio de la Encarnación
12 Mercado de San Miguel
13 Edificio Grassy
14 Palacio de Santa Cruz
15 Basílica Pontificia de San Miguel
16 Real Academia de Bellas Artes de San Fernando
17 Monasterio de las Descalzas Reales
18 Muralla Árabe
19 Gran Vía
20 Plaza de España
21 Plaza de Santa Ana
22 Calle de Preciados
23 Telefónica
24 Plaza del Callao
25 Iglesia de San Ginés de Arlés
26 Teatro Real
27 Palacio del Senado
28 La Latina
29 El Rastro
30 Plaza de la Paja
31 Museo Cerralbo

Eat
1 Botín
2 Chocolatería San Ginés
3 Casa Ciriaco
4 NA!A

Drink
5 La Fontanilla
6 Café de l'Opera
7 Delic

Stay
8 Dear Hotel
9 Gran Meliá Palacio de los Duques
10 The Hat
11 Posada del Dragon
12 Room Mate Mario

Shop
13 Guantes Luque
14 La Violeta
15 Antigua Casa Talavera
16 Desperate Literature

INSIDER TIP
Changing of the Guard

Every Wednesday and Saturday, soldiers march on the Plaza de la Armería, in front of the palace, to the sound of fifes, drums and horses' hoofs. Get there early to grab the best spot.

The sun bathing the limestone north façade of the Palacio Real ↑

❶ ✒️ Ⓜ️ 🖥️

PALACIO REAL

📍 C9 🚪 Calle de Bailén 🚌 Ⓜ️ Ópera, Príncipe Pío, Plaza de España
🕐 Palace: Apr-Sep: 10am-7pm Mon-Sat, Oct-Mar: 10am-6pm Mon-Sat (10am-4pm Sun year round); Changing of the Guard: 11am-2pm Wed & Sat (every 30 min) 🚫 For official functions, some public hols
🌐 patrimonionacional.es

Madrid's vast and lavish Royal Palace was built to impress. The site was originally occupied for centuries by a royal fortress, but after a fire in 1734, Felipe V commissioned a palatial replacement.

This splendid Royal Palace stands on the site of the original Moorish fortress. After the *reconquista* of Madrid in 1085, this *alcázar* served as a residence for visiting royals. But, following extensive modifications in 1561, it became the residence of Felipe II until the completion of El Escorial (*p174*) in 1584.

A fire on Christmas Eve 1734, during the reign of Felipe V, all but destroyed the castle. This suited Spain's first Bourbon king well – Felipe's idea of a royal palace was the Versailles of his childhood, and so he commissioned a new royal palace decorated in the French style.

Most of the limestone building is the work of Giovanni Battista Sachetti, with later modifications by other architects. So vast was the plan that construction lasted from 1738 to 1755, by which time Felipe V was dead. His son, Carlos III, became the first royal resident and the palace was the home of the Spanish royal family until Alfonso XIII went into exile in 1931.

> **Felipe's idea of a royal palace was the Versailles of his childhood, and so he commissioned a new royal palace decorated in the French style.**

↑ The landscaped gardens in the Plaza de Oriente, next to the palace

↑ The painted ceiling crowning the central staircase of the Palacio Real

Timeline

1000
△ 9th-century *alcázar* is built.

1561
▽ King Felipe II moves his court to Madrid.

1734
The old *alcázar* burns down.

1738
▽ Construction of the palace begins under the orders of King Felipe V.

1764
King Carlos III moves into the newly built palace.

1931
△ King Alfonso XIII - the last monarch to live in the palace - decides on voluntary exile.

↑ Crystal chandeliers illuminating the long table in the dining room

Inside the Palace

Unsurprisingly, the interior of the Palacio Real matches the grandeur of its façade. It is remarkable both for its size and for the exuberant furnishings found in many of the rooms, including luxurious carpets, massive tapestries and glittering silverware. Take a guided tour or carve your own route through some of the 2,800 rooms to see this decor and some fascinating treasures from the royal collection, including formidable suits of armour, masterpieces by Goya and finely tuned violins.

Did You Know?

The Palacio Real is the largest castle in Europe by floor area.

Visitors climbing the Palacio Real's grand marble staircase ↑

Palace Rooms

Entrance Rooms

The first port of call is the Salón de los Alabarderos (Hall of the Palace Guards), decorated with a fresco by Tiépolo. Adjoining it is the Salón de Columnas (Hall of Columns), which served as the banquet hall until the new dining hall was incorporated in the 19th century. Today it is used for receptions and functions. Next, enter the Rococo Salón del Trono (Throne Room). Completed in 1772, it has two rock crystal chandeliers, numerous candelabra and mirrors, and walls of crimson velvet with silver embroidery. The twin thrones are recent (1977), while the bronze lions that guard them date from 1651. The room is still used for functions, such as the royal reception on the Día de la Hispanidad or the yearly reception for the diplomatic corps posted in Madrid.

Carlos III Rooms

▷ Leading off from the Salón del Trono are the king's private chambers. He would take his meals in the Sala de Gasparini - lonely affairs considering the queen had her own dining room. In the Cámara de Gasparini, with its stucco ceiling and embroidered silk walls, the king would be dressed in the presence of courtiers.

Dining Room

This 400-sq-m (4,300-sq-ft) banquet hall was formed in 1879 when the queen's private chambers were joined together, during the reign of Alfonso XII. It is richly adorned with gold plate decoration on the ceiling and walls, frescoes, chandeliers, Flemish tapestries, Chinese vases and embroidered curtains. The table can accommodate up to 160 diners. The room immediately off the dining hall is devoted to commemorative medals, and also contains the elaborate centrepiece used during banquets. Other rooms contain silverware, china, crystal and an extraordinary collection of musical instruments.

Chapel Rooms

Built in 1749-57, the chapel is still used for religious services, and also for musical soirées. While the decor is luxurious, it is the dome, with its murals by Giaquinto, that immediately catches the eye. Next, visitors pass through the Salón de Paso and into María Cristina's chambers. During the reign of Alfonso XII these four small rooms served as an American-style billiards room, Asian-style smoking room, the *Salón de Estucos* (queen's bedroom) and the Gabinete de Maderas de Indias, used as an office.

Royal Armoury

◁ Returning to the Plaza de la Armería, near the ticket office, you come to the Real Armería (Royal Armoury), which is housed in a pavilion built in 1897 after the original armoury was destroyed by fire. It contains weapons and royal suits of armour. On display is an elaborate suit of armour which once belonged to Carlos I. The armoury could be considered as Madrid's first museum because it has been open to the public since Felipe II inherited the collection from his father.

2 🍴 ☕ 🛍️

PLAZA MAYOR

📍 E9 🚇 Ópera, Sol, Tirso de Molina

At the very heart of Madrid life for centuries, the Plaza Mayor has seen it all, from *autos-da-fé (p73)* to coronations to Christmas markets. In an ongoing tradition, residents of this grand arcaded square have long rented out balcony space to *Madrileños* wanting ringside seats to the city's big events.

The splendid rectangular square, lined with pinnacles and dormer windows, was started in 1617, and built in just two years, replacing slum houses. Its architect, Juan Gómez de Mora, was successor to Juan de Herrera, designer of Felipe II's austere monastery-palace, El Escorial *(p174)*. Gómez de Mora echoed the style of his master, softening it slightly. The square was later reformed by Juan de Villanueva. The fanciest part of the arcaded construction is the Casa de la Panadería – the bakery. Its façade, now crudely reinvented, is decorated with allegorical paintings. The equestrian statue in the centre is of Felipe III, who ordered the square's construction. Today the square is lined with cafés, and hosts a collectors' market on Sundays, as well as pageants and rock concerts.

→ The elaborately painted façade of the Casa de la Panadería

A HISTORIC SQUARE

Plaza Mayor has been witness to a number of historical events. The canonization of Madrid's patron, San Isidro, took place here in 1622, and the square was Carlos III's first stop after arriving from Italy in 1760. But what lives on most in popular culture is the 1621 execution of Rodrigo Calderón, secretary to Felipe III, held here. Although hated by the Madrid populace, Calderón bore himself with such dignity on the day of his death that the phrase "proud as Rodrigo on the scaffold" survives today.

↑ The square at dusk, seen through one of its gates

237

The number of
decorative balconies
that surround the
Plaza Mayor.

↑ One of the many cafés on
Plaza Mayor, spilling out
onto the square's cobbles

3 ⊕ ⊕

SAN FRANCISCO EL GRANDE

📍 B11 🏛 Plaza de San Francisco 🚇 Ⓜ La Latina, Puerta de Toledo 📞 913 65 38 00 🕐 Jul-Sep: 10:30am-3:30pm Tue-Sat; Oct-Jun: 10:30am-2:30pm & 4-6:30pm Tue-Sat 🚫 During services on Sat

Richly endowed with the work of great artists, the magnificent Basílica de San Francisco el Grande is one of Madrid's most iconic churches. The large dome is a work of art in itself, with eight main panels decorated with majestic frescoes.

Founded in 1760 by Carlos III, this basilica was once occupied by a Franciscan convent. The remarkable dome was designed by Francisco Cabezas to measure over 33 m (108 ft) in diameter, but work had to be halted due to complications with the size; it was finally completed in 1784 by Francesco Sabatini. Following a renovation project in 1878, the façade is now dominated by the dome and twin towers, which house 19 bells.

↑ The basilica's façade is dominated by the dome, one of the largest in the world

Inside, the seven main doors were carved in walnut by Juan Guas. On each side of the basilica are three chapels, the most famous being the one to the left of the main entrance. This chapel boasts a painting dating from 1784 by Goya of San Bernardino de Siena, with the painter himself appearing on the right of the picture. Work by Andrés de la Calleja and Antonio González Velázquez is also featured.

The adjoining Capilla del Cristo de los Dolores, dating from 1162, was designed by Hermano Francisco Bautista. In it is the sculpture of Cristo de los Dolores, with holes in Christ's hands from the nails on the cross.

↑ Attending a church service in one of the lavishly decorated chapels

Timeline

1561

▽ After Felipe II made Madrid Spain's capital, the convent became custodian of the "Holy Places" conquered by the crusaders.

1878

A renovation project was initiated and the church was decorated extravagantly.

1217

▲ The site of the basilica was previously occupied by a Franciscan convent founded, according to legend, by St Francis of Assisi in 1217.

1760

▲ Carlos III ordained that the convent be replaced by a Neo-Classical basilica, and appointed Francisco Cabezas architect.

1835

The basilica was taken over by the Foreign Ministry and used as an army barrack. A few years later it was made into a national pantheon.

↑ The breathtaking frescoes that decorate the interior of the dome

EXPERIENCE MORE

❹
Colegiata de San Isidro

📍E10 🏛Calle de Toledo 37
📞913 69 20 37 Ⓜ La Latina,
Tirso de Molina 🕐Summer:
7:30am–1pm & 7–9pm daily;
winter: 7:30am–1pm,
6–9pm daily

The Baroque-style Colegiata
de San Isidro was built for the
Jesuits in the mid-17th century.
This twin-towered church was
Madrid's cathedral until La
Almudena (p74) was completed
in 1993. After Carlos III expelled
the Jesuits from Spain in 1767,
it was rededicated to Madrid's
patron saint, St Isidore. Two
years later, the saint's remains
were brought here from the
Iglesia de San Andrés.

---

❺
Puerta del Sol

📍F9 Ⓜ Sol

One of the city's most popular
meeting places, the Puerta
del Sol is crowded and noisy

↓ Crowds gathering in
the Puerta del Sol on
a clear day

with chatter. The square marks
the site of the original eastern
entrance to the city, once
occupied by a gatehouse
and castle. These disappeared
long ago and a succession of
churches came in their place.
In the late 19th century the
area was turned into a square
and became the centre of
café society.

Today the "square" is shaped
like a half-moon, with a modern glass train station in front
of the statue of Carlos III. The
southern side of the square
is edged by an austere
red-brick building, home to
the regional government. The
buildings opposite it are arranged in a semicircle and contain
modern shops and cafés.
Originally the city's post office,
the regional government
building was built in the 1760s
under Carlos III. In 1847 it
became the headquarters of
the Ministry of the Interior.
The clocktower, which gives
the building much of its
identity, was added in 1866.
During the Franco regime,
the police cells beneath the
building were the site of many
human rights abuses. In 1963,
Julián Grimau, a member of
the underground Communist
party, allegedly fell from

an upstairs window and
miraculously survived, only to
be executed soon afterwards.

The Puerta del Sol itself has
witnessed many important
historical events. On 2 May
1808 the uprising against the
occupying French forces
began here, but the crowd
was crushed. In 1912 the
liberal prime minister José
Canalejas was assassinated
in the square and, in 1931,
the Second Republic was
proclaimed from the balcony
of the Ministry of the Interior.

The Puerta del Sol is the
focus of many festive events
today, and brings locals and
visitors together. At midnight
on New Year's Eve, crowds
fill the square to eat a grape
on each stroke of the clock,
a tradition supposed to bring
good luck for the rest of
the year.

> **Did You Know?**
>
> The statue of the bear
> and the strawberry
> tree on the Puerta del
> Sol represents the
> symbol of Madrid.

↑ Francisco de Ricci's *Auto-da-fé* painting of a trial held in the Plaza Mayor

THE SPANISH INQUISITION

The Spanish Inquisition was set up by King Fernando and Queen Isabel in 1478 to create a single, monolithic Catholic ideology in Spain. Protestant heretics and alleged "false converts" to Catholicism from the Jewish and Muslim faiths were tried, to ensure the religious unity of Spain.

AN UNFAIR TRIAL

Beginning with a papal bull, the Inquisition was run like a court, presided over by the Inquisitor-General. However, the defendants were denied counsel, not told the charges facing them and tortured to obtain confessions. Punishment ranged from imprisonment to beheading, hanging or burning at the stake. A formidable system of control, it gave Spain's Protestant enemies abroad a major propaganda weapon. The Inquisition lasted into the 18th century.

AUTO-DA-FÉ IN THE PLAZA MAYOR

The above painting by Francisco de Ricci (1683) depicts a trial, or *auto-da-fé* - literally, "show of faith" - held in Madrid's main square on 30 June 1680. Unlike papal inquisitions elsewhere in Europe, this trial was presided over by the reigning monarch, Carlos II, accompanied by his queen. The painting shows a convicted defendant, forced to wear a red *sanbenito* robe, being led away to prison after refusing his last chance to repent and convert. Those who didn't confess were sentenced by day, and then executed.

 INSIDER TIP
Walk on the Wild Side

Sandemans offers informative 3-hour walking tours that take you to the sites where the Inquisition played out *(neweurope tours.eu)*. Starting and finishing in the Plaza Mayor *(p68)*, you'll be taken back to dark days of trials and torture, exorcisms and executions.

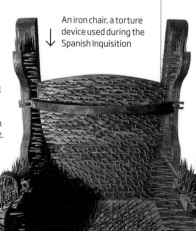
An iron chair, a torture device used during the Spanish Inquisition

Visitors admiring the altar at the far end of the Catedral de la Almudena

❽ Plaza de Oriente

⑨C9 ⓂÓpera

While King of Spain, Joseph Bonaparte (José I) carved out this stirrup-shaped space from the jumble of buildings to the east of the Palacio Real, providing the view of the palace enjoyed today.

The square was once an important meeting place for state occasions: kings, queens and dictators all made public appearances on the palace balcony facing the plaza. The many statues of early kings which stand here were originally intended to adorn the roofline of the Palacio Real, but proved to be too heavy. The equestrian statue of Felipe IV in the centre of the square is by Italian sculptor Pietro Tacca, and is based on drawings by Velázquez.

In the southeast corner of the plaza is the Café de Oriente, with outdoor tables for enjoying the view.

❻ Catedral de la Almudena

⑨B9 ⚐Calle de Bailén 10 ⓂÓpera ⏰9am-8:30pm daily (Jul & Aug: 10am-9pm); Museum & Dome: 10am-2:30pm Mon-Sat 🌐catedraldelaalmudena.es

Dedicated to the city's patron, Madrid's cathedral was begun in 1883, but it was not until 1993 that it was completed and subsequently inaugurated by Pope John Paul II. The slow construction, which ceased completely during the Spanish Civil War, involved several architects. The cathedral's Neo-Gothic grey and white façade resembles that of

the Palacio Real (*p64*), which stands opposite. Highlights include the beautiful bronze entrance doors, a 16th-century image of the Virgen de la Almudena inside the crypt and the striking double dome, which offers excellent views over the city.

❼ Iglesia de San Nicolás de Bari

⑨C9 ⚐Plaza de San Nicolás 6 ☎915 59 40 64 ⓂÓpera ⏰8:30am-1pm & 7-8:30pm Mon, 8:30-9:30am & 6:30-8:30pm Tue-Sat, 10am-1:45pm & 6:30-8:45pm Sun & public hols

The first mention of the church of San Nicolás de Bari is in a document written in 1202. Its brick tower, which is decorated with horseshoe arches, is the oldest surviving religious structure in Madrid. Thought to date from the 12th century, the tower is Mudéjar in style (*p49*), and may well have originally been the minaret of a Moorish mosque.

2004

The year that King Felipe VI and Letizia Ortiz wed at the Catedral de la Almudena.

❾ Campo del Moro

⑨B9 ⚐Paseo de la Virgen del Puerto s/n ⓂÓpera, Príncipe Pío ⏰10am-midnight ⏹1 & 6 Jan, 1 & 15 May, 12 Oct, 9 Nov, 24, 25 & 31 Dec and for official functions 🌐patrimonionacional.es

The Campo del Moro (the "Field of the Moor") is a pleasing park, rising steeply from the Río Manzanares to offer one of the finest views of the Palacio Real. The park

The old *ayuntamiento*, or Town Hall, on Madrid's Plaza de la Vil

> The much restored and remodelled Plaza de la Villa is one of the most atmospheric spots in Madrid. Some of the city's most historic secular buildings are situated around this square.

has a varied history. In 1109, a Moorish army, led by Ali ben Yusuf, set up camp here – hence the name. The park later became a jousting ground for Christian knights.

In the late 19th century, it was used as a playground for royal children and landscaped in what is described as the English style – with winding paths, grass and woodland, fountains and statues. In 1931, under the Second Republic, it was opened to the public. Under Franco it was closed again and was not reopened until 1978.

 10

Plaza de la Villa

D10 Ópera, Sol

The much restored and remodelled Plaza de la Villa is one of the most atmospheric spots in Madrid. Some of the city's most historic secular buildings are situated around this square.

The oldest building is the early 15th-century Torre de los Lujanes, with its Gothic portal and Mudéjar-style horseshoe arches. France's François I was allegedly imprisoned in it following his defeat at the Battle of Pavia in 1525. The Casa de Cisneros was built in 1537 for the nephew of Cardinal Cisneros, who was the founder of the historic University of Alcalá (p198). The main façade on Calle de Sacramento is an excellent example of the Plateresque style – early Spanish Renaissance with fine detail.

Linked to this building by an enclosed bridge is the Old Town Hall (ayuntamiento). Designed in the 1640s by Juan Gómez de Mora, architect of the Plaza Mayor, it exhibits the same combination of steep roofs with dormer windows, steeple-like towers at the corners and an austere brick-and-stone façade. Before construction was completed, more than 30 years later, the building had acquired handsome Baroque doorways. A balcony was later added by Juan de Villanueva, the architect of the Prado (p100), so that the royal family could watch Corpus Christi processions passing by.

 11

Monasterio de la Encarnación

C8 Plaza de la Encarnación 1 Ópera, Santo Domingo 10am-2pm, 4-6:30pm Tue-Sat, 10am-3pm Sun & public hols Easter, 17-20 Apr, 1 May, 24, 25 & 31 Dec patrimonionacional.es

Set in a lovely tree-shaded square, this Augustinian convent was founded in 1611 for Margaret of Austria, wife of Felipe III. The architect, Juan Gómez de Mora, also built the Plaza Mayor (p68).

Still inhabited by nuns, the convent has the atmosphere of old Castile, with its Talavera tiles, exposed beams and portraits of royal benefactors. It also contains a collection of 17th-century art, with paintings by José de Ribera and a polychrome wooden statue, *Cristo Yacente* (*Lying Christ*), by Gregorio Fernández.

The Monasterio de la Encarnación's main attraction is the reliquary chamber with a ceiling painted by Carducho. A phial containing St Pantaleon's dried blood can be found here. According to legend, the blood liquifies every 27 July, the anniversary of the saint's death. Should the blood fail to liquefy, it is said that disaster will befall Madrid.

🔴12
Mercado de San Miguel

🔲 D9 🏠 Plaza de San Miguel Ⓜ Sol, Ópera 🕐 10am–midnight daily (to 1am Fri & Sat) 🌐 mercadodesan miguel.es

While there are larger markets in Madrid, the Mercado de San Miguel is the city's last surviving example of a marketplace constructed from iron. The unique single-level, glassed-in market was built in 1914–15. It stands on the site of the former Iglesia de San Miguel de los Octoes, which was demolished in 1810 during the reign of Joseph Bonaparte (José I). The market is home to excellent stalls serving food prepared on site. There is a wine bar, vermouth bar and

---

🔍 HIDDEN GEM
Sweet Nuns

A one-minute walk from the Mercado de San Miguel, the cloistered nuns at the Convento de las Carboneras *(Plaza del Conde Miranda 3)* bake and sell biscuits. Ring the bell 9:30am–1pm and 4:30–6:30pm.

---

a flamenco venue and it also hosts live music performances.

At the front entrance, look up to see the fallen angel statue called Accidente Aereo. While not as famous as the one in the Parque del Retiro *(p108)*, it is just as spectacular.

🔴13
Edificio Grassy

🔲 G8 🏠 Gran Vía 1 Ⓜ Banco de España, Sevilla 🕐 Museum: by appt only 🌐 grassy.es

Designed by Eladio Laredo on a small sliver of land between the Gran Vía and the Calle de Caballero de Gracia, the Grassy building has a circular end-tower similar to that of the nearby Edificio Metrópolis *(p120)*. It is crowned by a round, two-tiered colonnade. It was built in 1917, but became known as the Grassy building in the 1950s, after the jewellery shop that has occupied the ground floor since then. The prestigious jewellery firm, established in 1923, specializes in watches and, in the basement, is the Museo de Reloj Grassy, a collection of 500 timepieces from the 16th to 19th centuries, including rare

clocks that belonged to European royalty. Be sure to book ahead to visit the museum.

🔴14
Palacio de Santa Cruz

🔲 E10 🏠 Plaza de Santa Cruz Ⓜ Sol, Tirso de Molina 🔒 To the public

Commissioned by Felipe IV and constructed between 1629 and 1643 by Juan Bautista Crescendi, this Baroque building is one of the finest examples of Habsburg architecture. Since 1901 it has been the Ministry of Foreign Affairs, but it originally housed the Carcel de la Corte (city prison). It was here that the participants in the *autos-da-fé* (Spanish Inquisition trials), held in the nearby Plaza Mayor *(p68)*, awaited their fate. More famous inmates include the playwright Lope de Vega (1562–1635), imprisoned for libelling his former lover, the actress Elena Osorio. General Rafael de Riego, who led an uprising against Fernando VII in 1820, and the famous bandit Luis Candelas spent their last hours in its cells. Candelas was a Robin Hood-like character

↑ Interior of the Basílica Pontificia de San Miguel, a curious blend of old and modern

who rubbed shoulders with the aristocracy (and stole their jewels).

The palace underwent an extensive restoration in 1846, following a fire, and further renovations in the aftermath of the Spanish Civil War, but its original architecture remains essentially intact. The style of the building is in keeping with the area around the Plaza Mayor, with spired towers on its corners and two interior courtyards. The building only became known as the Palacio de Santa Cruz after 1846, when it was made the headquarters of Spain's Overseas Ministry.

15

Basílica Pontificia de San Miguel

📍 D10 🏛 Calle de San Justo 4 Ⓜ Sol 🕐 Times vary, check website 🌐 bsmiguel.es

Standing on the site of an old Romanesque church dedicated to two local child-martyrs put to death by the Romans, this building is a rare example of Bourbon-inspired Baroque in

The ornate iron-and-glass Mercado de San Miguel, a popular covered market

the middle of old Madrid. It was built for Don Luis de Borbón y Farnesio, the youngest son of Felipe V, and Archbishop of Toledo at only five years of age.

Several architects had a hand in its design and construction between 1739 and 1746. The pediment and twin bell towers topping its convex façade were, however, added later. The façade is graced with four allegorical statues, representing Charity, Faith, Fortitude and Hope. There are also carvings depicting the two child-martyrs, Justo and Pastor.

Inside, there is a single nave, and the roof is supported only by the curved and crossing arches sprouting from the exterior walls. The decor is a curious mixture of old and new – the frescoes on the ceiling and the organ in the choir date from the 18th century, but many of the paintings and stained-glass windows are contemporary. Today the church is administered by the Catholic organization Opus Dei, who use it for some of their activities. One of the side chapels, which is dedicated to the organization's founder, Monsignor José María Escrivá de Balaguer (1902–75), houses an eerily lifelike statue of him. Classical music concerts are held some evenings.

EAT

Botín
The world's oldest restaurant, set in rustic interconnected dining rooms, is justly lauded for its excellent *cochinillo* (roast suckling pig).

📍 D10 🏛 Calle Cuchilleros 17 🌐 botin.es

€€€

Chocolatería San Ginés
This beloved spot has been satisfying Madrid's cravings for hot *churros* and rich hot chocolate since 1894. The combination is equally satisfying at breakfast, for an afternoon break or after a late night at the clubs.

📍 E9 🏛 Pasadizo de San Ginés 5 🌐 chocolateriasan gines.com

€€€

Casa Ciriaco
A Madrid institution serving traditional dishes since before the Civil War. Once a meeting place for the literary set.

📍 C9 🏛 Calle Mayor 84 🌐 casaciriaco.es

€€€

NA!A
This chic but relaxed bistro is popular with actors and artists and serves fresh cuisine with a creative twist. Dishes range from gnocchi to Iberian pork.

📍 C10 🏛 Plaza de la Paja 3 🌐 naiabistro.com

€€€

Quaint alleyway next to the historic Chocolatería San Ginés

↑ Bronze bust of Francisco de Goya, Real Academia de Bellas Artes

Real Academia de Bellas Artes de San Fernando

📍G9 🏛Calle de Alcalá 13 Ⓜ Banco de España, Gran Vía, Sevilla, Sol ⏰10am-3pm Tue-Sun ❌Aug & some public hols 🌐real academiabellasartes sanfernando.com

Dalí and Picasso are among the former students of this fine arts academy, which is housed in an 18th-century building by José Benito de Churriguera. Its art gallery displays a large selection of works, including drawings by Raphael and Titian. A superb collection of old masters includes paintings by Rubens and Van Dyck. Spanish artists from the 16th to the 19th centuries are particularly well represented, including Alejandrina Gessler y Lacroix, one of the first female painters admitted to the academy.

An entire room is devoted to Goya, a former director of the academy. On display are his paintings of Manuel Godoy and a self-portrait painted in 1815. The building also houses the National Chalcography Museum, with plates used by painters such as Goya to engrave on copper or brass.

Monasterio de las Descalzas Reales

📍E8 🏛Plaza de las Descalzas 3 Ⓜ Sol, Callao ⏰10am-2pm & 4-6:30pm Tue-Sat, 10am-3pm Sun & public hols ❌1 & 6 Jan, Easter, 1 May, 24, 25 & 31 Dec 🌐patrimonionacional.es

Madrid's most notable religious building is also a rare surviving example of 16th-century architecture in the city. Around 1560, Felipe II's sister Doña Juana converted the medieval palace that stood here into a convent for nuns. Her rank accounts for the vast collection of art and wealth of the Descalzas Reales (Royal Barefooted).

The stairway has a fresco of Felipe IV with his family, and a fine ceiling by Claudio Coello. It leads to a first-floor cloister, ringed with chapels containing paintings and precious objects. The main chapel houses Doña Juana's tomb.

Muralla Árabe

📍B10 🏛Parque del Emir Mohamed I, Cuesta de la Vega Ⓜ Ópera ⏰Dawn-dusk

Other than the city's name, which comes from the Arabic *Mayrit*, a small stretch of outer

---

🔺 GREAT VIEW
Staircase to Heaven

Inside the decadent Monasterio de las Descalzas Reales, no angle is more striking than the view up the staircase, with its 17th-century frescoes.

---

defence wall is all that is left of Madrid's Moorish heritage. The Muralla Árabe (Arab Wall) stands to the south of the Catedral de la Almudena, down the steep Cuesta de la Vega street. It is believed that one of the main gateways to the Moorish town stood near this site. The wall, constructed from flintstone blocks of various shapes and sizes, rises over 3 m (10 ft) along one side of the Parque del Emir Mohamed I. The park is named after the Moorish leader who founded Madrid.

The site was discovered while excavations were being carried out in 1953. As well as Moorish ruins dating from the ninth century, there is also a segment of a 12th-century Christian wall. On the other side of the wall are examples of typically Moorish brick horseshoe arches.

Across the street, a plaque and an image of the Virgin identify this as the spot where the statue of the Virgen de la Almudena was discovered in 1085 (*almudena* is from the Arabic for "outer wall"), possibly hidden from the Moors.

In summer, outdoor concerts and plays have been held in the Parque del Emir Mohamed I.

→ The huge stone obelisk marking the centre of Plaza de España

> **The city fathers saw the need for a new thoroughfare – a Gran Vía. This architectural showpiece was to be a symbol of modern Madrid.**

 19

Gran Vía

📍 F8 🚇 Plaza de España, Santo Domingo, Callao, Gran Vía

In the mid-1800s, Madrid's burgeoning middle class was pushing the city's limits outwards, destroying houses and poor districts to allow for the *Ensanche* (expansion). The city fathers saw the need for a new thoroughfare – a Gran Vía. This architectural showpiece was to be a symbol of modern Madrid.

On the drawing board since 1860, the project was not approved until 1904. Inaugurated by Alfonso XIII in 1910, the street was built in three stages, each segment bearing a different name, although they are no longer used. The first, and most elegant – Avenida Conde de Peñalver (after the Mayor) – ran from Calle de Alcalá to Red de San Luis. The second phase, to the Plaza de Callao, was completed in 1922, while the final segment, ending in the Plaza de España, was built between 1925 and 1929. The new street gave architects an opportunity to prove their skill, providing a survey of early 20th-century design trends, including some of the best examples of modern architecture in the city.

 20

Plaza de España

📍 C7 🚇 Plaza de España

One of Madrid's popular meeting places is the Plaza de España. The square acquired its present appearance during the Franco period, with the construction of the massive Edificio España, on the northern side, between 1947 and 1953. Across the square is the Torre de Madrid, completed in 1957. It was nicknamed *La Jirafa* (the Giraffe), for a time it was the tallest concrete structure in the world.

TOP 3 GRAN VÍA BUILDINGS

Museo Chicote
🏠 Ground floor of Gran Vía 12
A cocktail bar that features an immaculately preserved Art Deco interior.

Edificio la Estrella
🏠 No. 10
This building is an eclectic mix of Neo-Classical design and ornamental touches.

La Gran Peña
🏠 No. 12
Noteworthy is the curved Art Deco façade.

The most attractive part of the square is its centre, with a massive stone obelisk, which was built in 1928. In front of the obelisk is a statue of Cervantes. Below him, Don Quixote rides his horse Rocinante while Sancho Panza trots alongside on his donkey.

The square has now been renovated to include 1,300 new trees and two exciting playgrounds for children.

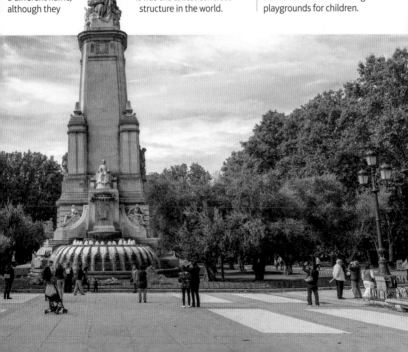

Plaza de Santa Ana

G10 **M**Sevilla, Antón Martín

This large pedestrian square, just four blocks southeast of the Puerta del Sol (p72), is a popular gathering place with a lively, at times rowdy, atmosphere. Built during the reign of Napoleon Bonaparte's brother Joseph (1808–13), the square took its name from the 16th-century Convent of Santa Ana that stood here, demolished to make way for the square.

Monuments to two of Spain's most famous writers testify to the square's strong literary connections. At one end is the brooding marble figure of Pedro Calderón de la Barca (1600–81). Madrid-born, he was the leading playwright in the twilight years of Spain's *Siglo de Oro* (Golden Century) of arts. His best-known work is *La Vida es Sueño* (Life is a Dream). The monument, with scenes from four of Calderón's plays adorning the pedestal, was sculpted by Juan Figueras in 1878. At the other end of the

PICTURE PERFECT
From Above

It's worth paying €8 to access The Radio Rooftop, a cocktail bar that overlooks Plaza de Santa Ana. Take a snapshot of local life on the bustling square below or use a wide lens to get a photo of the city beyond the square.

square, a statue of the poet Federico García Lorca, erected in 1998, commemorates the centenary of his birth and faces the Teatro Español (p116). Built in 1745, the theatre was originally known as the Teatro del Príncipe. It had to be restored in 1980 after a devastating fire.

The square's theatrical links go back even earlier, as the theatre stands on the spot of the Corral del Príncipe, one of Madrid's popular, 16th-century *corrales de comedias* (open courtyards where plays were staged). These tended to be boisterous affairs, often culminating in fights between the actors and the audience.

Across from the theatre are the glass balconies of ME Madrid Reina Victoria, one of Madrid's luxury hotels.

The other two sides of Plaza de Santa Ana and adjoining streets are home to some of the city's most popular bars and restaurants. The classic Cervecería Alemana, built in 1904 and once frequented by author Ernest Hemingway, is always packed with customers.

Around the corner from the theatre is the Viva Madrid. This well-known *taberna* is popular with the young and fashionable, and features notable 19th-century ceramic tableaux.

Calle de Preciados

E8 **M**Sol, Callao

This pedestrian street leading north from Puerta del Sol to the Plaza de Santo Domingo is now the domain of shoppers. It was originally a country path from the centre of old Madrid to the orchards of the Convent of San Martín which, until 1810, faced the Monasterio de las

A traditional tapas bar on Calle Nunez de Arce, just off the Plaza de Santa Ana

↑ The Manhattan-style Telefónica skyscraper set against the night sky

Descalzas Reales. Calle de Preciados acquired its contemporary look during the *Ensanche* (expansion) of the mid-19th century. It is the birthplace of Spain's most successful department store chain, El Corte Inglés. Adjoining the Plaza del Callao is a modern building occupied by FNAC, one of the city's best sources for music, DVDs and books. Between the two superstores, trendy boutiques share space with old-fashioned shops.

 23

Telefónica

📍 F8 🏠 Gran Vía 28
Ⓜ Gran Vía, Callao
🕐 Museum: 10am-8pm
Tue-Sun 🌐 espacio.funda
ciontelefonica.com

If the Telefónica building has an American look to it, it is because it was inspired by Manhattan's skyscrapers and designed by an American – Louis S Weeks – although the Spanish architect Ignacio de Cárdenas was made responsible for securing planning permission. Built between 1926 and 1929 to house the Spanish telephone company, its façade consists of tapered setbacks, ending in a central tower 81 m (266 ft) tall. The

little exterior ornamentation it has was added by Cárdenas so that the building would seem less out of place amid the neighbouring architecture. The clear view from the upper floors enabled the Republican defenders of the city to monitor the movements of besieging Nationalists in the Spanish Civil War.

The building and its history are the focal points of the Spanish TV show *Las Chicas del Cable* (The Cable Girls), a dramatic story about young women who worked as phone operators during an unstable political era, at the turn of the 20th century.

Part of the building is used for exhibitions; there is one that shows the evolution of telecommunications. Displays range from old phones to a bank of switchboards. Some of the Foundation's collection of modern art is now on long-term loan to the Museo Reina Sofía (p104).

24

Plaza del Callao

📍 E8 🏠 Plaza del
Callao Ⓜ Callao

Situated at the junction of Gran Vía and Calle de Preciados, the Plaza del Callao was named

DRINK

La Fontanilla
Look out for the shamrocks above the door of this Irish pub, which offers a broad selection of beer.

📍 D10 🏠 Calle Puerta
Cerrada 13 🌐 la
fontanillamadrid.com

Café de l'Opera
Tables under big white umbrellas on the terrace in front of the Teatro Real (p84) are ideal for a glass of cava before or after a production.

📍 D8 🏠 Calle Arrieta 6
🌐 elcafedelaopera.com

Delic
Bar/delicatessen with a global perspective that pours biodynamic wines and satisfies Madrid's passion for gin and tonics with several inventive offerings.

📍 C10 🏠 Costanilla de
San Andrés 14
🌐 delic.es

after a naval battle off the coast of Callao, Peru, in 1866. This square was once the movie mecca of film-loving Madrid, but today the only two surviving cinemas are the Art Deco Cine Callao, completed in 1927, and the Capitol. Most of the other cinemas along the Gran Vía have been converted into musical theatres or shops.

The Capitol cinema, housed in the Capitol building, was constructed in 1933. A superb example of Art Deco architecture, its features include a covered entrance and a vast, box-like interior, 35 m (115 ft) wide, adorned with simple lines and curves.

SHOP

Guantes Luque

This old-fashioned shop sells beautiful leather gloves in a rainbow of colours and gives a real taste of traditional Madrid.

Q F9 **A** Calle Espoz y Mina 3 **C** 915 22 32 87

La Violeta

The candied violets sold at this charming little shop are a favourite gift for special occasions.

Q F/G9 **A** Plaza de Canalejas 6 **W** lavioletaonline.es

Antigua Casa Talavera

A beautifully tiled exterior only hints at the richness of the Spanish ceramics to be discovered inside this quaint shop.

Q D8 **A** Calle Isabel la Católica 2 **W** antigua casatalavera.com

Desperate Literature

If you're looking for a large selection of used books, browse this eclectic collection, primarily in Spanish, French and English. Titles range from fiction and poetry to art and history.

Q D8 **A** Calle Campomanes 13 **W** desperate literature.com

Iglesia de San Ginés de Arlés

Q E9 **A** Calle Arenal 13 **C** 913 66 48 75 **M** Ópera, Callao, Sol **Ⓞ** 8:45am-1pm & 6-8:45pm Mon-Sat, 9:45am-1:45pm & 5:45-8:45pm Sun

This 17th-century church has numerous chapels with some of Madrid's most outstanding frescoes, sculptures and paintings. El Greco, Luca Giordano and Alonso Cano are a few of the artists displayed. Legend has it that an alligator, brought by Alonso de Montalbán (Isabel la Católica's admiral) in 1522, rested under the altar.

Teatro Real

Q D9 **A** Plaza de Oriente **M** Ópera **Ⓞ** 10:30am-4:30pm daily **◻** Aug **W** teatroreal.es

Madrid's opera house is an imposing six-sided grey building, made all the more impressive by the six floors below street level as well as the nine floors visible above ground. It was originally built around

1850. However, much of the structure that exists today is the result of a massive project to renovate the theatre, which took place between 1991 and 1997. The horseshoe-shaped main theatre area, decorated beautifully in red and gold with seating on five levels, holds 1,630 spectators and the stage area measures 1,430 sq m (15,400 sq ft). This, together with the curtain and the magnificent crystal chandelier weighing 2.5 tonnes, is among the theatre's noteworthy features.

On the second floor, there are four large foyers arranged around the main hall. They contain tapestries, paintings, mirrors, chandeliers and antiques. All of them are laid with carpets produced especially for the theatre by the Manuel Morón workshop in Ciudad Real, south of Madrid.

The second-floor restaurant has a ceiling representing Madrid's starlit sky as it was on the night of the theatre's inauguration (open for both lunch and dinner, but reserved for theatregoers on performance nights). The restaurant is in what was originally the ballroom, where Isabel II would often throw lively parties. On display are costumes from the operas *Aïda* and *Anne Boleyn*.

→ The awe-inspiring façade of Madrid's opera house, the Teatro Real

Madrid's opera house is an imposing six-sided grey building, made all the more impressive by the six floors below street level as well as the nine floors visible above ground.

On the sixth floor there is a cafeteria which has a good view overlooking the Plaza de Oriente (reserved for those who attend a performance).

The site has always been associated with the stage. In 1708, an Italian company built a small theatre here, which was demolished in 1735 to be replaced by a more ambitious building. However, due to the presence of underground streams, this theatre suffered severe structural problems. In 1816, it was torn down to make way for a modern opera house instigated by Fernando VII. Construction dragged on for 32 years and the theatre was finally inaugurated in 1850 by Isabel II on her 20th birthday. A production of Gaetano Donizetti's *La Favorita* marked the occasion, and the theatre became a centre of Madrid culture until the late 1920s. It appeared, however, that the new building was beset

with problems just like its predecessor, and needed constant repair work – finally it closed in 1988.

In 1991, an ambitious project to renovate the building was also plagued with problems. The architect died of a heart attack while inspecting the works and, when the theatre finally opened in October 1997 with a performance of Falla's *The Three-Cornered Hat*, it was way over budget and five years behind schedule.

27

Palacio del Senado

📍C8 🏛Plaza de la Marina Española 🚇Plaza de España, Ópera 🕐For tours only: 10am, 11am, noon, 1pm, 4pm, 5pm & 6pm Mon-Fri 🌐senado.es

The upper house of the Cortes (Spanish parliament) is installed in a 16th-century monastery, adapted in 1814 for the purpose. It became

the Senate headquarters when a two-chamber system was introduced 23 years later.

The monastery's courtyards were covered to create more meeting rooms. Some, such as the Salón de los Pasos Perdidos (Hall of the Lost Footsteps), contain paintings depicting great moments in Spanish history. Among these are the surrender of Granada, and Queen Regent María Cristina swearing to uphold the Constitution in 1897.

The library is a magnificent example of English Gothic style, dating from the turn of the 20th century. Ornate tiers of black metal bookcases contain 14,000 volumes, including a copy of Nebrija's *Gramática*, the first Spanish grammar book. In 1991 a granite-and-glass circular wing was added at the back of the building.

🏔 GREAT VIEW
Evening Colours

Join *Madrileños* on the terraces at the Jardínes de Las Vistillas, a 10-minute walk from the Teatro Real, for a bird's-eye view of the sun setting over the Río Manzanares and Casa de Campo.

28
La Latina

 C10 Ⓜ **La Latina**

The district of La Latina, together with the adjacent Lavapiés, is considered to be the heart of *castizo* Madrid *(p153)*. This term describes the culture of the traditional working classes of Madrid – that of the true *Madrileño*.

La Latina runs along the city's southern hillside from the Plaza Puerta de Moros through the streets where El Rastro flea market is held. To the east it merges with Lavapiés.

La Latina's steep streets are lined with tall, narrow houses, renovated to form an attractive neighbourhood. There are a number of trendy bars around

 HIDDEN GEM
San Pedro el Viejo

La Latina is home to one of Madrid's oldest churches *(Calle Nuncio 14)*, known for its 14th-century brick tower with distinctive horseshoe-arch windows in the Mudéjar style.

the Plaza de la Cebada, which add to the charm of this part of Madrid. It is worth wandering through simply to savour its atmosphere and authenticity.

29
El Rastro

E11 **Calle de la Ribera de Curtidores** Ⓜ **La Latina, Tirso de Molina** ⏰ **9am-3pm Sun & public hols**

Madrid's flea market, established in the Middle Ages, has its hub in the Plaza de Cascorro and sprawls downhill towards the Río Manzanares. The main street is the Calle de la Ribera de Curtidores, or "Tanners' Riverbank", once the centre of the slaughterhouse and tanning industries.

Although some people claim that El Rastro has changed a great deal since its heyday during the 19th century, plenty of *Madrileños*, as well as tourists still shop here. They come in search of a bargain from the stalls, which sell anything from new furniture to second-hand clothes. For crafts and antiques head to the Plaza de General Vara del Rey and the Galerías Piquer *(Calle Ribera de*

↑ A stall crammed with household goods at El Rastro flea market

Curtidores 29). The Calle de Embajadores is the area's other main street. It runs down past the dusty Baroque façade of the Iglesia de San Cayetano, designed by José Churriguera and Pedro de Ribera. Its interior has been restored since fire destroyed it during the Civil War.

30
Plaza de la Paja

C10 Ⓜ **La Latina** ⏰ **Iglesia de San Andrés: 9am-1pm & 6-8pm Mon-Sat, 9am-1pm Sun & public hols; Capilla del Obispo: for tours only at 10am, 10:45am & 11:30am Tue, 4pm & 4:45pm Thu**

Once the focus of medieval Madrid, the area around the Plaza de la Paja – literally "Straw Square" – is still atmospheric. With many interesting buildings nearby, the area is pleasant to walk around.

As you climb upwards from the Calle de Segovia, a glimpse left along Calle del Príncipe

Anglona yields a view of the Mudéjar-style brick tower of the Iglesia de San Pedro, dating from the 14th century. Ahead is the Capilla del Obispo (Bishop's Chapel), which first belonged to the adjoining Palacio Vargas. One of the few examples of Gothic architecture in Madrid, the chapel has an inner door made of walnut, decorated with reliefs depicting biblical scenes. The adjacent Baroque-style Iglesia de San Andrés, with its cherub-covered dome, can also be visited. Since it was partially destroyed during the Spanish Civil War, little remains of the original 12th-century church. It was frequented by the patron saint of Madrid, San Isidro, who was also buried here. His remains were moved to the Basílica de Nuestra Señora del Buen in the 18th century.

Museo Cerralbo

C7 Calle de Ventura Rodríguez 17 Plaza de España, Ventura Rodríguez 9:30am–3pm Tue–Sat (also 5–8pm Thu), 10am–3pm Sun Mon, 1 & 6 Jan, 1 May & some public hols culturaydeporte.gob.es/mcerralbo

This 19th-century mansion is a monument to Enrique de Aguilera y Gamboa, the 17th Marquis of Cerralbo. He bequeathed his lifetime's collection of art and artifacts to the nation in 1922, which ranges from Iberian pottery to 18th-century marble busts. One of the star exhibits is El Greco's *The Ecstasy of Saint Francis of Assisi*. There are also paintings by Ribera, Zurbarán, Alonso Cano and Goya. The focal point of the main floor is the ballroom, which is lavishly decorated.

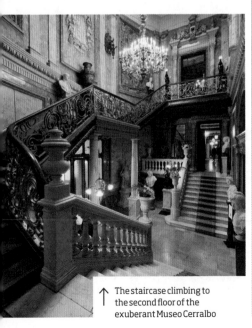

↑ The staircase climbing to the second floor of the exuberant Museo Cerralbo

STAY

Dear Hotel
Rooms with simple decor look towards Gran Vía or Plaza de España. There is a rooftop pool with panoramic views.

D7 Gran Vía 80 dearhotelmadrid.com

Gran Meliá Palacio de los Duques
A 19th-century palace-turned-hotel featuring a historic garden as well as a modern pool and wellness centre.

D8 Cuesta de Santo Domingo 5–7 melia.com

The Hat
Hostel with private and shared rooms (including some for women only); a good value option behind Plaza Mayor.

E10 Calle Imperial 9 thehatmadrid.com

Posada del Dragon
A stylish hotel in a historic inn, with cosy rooms. It has a tapas bar and a restaurant.

D10 Calle de la Cava Baja 14 posadadeldragon.com

Room-Mate Mario
Expect minimalist, chic design at this no-frills hotel on a quiet street near the Teatro Real.

D8 Calle de Campomanes 4 room-matehotels.com

A SHORT WALK
WEST MADRID

Distance 2 km (1 mile) **Time** 30 minutes
Nearest metro Tirso de Molina, Sol

Stretching from the charming Plaza de la Villa to the busy
Puerta del Sol, the compact heart of West Madrid is steeped
in history and full of interesting sights. As you walk through the
area, you'll feel poignant moments in the city's history seeping
through the streets. This is nowhere more apparent than in
the Plaza Mayor, which you'll cross more than once. Trials and
executions under the orders of the Inquisition *(p73)* were held
in this porticoed square. Despite this gruesome past, it is
West Madrid's finest piece of architecture, a legacy of the
Habsburgs. Other buildings of note are the Colegiata
de San Isidro and the Palacio de Santa
Cruz. Although the route is short
in length, take your time,
stopping to sit in one of
the area's numerous cafés
and browsing among the
stalls of the Mercado de
San Miguel.

*The beautiful **Plaza Mayor**
(p68) competes with the
Puerta del Sol as the focus of
West Madrid. The arcades at
the base of the three-storey
buildings are filled with cafés
and craft shops.*

*The **Mercado de San Miguel** (p76) is
housed in a 19th-century building with
wrought-iron columns. It's a great
place to stop for a snack.*

PLAZA
COMMANDANT
MORENAS

CALLE MAYOR

PLAZA
DE LA
VILLA

START

CORDÓN

PUÑONROSTRO

*Old Town Hall
(ayuntamiento)*

Casa de Cisneros

*A statue of Álvaro
de Bazán stands in the
centre of the **Plaza de
la Villa** (p75).*

0 metres   100   N
0 yards   100   ↑

Arco de Cuchilleros

*The **Basílica Pontificia de
San Miguel** (p77) is an
imposing 18th-century
church with a beautiful
façade and a graceful
interior. It is one of very few
churches in Spain inspired by
the Italian Baroque style.*

←

People visiting the
Mercado de San Miguel
for a bite to eat at dusk

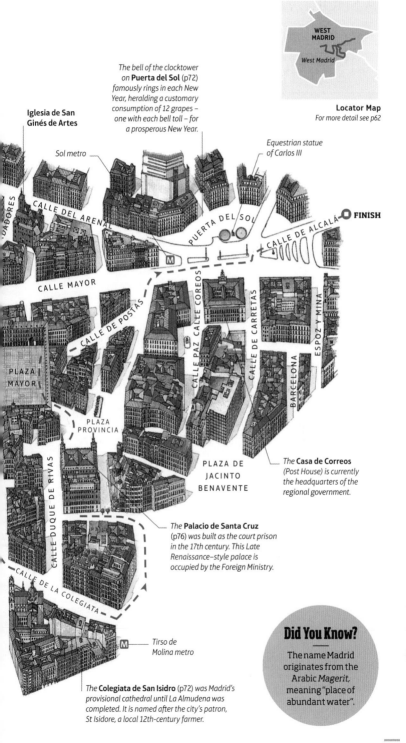

Locator Map
For more detail see p62

WEST MADRID
West Madrid

Iglesia de San
Ginés de Artes

Sol metro

The bell of the clocktower
on **Puerta del Sol** (p72)
*famously rings in each New
Year, heralding a customary
consumption of 12 grapes –
one with each bell toll – for
a prosperous New Year.*

Equestrian statue
of Carlos III

FINISH

CALLE DEL ARENAL

PUERTA DEL SOL

CALLE DE ALCALÁ

CALLE MAYOR

CALLE DE POSTAS

CALLE CORREOS

CALLE PAZ

CALLE DE CARRETAS

ESPOZ Y MINA

BARCELONA

PLAZA
MAYOR

PLAZA
PROVINCIA

PLAZA DE
JACINTO
BENAVENTE

CALLE DUQUE DE RIVAS

*The **Casa de Correos**
(Post House) is currently
the headquarters of the
regional government.*

*The **Palacio de Santa Cruz**
(p76) was built as the court prison
in the 17th century. This Late
Renaissance–style palace is
occupied by the Foreign Ministry.*

CALLE DE LA COLEGIATA

Tirso de
Molina metro

*The **Colegiata de San Isidro** (p72) was Madrid's
provisional cathedral until La Almudena was
completed. It is named after the city's patron,
St Isidore, a local 12th-century farmer.*

Did You Know?

The name Madrid
originates from the
Arabic *Magerit*,
meaning "place of
abundant water".

A SHORT WALK
AUSTRIAS DISTRICT

Distance 2 km (1 mile) **Walking time**
30 minutes **Terrain** Easy, generally flat
and paved **Nearest metro** La Latina
Stopping-off point Café de Oriente

West Madrid was mostly built on a plateau, and
because of its superb vantage point, the Moors
built their *alcázar* (fortress) on the ridge. The
magnificent Palacio Real – one of the most
illustrious and renowned sights in the city – now
stands on the site. This walk takes in the best of
the west of the city, with its contrast between
wide, majestic boulevards and grand squares,
and follows the ridge and Calle de Bailén past
monuments such as the Arab city walls, two
cathedrals, the Royal Palace, a Habsburg convent
and an incongruous Egyptian temple. For
something spectacular, plan this walk in the
early evening, reaching the Templo de Debod
just in time to watch the sun set.

↑ A view of the Catedral de la Almudena
from the Terraza de las Vistillas

Continue up Ferraz to the
Templo de Debod (p158),
a 2nd-century-BC Egyptian
temple presented to Spain
in 1968. Get some photo-
graphs of the temple, then
relax and watch the sun set
over the city.

FINISH

Templo de
Debod

Parque de la
Montaña

Jardines
de Fer

Príncipe
Pío Ⓜ

CUESTA DE SAN VICENTE

Jardines del
Palacio Real

Campo del
Moro

Catedral de la
Almudena

Parque
de Atenas

CUESTA DE LA VI
Parque del
Mohame

CALLE DE SEGOVIA

Jardines
las Visti

The **Basílica de
San Francisco el Grande**
(p70) *features the largest
dome in Madrid.*

San Franc
el Gra

START

0 metres 300 N
0 yards 300 ↑

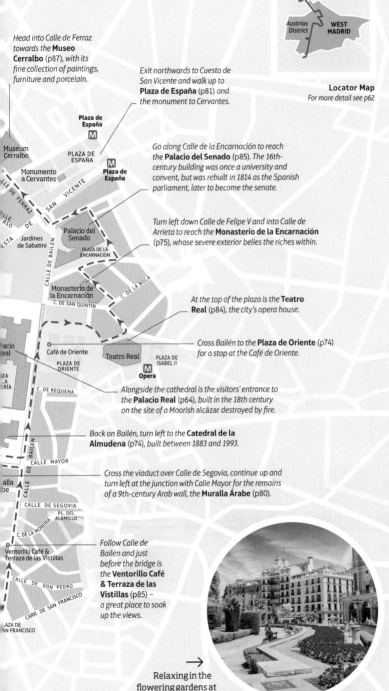

Head into Calle de Ferraz towards the **Museo Cerralbo** (p87), with its fine collection of paintings, furniture and porcelain.

Exit northwards to Cuesta de San Vicente and walk up to **Plaza de España** (p81) and the monument to Cervantes.

Go along Calle de la Encarnación to reach the **Palacio del Senado** (p85). The 16th-century building was once a university and convent, but was rebuilt in 1814 as the Spanish parliament, later to become the senate.

Turn left down Calle de Felipe V and into Calle de Arrieta to reach the **Monasterio de la Encarnación** (p75), whose severe exterior belies the riches within.

At the top of the plaza is the **Teatro Real** (p84), the city's opera house.

Cross Bailén to the **Plaza de Oriente** (p74) for a stop at the Café de Oriente.

Alongside the cathedral is the visitors' entrance to the **Palacio Real** (p64), built in the 18th century on the site of a Moorish alcázar destroyed by fire.

Back on Bailén, turn left to the **Catedral de la Almudena** (p74), built between 1883 and 1993.

Cross the viaduct over Calle de Segovia, continue up and turn left at the junction with Calle Mayor for the remains of a 9th-century Arab wall, the **Muralla Árabe** (p80).

Follow Calle de Bailén and just before the bridge is the **Ventorillo Café & Terraza de las Vistillas** (p85) – a great place to soak up the views.

→ Relaxing in the flowering gardens at the Plaza de Oriente

Map labels:
Museum Cerralbo
PLAZA DE ESPAÑA
Plaza de España M
Monumento a Cervantes
SAN VICENTE
CALLE DE FERRAZ
Palacio del Senado
PLAZA DE LA ENCARNACION
Jardines de Sabatini
CALLE DE BAILEN
Monasterio de la Encarnación
C. DE SAN QUINTIN
C. DE LA BOLA
Palacio Real
Café de Oriente
Teatro Real
PLAZA DE ORIENTE
PLAZA DE ISABEL II
Opera M
C. DE REQUENA
BAILEN
CALLE MAYOR
CALLE DE
CALLE DE SEGOVIA
PL. DEL ALAMILLO
C. DE LA MORERIA
Ventorillo Café & Terraza de las Vistillas
CALLE DE DON PEDRO
CARR. DE SAN FRANCISCO
PLAZA DE SAN FRANCISCO

EAST MADRID

To the east of the city centre, there once lay an idyllic district of market gardens known as the Prado, the "Meadow". In the 16th century a monastery was built here and later the Habsburgs extended it to form a palace, of which only fragments still remain; the palace gardens are now the popular Parque del Retiro.

This development attracted intellectuals to this corner of the city and the Huertas district, which had once been farmland, soon became the haunt of Spain's most famous writers of the time. During the 17th century, the Barrio de Las Letras (Writers' Quarter) played host to everyone from Miguel de Cervantes to Lope de Vega.

The Bourbon monarchs chose this eastern area to expand and embellish the city in the 18th century. They built grand squares with fountains, a triumphal gateway, and, in 1785, work began on a Neo-Classical building that was set to house a museum of natural history. The ambition never came to fruition and the Museo del Prado opened here instead in 1819, housing works from the former Spanish Royal Collection. In the 20th century, the Prado was joined by the Museo Nacional Centro de Arte Reina Sofía, a collection of modern Spanish and international art, and the Museo Nacional Thyssen-Bornemisza, displaying works from across the centuries, to form the "Golden Triangle of Art".

CHUECA

C. DE BARBARA DE BRAGANZA

Biblioteca
Nacional
de España

Estación de
Recoletos

RECOLET

MALASAÑA, CHUECA
AND SALAMANCA
p130

EAST
MADRID

Cuartel General
del Ejército
de Tierra

8

GRAN VIA

Iglesia de
San José

Plaza de
Cibeles
7

CALLE DE ALCALA

Puert
Al

Edificio
Metrópolis **22**

Círculo de
Bellas Artes
8 **19**

Banco de
España **M**

Banco de
España **9**

7 **11**
Palacio de
Comunicaciones

CALLE DE
VALENZUELA

Museo
Nacional
de Artes
Decorativa

8

WEST
MADRID
p60

M Sevilla

CALLE DE ALCALA

CALLE DE LOS MADRAZO

Teatro de la
Zarzuela

CALLE DE ZORRILLA

Museo
Naval **10**

CALLE DE
MONTALBAN

CALLE DE ARLABAN

CALLE DE SAN JERONIMO

9

Congreso de
los Diputados
23

Museo Nacional
Thyssen-
Bornemisza **1**

CALLE DE

JUAN DE MENA

Bolsa de
Comercio **15**

ANTONIO MAURA

Salón de
Reinos **13**

Casón
Bue
Reti **24**

6

Ateneo
de Madrid
16 **9**

PLAZA
DE LAS
CORTES

Fuente de
Neptuno **18**

6
Hotel
Ritz

Real Academia
Española **26**

CALLE DE FELIPE IV

21
Westin
Palace **2**

PLAZA CANOVAS
DEL CASTILLO

CALLE DE LA ACADEM

Teatro
Español **20**
5 **10**

Casa-Museo de
Lope de Vega **14**

CALLE DE CERVANTES

Edificio
Jerónimos

Parroquia de
Jerónimo el R

12

PLAZA DE
MATUTE

CALLE DE LOPE DE VEGA

Museo
del Prado **2**

CALLE DE MORETO

CALLE DE ALBERTO BO

Real Academia
de la Historia **17**

CALLE DE LAS HUERTAS

PLAZA
JESUS

CALLE DE ESPALTER

Antón
Martín **M**

CALLE DE SANTA MARIA

PLAZA DE
SAN JUAN

PLAZA DE
PLATERIA DE
MARTINEZ

PLAZA DE
MURILLO

Cine Doré
11

CALLE DE MORATIN

3

VERONICA

Real Jardín
Botánico **28**

CALLE DE ATOCHA

10

CALLE DE LA
MAGDALENA

PLAZA DE
ANTON
MARTIN

1

5

3

GOBERNADOR

CaixaForum **25**

CALLE DE FUCAR

CALLE DE ALMADEN

Real Jardín
Botánico

M
Lavapies

Palacio de
Fernán Núñez **32**

Convento
Santa Isabel

CALLE DE SANTA ISABEL

Estación del
Arte **M**

CALLE DE CLAUDIO MOYAN

Ministerio de
Agricultura **27**

Mu
Nacio
Antro

CALLE DE ARGUMOSA

CALLE DEL DOCTOR FORQUET

CALLE DEL HOSPITAL

PLAZA
SANCHEZ
BUSTILLO

PLAZA DEL
EMPERADOR
CARLOS V

Estación de
Atocha

Atocha
RENFE **M**

12

Museo Nacional
Centro de
Arte Reina Sofía **3**

30
Estación de
Atocha

RONDA DE ATOCHA

CALLE DE MENDEZ ALVARO

Palos de la
Frontera **M**

CALLE DE SEBASTIÁN ELCANO

CANARIAS

EAST MADRID

Must Sees

1 Museo Nacional Thyssen-Bornemisza
2 Museo del Prado
3 Museo Nacional Centro de Arte Reina Sofía
4 Parque del Retiro

Experience More

5 Puerta de Alcalá
6 Hotel Ritz
7 Plaza de Cibeles
8 Museo Nacional de Artes Decorativas
9 Banco de España
10 Museo Naval
11 Palacio de Comunicaciones
12 Parroquia de San Jerónimo el Real
13 Salón de Reinos
14 Casa-Museo de Lope de Vega
15 Bolsa de Comercio
16 Ateneo de Madrid
17 Real Academia de la Historia
18 Fuente de Neptuno
19 Círculo de Bellas Artes
20 Teatro Español
21 Westin Palace
22 Edificio Metrópolis
23 Congreso de los Diputados
24 Casón del Buen Retiro
25 CaixaForum
26 Real Academia Española
27 Ministerio de Agricultura
28 Real Jardín Botánico
29 Museo Nacional de Antropología
30 Estación de Atocha
31 Real Observatorio Astronómico de Madrid
32 Palacio de Fernán Núñez

Eat

1 TriCiclo
2 Estado Puro
3 Vinoteca Moratín

Drink

4 Salmón Guru
5 Jazz Bar
6 La Venencia
7 CentroCentro Terrace Bar
8 La Pecera

Stay

9 One Shot Prado 23
10 Room Mate Alicia
11 Catalonia Atocha

❶ 🎨 🎭 🍴 🖥 🛍

MUSEO NACIONAL THYSSEN-BORNEMISZA

📍H9 🚍Paseo del Prado 8 🚌001, 10, 14, 27, 34, 37, 45, C03 Ⓜ Banco de España, Sevilla
🕐 Jun-mid-Sep: 10am-10pm Tue-Sat, 10am-7pm Sun & Mon for temp exhibs; mid-Sep-May: noon-4pm Mon, 10am-7pm Tue-Sun 🚫1 Jan, 1 May & 25 Dec 🌐museothyssen.org

Regarded by many critics as the most important privately assembled art collection in the world, the Museo Nacional Thyssen-Bornemisza illustrates the history of European art, from European primitives through to 20th-century works. The museum's excellent collection, consisting of more than 1,000 paintings, includes masterpieces by the likes of Titian, Goya, Van Gogh and Picasso.

This magnificent museum is based on the fine collection assembled by Baron Heinrich Thyssen-Bornemisza and his son, Hans Heinrich. In 1992 it was installed in Madrid's 18th-century Villahermosa Palace, and was sold to the nation the following year. A collection of mainly Impressionist works acquired by Carmen Thyssen-Bornemisza,

Hans Heinrich's wife, opened in 2004. The museum's galleries are arranged around a covered central courtyard, which rises the full height of the building. The top floor exhibits early Italian art through to 17th-century works, while the first floor continues with 17th-century Dutch art and Expressionism. The ground floor displays 20th-century paintings.

This magnificent museum is based on the fine collection assembled by Baron Heinrich Thyssen-Bornemisza and his son, Hans Heinrich.

Once housed in the Villahermosa Palace, the museum has a Neo-Classical façade and *(inset)* a modern extension ↑

Walking through the museum's salmon-pink interior ↓

TOP 7 MUSEUM HIGHLIGHTS

Portrait of Giovanna degli Albizzi Tornabuoni (1489-90)
A symbolic painting by Domenico Ghirlandaio.

Venus y Cupido (1606-11)
Peter Paul Rubens' depiction of a reflection of ideal beauty.

The Grand Canal From San Vio, Venice (c 1723-24)
This Canaletto painting is prized for its topographic accuracy.

Les Vessenots in Auvers (1890)
A painting of old country cottages by Van Gogh.

Swaying Dancer (1877-79)
Degas conveys the ballerina's movement.

Hotel Room (1931)
Edward Hopper's study of urban isolation.

Woman in Bath (1963)
Roy Lichtenstein's iconic comic-strip-style painting.

Exploring the Collection

The museum's collection provides a sweeping overview of Western art between the 14th and 20th centuries, touching on every school and trend in European art over the last 500 years. It is distinctive from the Prado in areas, such as in Italian and Dutch primitives, 19th-century American painting, Impressionism and Expressionism. Portraiture from different periods is also well represented. The Carmen Thyssen Collection contains mainly landscapes, from 17th-century Dutch examples to Impressionist and Expressionist works.

↑ Degas' *Swaying Dancer*, a modern masterpiece

←
Roy Lichtenstein's *Woman in Bath*, a popular work of Pop Art on display

The Collection

The Birth of the Renaissance

The works on display range from early Italian art with a return to naturalism, to medieval art that illustrates how Italian influences combined with the Gothic style popular in Europe, such as *Koerbecke's Assumption of the Virgin* (c 1457). The collection of early Dutch art includes two jewels, Jan van Eyck's *The Annunciation* (c 1433-35) and Petrus Christus's *Our Lady of the Dry Tree* (c 1465).

Renaissance to Baroque

▷ This section encompasses the height of the Renaissance, ending with Baroque art and 18th-century Italian painting. An outstanding example of high Renaissance art in Italy is Carpaccio's *Young Knight in a Landscape* (1510, right). Room 12 begins with early Baroque, when artists started to break with the rigid Classical rules of the Renaissance and introduce elements of drama and pathos into their work. This new trend flourishes in rooms 13-15.

Dutch and Flemish Painting

The remarkable series of Dutch and Flemish art is a strong point of the collection. Room 19 features 17th-century Flemish painting, though the big attraction is Rubens' *Venus y Cupid* (c 1606-11). Some of the most interesting works are in rooms 22-26, where everyday scenes, landscapes and informal portraits reveal the unique quality of Dutch art. Excellent examples are Frans Hals' *Family Group in a Landscape* (c 1645-8) and Nicholas Maes's *The Naughty Drummer* (c 1655).

Rococo to Realism

◁ Rococo took Europe by storm in the early 18th century, and is best represented by François Boucher's *La Toilette* (1742, left). Meanwhile, the development of landscape art in America fulfilled a need to express the country's romantic spirit and pride, and is best illustrated through the paintings of Winslow Homer, especially *Waverly Oaks* (1864). In Europe, the 19th century saw the dawn of Romanticism, a transition clearly seen in Goya's works. The series also demonstrates a trend towards Realism, a shift that is depicted in Corot's *The Parc des Lions at Port-Marly* (1872).

Modern Masters

▷ Some of the most highly regarded exponents of the Impressionist movement are represented in rooms 32-33, including Manet, Degas with *Swaying Dancer* (1877-79), Renoir and Sisley. A development that came from Impressionism was Post-Impressionism, of which Gauguin's *Mata Mua* (c 1892, right), part of the Carmen Thyssen-Bornemisza Collection, is a fine example. Eight ground floor rooms deal with modern and contemporary art, from the avant-garde to Surrealism and Pop Art. Among the gems are Picasso's *Harlequin with a Mirror* (1923) and portraits by Lucian Freud.

↑ Admiring Caravaggio's *Saint Catherine* (1598) oil painting

THE EVOLUTION OF MODERN ART

In 1863, artists whose work was rejected by Paris's art salon were displayed in a parallel Salon des Refusés. This show of "discarded art" marked the birth of Impressionism, which freed the artist and led to Post-Impressionism and Symbolism, which centred on the artist as an individual. A name that did endure was Expressionism, which started in Germany. This school drew on the artist's emotions, and sought to precipitate an emotion in the viewer. Early practitioners were centred around the Dresden group, "The Bridge", founded in 1905. Among its members was Karl Schmidt-Rottluf, whose work can be seen in the museum.

② ⊗ ⊗ ⊗ ⊕ ⊕

MUSEO DEL PRADO

📍J10 🏠Paseo del Prado 🚌001, 6, 10, 14, 19, 26, 27, 32, 34, 37, 45, C03, E1 Ⓜ️Estación del Arte, Banco de España 🕐10am-8pm Mon-Sat, 10am-7pm Sun & public hols; reduced hours 10am-2pm on 6 Jan, 24 & 31 Dec 🚫1 Jan, 1 May, 25 Dec 🌐museodelprado.es

A must for any art fan, the Prado Museum contains the world's greatest assembly of Spanish painting – especially works by Velázquez and Goya – ranging from the 12th to 19th centuries. But that's not all – it also houses impressive foreign collections, particularly of Italian and Flemish works.

The Neo-Classical main building of the Museo Nacional del Prado, as it's formally known, was designed in 1785 by Juan de Villanueva on the orders of Carlos III. It was built to house the Natural History Cabinet, a museum of natural history, but it was under Carlos III's grandson, Fernando VII, that it opened as the Royal Museum of Paintings and Sculptures in 1819. The collection initially comprised 311 Spanish paintings, but the current collection of over 20,000 works reflects the historical power of the Spanish Crown. The Low Countries and parts of Italy were under Spanish domination for centuries and are well represented in the collection, while the 18th century was an era of French influence. The Prado is worthy of repeated visits, but if you go only once, see the Spanish works of the 17th century.

Upon the deposition of Isabella II in 1868, the museum was nationalized and the collection grew beyond its original building. The expansion has been ongoing since 1918. In 2007, a new building was constructed over the adjacent church's cloister to house temporary exhibitions. Norman Foster and Carlos Rubio Carvajal's redesign of the Salón de Reinos (p114), a building nearby, was chosen in 2016 as the museum's next expansion.

ART AT WAR

As tensions peaked and the Spanish Civil War commenced, the League of Nations recommended the removal of some of the Museo del Prado's most precious treasures. Museum staff sent 353 paintings, 168 drawings and the Dauphin's Treasure first to Valencia, then on to Girona, before they finally arrived safely in Geneva. Although the Spanish Civil War ended in 1939, the advent of World War II meant that the art had to travel back to the Prado – across French territory – under the cover of darkness.

→

The museum's imposing Goya Square entrance as the sun begins to set

↑ Art enthusiasts viewing Hieronymus Bosch paintings in one of the Prado's galleries

← Admiring the museum's collection of Muse sculptures

↑ Visitors taking in *The Clothed Maja*, an early 19th-century work by Goya

Exploring the Collection

The museum's extensive permanent collection is arranged chronologically over three main floors. Classical sculpture is on the ground floor, Velázquez on the first floor, and the extensive Goya collection across the Murillo side of all three floors. The museum is accessed via Puerta ed los Jerónimos, to the left of the ticket office. Visitors are encouraged to reserve their tickets online.

Did You Know?

Goya was accused of obscenity for his naked version of *The Clothed Maja*, exhibited beside it in the Prado.

The large interior of one of the Prado's many galleries ↓

The Collection

Spanish Painting

Right up to the 19th century, Spanish painting focused on religious and royal themes, offering a sharp focus that seems to have suited Spanish painters. What is often considered as a truly Spanish style - with its highly wrought emotion and deepening sombreness - first started to emerge in the 16th century in the paintings of the Mannerists, of which the Prado has an impressive collection. The 17th century is best represented by the work of Diego Velázquez.

Flemish and Dutch Painting

▷ Spain's long connection with the Low Countries naturally resulted in an intense admiration for the so-called Flemish primitives. Most notable are nearly 100 canvases by the 17th-century Flemish painter Peter Paul Rubens, including *The Adoration of the Magi (right)*. The most significant Dutch painting on display is Rembrandt's *Artemisia*.

Italian Painting

▷ Botticelli's dramatic wooden panels telling *The Story of Nastagio degli Onesti*, a vision of a knight condemned to kill his own beloved, were commissioned by two rich Florentine families and are a sinister high point. Raphael contributes the superb *The Holy Family with a Lamb (right)*, while *Christ Washing the Disciples' Feet*, an early masterpiece by Tintoretto, reveals the painter's brilliant handling of perspective. Titian, who served as court painter to Carlos I, and Caravaggio are also represented.

French Painting

Marriages between French and Spanish royalty in the 17th century, culminating in the 18th-century Bourbon accession to the throne, brought French art to Spain. The Prado has eight works attributed to Poussin, among them his serene *St Cecilia* and *Landscape with St Jerome*. The magnificent *Landscape with the Embarkation of St Paula Romana at Ostia* is the best work here by Claude Lorrain. Among the 18th-century artists featured are Antoine Watteau and Jean Ranc. *Felipe V* is the work of the royal portraitist Louis-Michel van Loo.

German Painting

◁ Although German art is not especially well represented in the Prado's collection, there are a number of paintings by Albrecht Dürer, including his classical depictions of Adam and Eve *(left)*. His lively *Self-Portrait* of 1498, painted at the tender age of 26, is undoubtedly the highlight of the small but valuable German collection in the museum. Lucas Cranach is also featured and works by the late 18th-century painter Anton Raffael Mengs include some magnificent portraits of Carlos III.

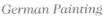

3 ⊘ Ⓜ 🍽 🖥 🏛

MUSEO NACIONAL CENTRO DE ARTE REINA SOFÍA

📍H12 🏠Calle de Santa Isabel 52 🚌 Ⓜ Estación del Arte
🕐10am-8pm Mon, Wed-Sat, 10am-2:30pm Sun ✕Tue,
1 & 6 Jan, 1 & 15 May, 9 Nov, 24, 25 & 31 Dec, some public
hols 🌐museoreinasofia.es

Perhaps most famous for Picasso's *Guernica*,
this museum of 20th-century art holds
other major works by influential artists,
including pieces by Miró and Dalí. The
museum has been at the cutting
edge since it opened in 1992 and
continues to reinvent itself.

Housed in Madrid's former General
Hospital, the museum's collection is as
exciting and impressive as its building. Built
in the late 18th century and designed by José
de Hermosilla and Francisco Sabatini, the
hospital was shut down in 1965, but survived
demolition as it was declared a national monument in
1977 due to its history and unique architecture. Restoration
of the building began under the direction of Antonio Fernández
Alba, and in April 1986 the Reina Sofía Art Centre opened. The
distinct steel and glass elevator towers, designed by Spanish
architects José Luis Iñiguez de Onzoño and Antonio Vázquez de
Castro in collaboration with British architect Ian Ritchie, were
added in 1988. The collection was finally inaugurated as a
permanent collection – now commonly referred to as simply
the Museo Reina Sofía – in 1992. The latest major extension,
designed by Jean Nouvel, was added in 2005. Named after
its architect, this stunning building increased the museum's
exhibition space and includes Collection 3: From Revolt to
Postmodernity, a library, a café and
auditoriums which host various events
such as film screenings and concerts.

Did You Know?

Jean Nouvel was
awarded the Pritzker
Prize, architecture's
highest honour,
in 2008.

← *Wheat & Steak*, a
sculpture by Spanish
artist Antoni Miralda

INSIDER TIP
Free Time

Entry to the museum is free after 6pm every day apart from Tuesday and Sunday. Certain professions can also get free admission with accreditation, regardless of the day. Check the website for details.

↑ Roy Lichtenstein's *Brushstroke* in Nouvel's extension, and *(inset)* the original building

Exploring the Collection

The 20th century has undoubtedly been the most brilliant period in the history of Spanish art since the 17th century. Many facets of the Spanish artistic genius are on show in the Museo Reina Sofía. Sculpture, paintings and even work by the Surrealist film-maker Luis Buñuel provide a skilfully arranged tour through an eventful century. The permanent collection, in the Sabatini Building, is arranged around an open courtyard. Collection 1, on the second floor, displays works dating from 1900 to 1945, and includes rooms dedicated to important movements such as Cubism and Surrealism; Collection 2, on the fourth floor, has works dating from 1945 to 1968, including representatives of Pop Art, Minimalism and more recent tendencies; Collection 3: From Revolt to Postmodernity is dedicated to art from the 1960s to the 1980s.

↑ A crowd gathering in front of Picasso's spectacular *Guernica*

Did You Know?

The museum is named after Queen Sofía of Spain, mother of the current King Felipe VI.

PICASSO'S GUERNICA

The most well-known single work of the 20th century, this Civil War protest painting was commissioned by the Spanish Republican government in 1937 for a Paris exhibition. Picasso found his inspiration in the mass air attack of the same year on the Basque town of Gernika-Lumo, by German pilots flying for the Nationalist air force. The painting hung in a New York gallery until 1981, reflecting the artist's wish that it should not return to Spain until democracy was re-established. It was moved to the Reina Sofía from the Prado (p100) in 1992.

The Collection

The Beginnings of Modern Spanish Art

▶ Following the storm of creativity that culminated with Goya in the 19th century, Spanish painting went through an unremarkable period. A few artists managed to break the mould, hinting at the dawn of a new era of artistic brilliance; the museum displays the brooding works of Gutiérrez Solana, whose favourite subjects are the people of his native Madrid. Influenced by the Spanish masters, his paintings include *La Tertulia del Café de Pombo* (1920, *right*).

Pablo Picasso

The works on display span five decades in the life of Pablo Picasso. The first image visitors notice is the haunting *Woman in Blue* (1901), one of Picasso's earliest works from his so-called "blue" period. In Room 206 is the most-visited piece in the collection – the vast *Guernica* (1937). Aside from its unquestionable artistic merits, the canvas has a deep historical significance for Spaniards.

Miró, Dalí and the Surrealists

Joan Miró turned his hand to many styles. His Surrealist experiments of the 1920s provide evidence of his love of the vivid colours and bold shapes of Catalan folk art. His fellow Catalan, Salvador Dalí, is especially well known as a member of the Surrealist movement, which depended on access to subconscious images without censorship by the rational mind. Other prominent Surrealists whose work is displayed here include Benjamín Palencia, Oscar Domínguez and Luis Buñuel. Dalí's Surrealist masterpiece, *The Great Masturbator* (1929), hangs in contrast to the realistic *Girl at the Window* (1925). Like many of his contemporaries, Dalí embraced widely differing styles during his career.

Julio González

◀ A friend and contemporary of Gargallo and Picasso, Julio González is known as the father of modern Spanish sculpture, chiefly because of his pioneering use of iron as a raw material. Look out for González' humorous self-portrait entitled *Tête dite "Lapin"*, or *Head called "Rabbit"* (1930, *left*).

The Paris School

The turbulent history of Spain in the 20th century resulted in a steady stream of talented Spanish artists leaving their homeland. Many of them, including Picasso, Dalí, Juan Gris and Miró, passed through Paris – some staying for a few months, others for years. Artists of other nationalities also congregated in the French capital, and all of these artists were part of the Paris School. It is possible to see the mutual influence of this closely knit, yet constantly evolving, group of young artists.

Franco and Beyond

The Civil War (1936–9) had an enormous effect on the development of Spanish art. Under Franco, the state enforced rigid censorship. In the rooms of the fourth floor, the Museo Reina Sofía displays pieces of modern art from the 20th century. Works span the period from the end of World War II in 1945 through to 1968, and the development of different movements is marked. Artists on show include Robert Delaunay, Max Ernst, Francis Bacon and Georges Braque. Later works by Picasso and Míro can also be found here, as can pieces by sculptors Julio López-Hernández and Jorge Oteiza.

↑ *Green-Blue* by Gerhard Richter and *Untitled* by Bruce Nauman

4 ⊡

PARQUE DEL RETIRO

📍L10 🏛Plaza de la Independencia 7 📞915 30 00 41 🚍 Ⓜ Retiro, Ibiza, Estación del Arte 🕐Apr-Sep: 6am-midnight daily; Oct-Mar: 6am-10pm daily

Strolling the manicured pathways of the Retiro was once the preserve of kings and queens, but nowadays it is a blissful pastime for *Madrileños* and visitors of the pleasure garden. At dusk, as the temperature drops, it feels as though half the city turns out to see and be seen.

The Retiro, which is situated in Madrid's smart Jerónimos district, takes its name from Felipe IV's royal palace complex, which once stood here. Today, all that is left of the palace is the Casón del Buen Retiro (p120)– now the Prado's library – and the Salón de Reinos (p114), both located just outside the park.

Used privately by the royal family from 1632, the park became the scene of elaborate pageants, bullfights and mock naval battles. In the 18th century it was partially opened to the public, provided visitors were formally dressed, and in 1869 it was fully opened.

A short stroll from the park's northern entrance down the tree-lined avenue leads to the bustling *estanque* (pleasure lake). This is a hub for much of the park's activity, and rowing boats can be hired here. On one side of the lake is a half-moon colonnade in front of which an equestrian statue of Alfonso XII rides high on a column. Opposite, portrait painters and fortune-tellers ply their trade.

To the south of the lake are two ornate palaces. The Neo-Classical Palacio de Velázquez and the Palacio de Cristal (Crystal Palace) were built by Ricardo Velázquez Bosco in 1883 and 1887 respectively and regularly hold contemporary art exhibitions.

The gardens are also home to many elegant marble monuments and statues. Among them is *El Ángel Caído* (Fallen Angel), which is a late 19th-century sculpture by Ricardo Bellver that crowns one of the park's fountains. It is one of perhaps three statues of Lucifer in the world.

 PICTURE PERFECT
Those in Glass Houses

The intricate iron architecture of the Palacio de Cristal can be perfectly captured reflected in the lake. Get the best shot of the east-facing structure at sunrise, when the light reflects off the hundreds of glass panels.

① Visitors can seek shade beneath the colonnade encircling Alfonso XII's monument.

② The park's turquoise pleasure lake is an especially popular spot to take a rest.

③ As well as rolling parkland, the Parque del Retiro is also home to a parterre garden of formal French design.

The Palacio de Cristal at sunset, in the southern part of the Parque del Retiro

EXPERIENCE MORE

5
Puerta de Alcalá

📍K8 🅰Plaza de la Independencia Ⓜ Retiro

This ceremonial gateway is the grandest of the monuments erected by Carlos III in his efforts to improve eastern Madrid. Designed by Francesco Sabatini, it replaced a smaller Baroque gateway, which had been built by Felipe III for his wife's entry into Madrid. Construction of the gate was

---

PICTURE PERFECT
Quirky Quotes

As you walk through the literary quarter Barrio de Las Letras, a five-minute walk west of Plaza Cánovas del Castillo, be sure to capture the brass letters embedded in the pavement. These recreate passages from great Spanish literature.

---

started in 1769 and lasted a total of nine years. It was built from granite in Neo-Classical style, with a lofty pediment and sculpted angels. It has five arches – three central and two outer rectangular ones.

Until the mid-19th century, the gateway marked the city's easternmost boundary. Visit at night when it is floodlit to fully appreciate its grandeur.

6
Hotel Ritz

📍J9 🅰Plaza de la Lealtad 5 Ⓜ Banco de España 🌐mandarinoriental.com/ritzmadrid

A short walk from the Prado (p100), this hotel is said to be Spain's most extravagant. It was commissioned in 1906, around the time that Alfonso XIII was embarrassed by the lack of luxury accommodation in the city for his wedding guests. At the start of the Civil War, the Ritz became a

---

Did You Know?

Real Madrid football fans celebrate major victories by jumping into in the Fuente de Cibeles.

---

hospital, and anarchist leader Buenaventura Durruti died here of his wounds in 1936.

The opulence of the Ritz is reflected in its prices and dress code. Each room is beautifully decorated in a different style, with carpets made by hand at the Real Fábrica de Tapices (p170).

7
Plaza de Cibeles

📍J8 Ⓜ Banco de España

The Plaza de Cibeles is one Madrid's best-known landmarks. The elegant and

General del Ejército de Tierra, housed in the buildings of the former Palacio de Buenavista. Commissioned by the Duchess of Alba in 1777, construction was twice delayed by fires.

Finally, occupying a whole block on the opposite corner is the Venetian-Renaissance Banco de España (p112), with delicate ironwork on the roof and windows. Renovation work has returned the bank to its 19th-century glory.

Museo Nacional de Artes Decorativas

K9 **Calle de Montalbán 12** **Retiro, Banco de España** **9:30am-3pm Tue-Sat (Thu also 5-8pm, except Jul & Aug), 10am-3pm Sun & public hols** **mnartesdecorativas.mcu.es**

Housed in an aristocratic residence built in the 19th century and near the Parque del Retiro (p108), the National Museum of Decorative Arts contains an interesting collection of furniture and *objets d'art*. The exhibits are mainly from Spain and date back to Phoenician times.

On show are excellent ceramics from Talavera de la Reina, a town that is famous for the craft, and a collection of jewellery and ornaments from the Far East. Several of the rooms on display recreate scenes from the past.

←

The Puerta de Alcalá, fronted by a carpet of yellow flowers

imposing Fuente de Cibeles stands in the middle of the busy traffic island at the junction of the Paseo del Prado and the Calle de Alcalá. This fine, sculpted fountain is named after Cybele, the Greco-Roman goddess of nature, and shows her sitting in her chariot, drawn by a pair of lions. Designed in the late 18th century by José Hermosilla and Ventura Rodríguez, it is considered a symbol of Madrid.

Four important buildings rise around the square, the most impressive being the Palacio de Comunicaciones (p113). On the northeast side is the Palacio del Marques de Linares (p141), built in 1873 about the time of the second Bourbon restoration.

In the northwest corner of the Plaza de Cibeles, surrounded by attractive gardens, is the heavily guarded army headquarters, the Cuartel

→

The beautiful Fuente de Cibeles on the Plaza de Cibeles

EAT

TriCiclo

At this popular restaurant, superb modern Spanish dishes come in three different sizes to fit every budget, and are served in an industrial-style setting.

H10 **Calle de Santa María 28** **eltriciclo.es**

€€€

Estado Puro

Tuck into gourmet tapas by celebrated chef Paco Roncero, who takes classic recipes such as *rabo de toro* (oxtail stew) and reinvents them.

H10 **Plaza de Cánovas del Castillo 4** **tapasenestadopuro.com**

€€

Vinoteca Moratín

Market-fresh bistro fare and a nicely curated list of mostly Spanish wines head the attractions at this atmospheric spot in the Barrio de Las Letras.

H10 **Calle de Moratín 36** **vinotecamoratin.com**

€€€

9

Banco de España

📍 H8 📍 Calle de Alcalá 48
Ⓜ Banco de España
🕐 Groups by appt only,
Tue & Thu 4pm 🌐 bde.es

Viewing this vast building, with façades facing Paseo del Prado, Plaza de Cibeles and Calle de Alcalá, you might wonder which is the main entrance. In fact it is the one on the Paseo del Prado, used only for ceremonial occasions nowadays. The original bank

---

> The Banco de España's various meeting rooms and hallways are decorated with the bank's collection of tapestries, vases, antique furniture and paintings.

dates from 1882–91 and occupied the corner of Cibeles, while new wings were added later. The Bank of Spain itself was founded in 1856.

The bank's vast main staircase, made of Carrara marble and overlooked by stained-glass windows with mythological and allegorical themes, leads to the Patio del Reloj, a glass-roofed central courtyard with the cashiers' windows. It is a striking example of Art Deco design. The library, which is open to researchers, is located in another large hall, the interior of which is made entirely of wrought-iron filigree, painted off-white. There is also an older, smaller library with glassed-in mahogany bookshelves.

The Banco de España's various meeting rooms and hallways are decorated with the bank's sizeable collection of tapestries, vases, antique furniture and paintings, including a first printing of Goya's series of etchings of bull-fighting, the *Tauromaquia*. In the circular Goya room are eight further paintings by the

Spanish master, including portraits of Carlos IV and various governors of the Bank of Spain. In *Conde de Floridablanca in the Artist's Studio*, rather than looking out at the viewer, Goya is seen gazing at his companion.

Beneath the Patio del Reloj, 30 m (98 ft) below street level and off limits to visitors, is a chamber with an island-like structure ringed by a moat. On it is the vault containing the bank's gold. Prior to sophisticated security gadgetry, this chamber would immediately flood were there any threat of a bank robbery.

10

Museo Naval

📍 J9 📍 Paseo del Prado 5
Ⓜ Banco de España 🕐 10am–
7pm Tue–Sun (Aug: to
3pm) 🌐 armada.mde.es/
museonaval

Added to the Ministry of Defence building in 1977, the copper-tinted

→ The distinctive Palacio de Comunicaciones is just as impressive inside *(inset)*

glass Naval Museum has 18 excellent display halls charting Spain's centuries-old history of seafaring. As well as a large collection of scale models of ships throughout the ages, often dating from the same period as the ships themselves, there are numerous figureheads, amphorae, globes, astrolabes, sextants, compasses and maps to examine. A range of weapons used during Spain's time in the Americas also feature here. One unusual exhibit is a map of the world dated 1500. It was drawn for the Catholic Monarchs Isabel and Fernando, and features the Americas for the first time. There is also a piece of the tree trunk upon which the Spanish conquistador Hernán Cortés is said to have rested after *La Noche Triste* (The Sad Night) in 1520, when he and his men fled from Montezuma's Aztec capital, Tenochtitlán. The Museo Naval has undergone a renovation, making it more accessible to the public.

Palacio de Comunicaciones

📍 J8 🏛 Plaza de Cibeles
Ⓜ Banco de España
🕐 10am–8pm Tue–Sun
🚫 Mon, 1 & 6 Jan, 1 May, 24, 25 & 31 Dec 🌐 centro centro.org

Occupying one corner of the Plaza de Cibeles, this impressive building was constructed to house the headquarters of Spain's postal service. Built between 1905 and 1917 by Antonio Palacios and Joaquin Otamendi, its appearance – white with tall pinnacles – is often likened to a wedding cake. In 2011, work was completed on a huge glass dome over the building's central courtyard. You can still see the old-fashioned brass letterboxes with the names of different Spanish cities and provinces that are embedded in the wall by the main entrance. The building now houses the offices of the Mayor of Madrid and the City Council,

> ⚠ GREAT VIEW
> ## Panorama Drama
>
> A ticketed lift will sweep you up to the eighth floor of CentroCentro inside the Palacio de Comunicaciones for the best panoramic view of Madrid.

which also occupies another historical building in Plaza de la Villa.

The building also houses CentroCentro, a fantastic cultural centre with a packed programme of fun activities, including workshops, exhibitions and concerts, that revolve around Madrid. It's also a hip place to sit back and relax, with a colourful lounge beside the entrance hall, looking onto the Plaza de Cibeles. The restaurant and terrace *(p116)* on the top floor offer fabulous panoramic views of Madrid and is a popular place to hang out in the early evening. On special occasions such as Christmas, the building is used as a backdrop for illuminations and projected images.

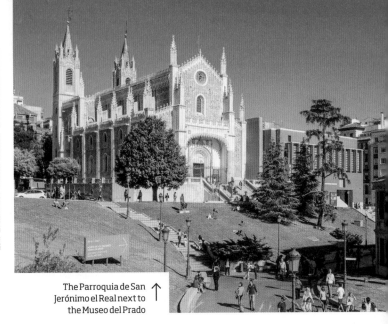

↑ The Parroquia de San Jerónimo el Real next to the Museo del Prado

12

Parroquia de San Jerónimo el Real

📍K10 🏠Calle del Moreto 4 Ⓜ Banco de España 🕐Jul-Sep: 10:30am-1pm & 6-8pm daily; Oct-Jun: 10am-1:30pm & 5:30-8:30pm daily 🌐par roquiasanjeronimoelreal.es

Built in the 16th century, but since remodelled, San Jerónimo is Madrid's royal church. From the 17th century it was virtually a part of the Buen Retiro palace which once stood here.

Originally attached to the Hieronymite monastery, which today stands beside it, the church was the location for the marriage of Alfonso XIII and Victoria Eugenia von Battenberg in 1906. The cloisters and part of the atrium form an annex of the Prado's extension.

13

Salón de Reinos

📍K9 🏠Calle de Méndez Núñez 1 Ⓜ Retiro, Banco de España 🕐For refurb

The Salón de Reinos (Hall of Kingdoms) is one of the

two remaining parts of the 17th-century Palacio del Buen Retiro and gets its name from the shields of the 24 kingdoms of the Spanish monarchy. These shields form part of the decor and were supervised by court painter Velázquez. In the time of Felipe IV, the Salón was used for diplomatic receptions and official ceremonies.

14

Casa-Museo de Lope de Vega

📍G10 🏠Calle de Cervantes 11 Ⓜ Antón Martín, Sevilla 🕐By appt only: 10am-6pm Tue-Sun 🗓1 & 6 Jan, 1 & 15 May, 24, 25 & 31 Dec 🌐casa museolopedevega.org

Félix Lope de Vega, who was a leading Golden Age writer, moved into this sombre house in 1610 and lived here until his death in 1635. Book lovers will rejoice at a visit to the house, as it was here that he wrote over two thirds of his large collection of plays.

The house was first opened to the public in 1935 after a meticulous restoration project, using some of Lope

de Vega's own furniture. It was also declared a national monument the same year. Casa-Museo de Lope de Vega gives a great feeling of Castilian life in the early 17th century. A dark chapel with no external windows occupies the centre, separated from the writer's bedroom by only a barred window. Be sure to visit the small garden at the rear, which, complete with the original well, is planted with the flowers and fruit trees mentioned by the writer in his many plays.

Lope de Vega died in this house in 1635. Across the street stands the 17th-century Convento de las Trinitarias, which can be visited to locate where the remains of Miguel de Cervantes and Félix Lope de Vega lie.

1,800

The estimated number of plays that Felix Lope de Vega wrote.

the Lost Steps). This gallery is often used for exhibitions on the history of the institution.

16

Ateneo de Madrid

📍 G9 🏛 Calle del Prado 21 Ⓜ Antón Martín, Sevilla 🕐 By appt only: 10am–1pm Mon–Fri 🌐 ateneode madrid.com

Formally founded in 1835, this learned association is similar to a gentlemen's club in atmosphere. It is housed in a Modernist building with a grand stairway and panelled hall hung with portraits of famous fellows.

Although often closed down during past periods of repression and dictatorship, the institution has remained a mainstay of liberal thought in Spain. It was also a gathering place for the *la tertulia* literary group in the 19th century. Many leading Socialists are members, along with writers and other intellectuals.

LA TERTULIA – LITERARY GROUPS IN MADRID

The Ateneo de Madrid was one of many homes for the unique Madrid institution of *la tertulia*. Groups of people with common interests gathered to discuss everything from politics or the arts to the finer points of bullfighting. Not a formal club, yet more than a casual conversation among friends, *tertulias* were a major source of news, ideas and gossip in the 19th century, and more than one political plot was hatched over cups of coffee. They were usually held at Madrid's 19th-century cafés. Those which occupied choice real estate, such as the Pombo, El Oriental and the Paix, have since disappeared, but there are a few survivors.

15 Ⓜ

Bolsa de Comercio

📍 J9 🏛 Plaza de la Lealtad 1 Ⓜ Banco de España 🕐 By appt only: Thu at noon; groups Mon–Fri at 10am & noon 🚫 Public hols 🌐 bolsamadrid.es

The Madrid Stock Exchange was established in 1831. It operated in 11 different, generally inadequate venues – it was once housed in a convent – before moving in 1893 to the headquarters it now occupies. Designed by Spanish architect Enrique María Repullés y Vargas, the building took more than six years to construct, at a cost of around three million pesetas. Nearly one third of this went on the concave, Neo-Classical façade and main entrance, with its six giant columns topped by Corinthian capitals.

Dealers occupy the Sala de Contratación (trading floor). This large, vaulted space of 970 sq m (10,400 sq ft) has an ornate Neo-Baroque clock on a marble plinth at its centre. You can watch the proceedings from the Salón de los Pasos Perdidos (Hall of

↑ The hallway at the Ateneo de Madrid, displaying portraits of its famous members

DRINK

Salmón Guru

Retro bar rooms, an inventive cocktail menu and custom glassware make this spot much more than a gin-and-tonic joint.

📍G10 🏠Calle de Echegaray 21
🌐salmonguru.es

Jazz Bar

The chilled ambience at this bar cannot be beaten. Leather booths make for cosy drinking spots, accompanied by jazz music.

📍H10 🏠Calle de Moratín 35 📞914 29 70 31

La Venencia

The one-time stronghold of Spanish leftists serves only sherry and a few tapas. Photos have been banned since the 1930s.

📍G9 🏠Calle de Echegaray 7
🌐lavenencia.com

CentroCentro Terrace Bar

One level down from the observation deck, this upscale bar is perfect to sip a glass of bubbly as the sun goes down.

📍J8 🏠Plaza de Cibeles 1
🌐centrocentro.org

La Pecera

Bartenders make a mean gin fizz at this elegant café-restaurant at the Círculo de Bellas Artes.

📍H9 🏠Calle de Alcalá 42
🌐circulodebellas artes.com

Real Academia de la Historia

📍G10 🏠Calle del León 21 Ⓜ Antón Martín 🕐To the public 🌐rah.es

The Royal Academy of History is an austere brick building built by Juan de Villanueva in 1788. In 1898, the intellectual and bibliophile Marcelino Menéndez Pelayo became director of the academy, living here until his death in 1912. The academy retains significant libraries and collections of antiquities, and holds more than 200,000 books.

Fuente de Neptuno

📍J9 Ⓜ Banco de España

Dominating the Plaza de Cánovas del Castillo is the majestic Fuente de Neptuno, a fountain with a statue of Neptune in his chariot, being pulled by two horses. The statue was designed in 1777 by Ventura Rodríguez as part of a grand scheme by Carlos III to beautify eastern Madrid.

The plaza itself takes its name from the historian Antonio Cánovas del Castillo, one of the leading statesmen in 19th-century Spain. He was assassinated in 1897.

Círculo de Bellas Artes

📍H8/9 🏠Calle de Alcalá 42 Ⓜ Banco de España, Sevilla 🕐9am-5pm Mon-Fri, 11am-9pm Sat-Sun; café 9am-1am 🌐circulobellasartes.com

The Círculo de Bellas Artes is a cultural foundation established in 1880. Since 1926, it has been housed in this building designed by Antonio Palacios. The building has a vast ballroom, exhibition halls, a theatre, library and studios for use by artists and sculptors. It also hosts cultural and social events, such as the Carnival Masquerade Ball held every February.

Although the foundation is for members only, the €5 admission fee gives visitors access to parts of the building, including exhibition halls, the rooftop terrace restaurant and the café. Known as La Pecera (Fishbowl) for its large windows, it is a great place to have breakfast while observing life on the Calle de Alcalá.

Teatro Español

📍G10 🏠Calle del Príncipe 25 Ⓜ Antón Martín, Sol, Sevilla 🕐Performances from 7pm Tue-Sun 🌐teatroespanol.es

Dominating the Plaza de Santa Ana (p82) is the Teatro Español, one of the oldest and most beautiful theatres in Madrid. In the late 16th century, many

← A statue of Neptune in his chariot, the centrepiece of the Fuente de Neptuno

of Spain's finest plays were performed in the Corral del Príncipe which originally stood here. Replaced by the Teatro del Príncipe in 1745, it underwent extensive restoration in the mid-19th century and was renamed Teatro Español. Names of great Spanish dramatists are engraved on the façade, including that of Federico García Lorca. Theatre lovers should book a guided tour to see the boxes, the stage and much more.

 21
Westin Palace

📍 H9 🏠 Plaza de las Cortes 7 Ⓜ Sevilla, Banco de España, Estación del Arte 🌐 westin palacemadrid.com

The former palace of the Duque de Medinaceli was torn down to build this hotel, which opened in 1912. Alfonso XIII wanted his capital to have elegant hotels to match those in other European cities, and actively encouraged the project. Its life as a luxury hotel was interrupted during the Civil War, when it housed a military hospital and refuge for the homeless – the famous glass-domed lounge was used as an operating theatre – as well as the Soviet Embassy.

For many years, the Westin and the Ritz (p110) were the only grand hotels in Madrid. However, while the Ritz was the exclusive reserve of its titled guests, none of whom would dare to venture from their rooms without a tie, the no less luxurious but more informal Westin was open to non-residents and was a lively meeting place for *Madrileños*. It was the first establishment in Madrid where ladies could take tea unaccompanied. It is still a favourite rendezvous, and the wood-panelled Palace Bar and Rotonda Hall lounge, with its huge glass dome, are Madrid landmarks.

Statesmen, spies, literati and film stars have all stayed at the Westin. Past guests include Henry Kissinger, Mata Hari, Ernest Hemingway, Orson Welles, David Bowie, Richard Attenborough, Michael Jackson and Salvador Dalí,

↑ Socializing over drinks at Azotea at the Círculo de Bellas Artes

who once drew lewd pictures on the walls of his hotel room. However, an over-zealous maid scrubbed the walls clean the next day.

The hotel's other facilities include a Royal Suite, solarium and fitness centre, and a wine cellar for tastings and sales.

↑ The elegance of the Westin's glass-domed Rotunda Hall lounge

 The iconic and dazzling Edificio Metrópolis illuminated at night

Edificio Metrópolis

H8 ☖ Calle de Alcalá 39 Ⓜ Sevilla ☒ To the public

Of unmistakable French inspiration, this building, jutting out like a ship's prow at the corner of Calle Alcalá and the Gran Vía (p79), is a Madrid landmark. Inaugurated in 1911, it was designed by Jules and Raymond Février for the Unión y el Fenix Español insurance company.

The restrained ground level is topped by ornate colonnaded upper floors, each pair of columns serving as a pedestal for allegorical statues that represent Commerce, Mining,

Did You Know?

The "La Violetera" statue that stood in front of the Edificio Metrópolis is now in Las Vistillas park.

Agriculture and Industry. The rounded corner tower is crowned by a double-layered dome of dark slate with gilded ornaments. It used to hold the symbol of the Unión y el Fenix Español company – a bronze statue representing the mythological Phoenix and, astride it, a human figure with upraised arm representing Ganymede. In the early 1970s, the company sold the building to the Metrópolis insurers. In a controversial move, they decided to take the statue – by then a familiar element of the Madrid skyline – to their new headquarters on the Paseo de la Castellana. Eventually the statue was replaced by a new one, representing Winged Victory; the original is in the garden of the Unión y el Fenix Español's building.

In front of the tower of the Edificio Metrópolis used to stand "La Violetera", a statue of a woman selling violets. It recalls a character from a Spanish light opera, which later inspired the film La Violetera. The violet-sellers would sell their flowers to theatregoers on the Gran Vía. An inscription on the statue bears the first two lines of the song La Violetera: "Como ave precursora de primavera, en Madrid aparece la violetera" ("The violet-seller appears in Madrid like a bird announcing spring").

Congreso de los Diputados

H9 ☖ Plaza de las Cortes 1 Ⓜ Sevilla ☒ By appt 9am-2:30pm, 4-6:30pm Mon-Thu, 9am-1:30pm Fri ☒ Aug ☒ congreso.es

This imposing yet attractive building is home to the Spanish parliament, the Cortes. Built in the mid-19th century, it is characterized by Classical columns, heavy pediments and bronze lions. It was here, in 1981, that Colonel Tejero of the Civil Guard held the deputies at gunpoint, as he tried to spark off a military coup. His failure was seen as an indication that democracy was firmly established in Spain.

LA ZARZUELA - SPANISH LIGHT OPERA

The *zarzuela*, a direct descendant of Italian light opera, started out as an amusement for kings in the 17th century, but was soon appropriated by the common people as Madrid's most characteristic performing art genre. Although no new *zarzuelas* have been written in decades, the genre has a tremendous following in Madrid, where there are regular performances and where music shops always have a section devoted to it.

ROYAL BEGINNINGS

The name *zarzuela* is derived from the Palacio de La Zarzuela, current home of the Spanish royal family, outside Madrid. *Zarzuelas* were initially performed during the reign of Felipe IV. With the ascendancy of the Bourbon kings, who preferred traditional Italian opera, the *zarzuela* was taken up in theatres. It was here that it evolved into the light-hearted spectacle we know today, halfway between opera and musical comedy.

↑ An early performance of Tomás Bretón's famous *La Verbena de la Paloma*

CONSTRUCTING A LEGACY

Calderón de La Barca, the famous 17th-century Spanish playwright, was one of the first great exponents of this type of opera. Others followed, most notably Tomás Bretón, who composed nearly 40, including *La Verbena de la Paloma*. The central theme of *zarzuelas* is life in *castizo* Madrid *(p153)*, with its streetwise *majas* (women) and cocky *chulos* (men) dressed in traditional costumes. It combines singing, spoken dialogue and dances.

↑ Rossy de Palma in *Le Chanteur de Mexico* at Madrid's Teatro de la Zarzuela in 2017

A *zarzuela* production of *A Midsummer Night's Dream* ↑

24
Casón del Buen Retiro

QK9 **A**Calle de Alfonso XII 28 **M**Retiro, Banco de España **O**Library only: by appt, 8:30am-2pm Mon-Fri (to 5pm Mon & Wed, to 3pm Tue)

The Casón del Buen Retiro is one of the remaining buildings of the 17th-century Palacio del Buen Retiro, designed by Alonso Carbonel. It was built in 1637 for Felipe IV on a stretch of land next to the Monastery of San Jerónimo (p114), but the structure of the building evolved over the years. It was remodelled in the 19th century, and two monumental façades were included.

Now part of the Prado (p100), the building houses the museum's library that has a collection of 70,000 books. On the ceiling in the main hall is *The Allegory of the Golden Fleece*, a magnificent painting by Luca Giordano.

25

CaixaForum

QJ11 **A**Paseo del Prado 36 **M**Estación del Arte **O**10am-8pm daily **C**1 & 6 Jan, 25 Dec **W**lacaixa.es/obrasocial

CaixaForum is a cultural centre with four floors dedicated to exhibitions of modern art and photography, educational workshops, conferences, music and poetry festivals and concerts. The eye-catching building – which appears as if it's levitating above ground – was built by Swiss architects Herzog & de Meuron in 2007 in a former electric power station. The cool industrial interior is a work of art in itself. The top-floor café and restaurant are highly recommended. Adjoining the building is an extraordinary vertical garden – a highly photographed spot in the city.

Nearby is **La Fábrica Galería**, an open space devoted to culture. It has an art gallery that caters to contemporary art, a photography bookshop and a café.

PICTURE PERFECT
CaixaForum Vertical Garden Wall

Designed by French botanist Patrick Blanc, the 24-m (79-ft) high vertical garden wall on CaixaForum's plaza is verdant with 250 species of plants that grow without soil. It's a can't-miss selfie.

La Fábrica Galería
ACalle Alameda 9 **O**10am-8pm daily (to 5pm Sun) **W**lafabrica.com

26
Real Academia Española

QJ10 **A**Calle de Felipe IV 4 **M**Banco de España, Retiro **O**Library: 9am-2pm Mon-Fri **W**rae.es

The motto of Spain's Royal Academy is "*Limpia, brilla y da esplendor*" ("Cleans, polishes and shines"). It describes the function of

The vertical garden, which puts its stamp on the CaixaForum

← The elaborate and impressive exterior of the Ministerio de Agricultura

by Agustín Querol. The three central figures represent Glory personified bestowing laurels on Science and Art. On either side are statues of Pegasus. Originally made of marble, these were replaced by bronze replicas when the stone deteriorated. The original statues are now at Plaza de Legazpi, south of the city.

the organization, which is to preserve the purity of the Spanish language.

Founded in 1713, the academy moved to this Neo-classical building in 1894. Only the library is open to visitors. The elegant façade has a majestic entrance with Doric columns and an impressive carved pediment. The members include scholars, writers and journalists – the post, which is for life, is unpaid – who occupy seats identified by a letter of the alphabet. They meet regularly to assess the acceptability of any new trends in the Spanish language.

27

Ministerio de Agricultura

📍 J11 📍 Paseo de la Infanta Isabel 1 Ⓜ Estación del Arte ⏱ For tours: noon Sat & Sun; dramatized tours: 8pm Fri & Sat 🌐 mapama.gob.es

This magnificent, imposing building was originally home to the Ministry of Development (Palacio de Fomento) whose 19th-century remit was to promote economic, industrial and scientific growth in Spain. Today it houses the Ministry of Agriculture, and as such is frequently the target of pro-tests by Spanish farmers and olive oil producers. The building itself is adorned with sculptures, friezes and painted tiles, bringing together elements of both Romantic and Neo-Classical styles. It was constructed between 1884 and 1886 by Ricardo Velázquez Bosco, architect of the Palacio de Velázquez in the Parque del Retiro (p108). The artist Ignacio Zuloaga was later involved in its design.

Gigantic Corinthian columns line the exterior walls, with areas of coloured bricks and decorative glazed tiles enhan-cing the spaces between them. The pediment above the columns is decorated with the Spanish coat of arms. Crowning the building are allegorical sculptures created

28

Real Jardín Botánico

📍 K11 📍 Plaza de Murillo 2 Ⓜ Banco de España, Estación del Arte ⏱ 10am-dusk daily 🔒 1 Jan, 25 Dec 🌐 rjb.csic.es

South of the Prado (p100), and a suitable place to rest after visiting the gallery, are the Royal Botanic Gardens. The idea of Carlos III, they were designed by Gómez Ortega, Francesco Sabatini and Juan de Villanueva, the architect of the Prado, in 1781.

Interest in the plants of the Philippines and South America took hold during the Spanish Enlightenment, and today the neatly laid out gardens offer a huge variety of trees, shrubs, medicinal plants and herbs.

The original 1755 location of the Jardín Botánico on the Manzanares riverbank con-tained more than 2,000 plants collected by botanist and surgeon José Quer y Martínez.

Did You Know?

The Real Jardín Botánico contains around 30,000 plants and flowers and 1,500 trees.

The industrial interior of the cutting-edge CaixaForum

㉙

Museo Nacional de Antropología

📍K12 🏛Calle de Alfonso XII 68 Ⓜ Estación del Arte, Atocha RENFE 🕐9:30am-8pm Tue-Sat, 10am-3pm Sun 🚫Mon & public hols 🌐mnantropologia.mcu.es

Previously known as the Museo Nacional de Etnología, this three-floor museum, which is built around a grand open hall, was inaugurated by Alfonso XII in 1875.

Through the displays, the anthropology and ethnology of geographical groups of people are studied. The ground floor houses an important collection from the Philippines. The centrepiece is a 10-m- (33-ft-) long dug-out canoe made from a single tree trunk. There are also some gruesome exhibits, such as deformed skulls from Peru and the Philippines, the mummy of a Guanche from Tenerife and the skeleton of Don Agustín Luengo y Capilla, a late 19th-century giant from Extremadura. He was 2.35 m (7 ft 4 in) tall and died aged 26.

> The older part of Atocha was one of the first big constructions in Madrid to be built from glass and wrought iron. Now, it houses a palm garden.

The first floor is dedicated to Africa. As well as clothing and ceramics, there is a reproduction of a Bubi ritual hut from Equatorial Guinea, in which tribal members met the *boeloelo* (witch doctor). On the second floor are exhibits on the lifestyles of Indigenous groups in America.

㉚

Estación de Atocha

📍J12 🏛Plaza del Emperador Carlos V Ⓜ Atocha RENFE 🕐5am-1am daily 🌐renfe.com

Madrid's first rail service, from Atocha to Aranjuez, was inaugurated in 1851.

Forty years later, the original station at Atocha was replaced by the present one. The older part of Atocha was one of the first big constructions in Madrid to be built from glass and wrought iron. Now, it houses a palm garden. Next to it is the modern AVE terminus, providing high-speed links to various towns including Toledo, Seville, Córdoba, Zaragoza, Valladolid, Valencia and Barcelona.

㉛

Real Observatorio Astronómico de Madrid

📍L12 🏛Calle de Alfonso XII 3 Ⓜ Estación del Arte 🕐Fri-Sun; booking essential 🚫Public hols 🌐ign.es

When building began in 1790, this was one of only four observatories in Europe. It was designed by Juan de Villanueva along Neo-Classical lines; the vertical slit window was used for telescopes, and the colonnaded roof cupola for weather observation.

IN SOLEMN MEMORY

The Atocha Bombing Victims Memorial outside Estación de Atocha commemorates the victims of "11-M", as the Spanish refer to the 11 March 2004 bombing of four commuter trains bound for Atocha station. The memorial is a simple 11-m- (36-ft-) tall cylinder containing hundreds of messages of grief, solidarity and compassion. At least 1,800 people were injured in addition to the 191 killed. A special forces agent was also killed in a 2 April 2004 raid on an apartment used by the bombers when seven suicide bombers blew themselves up. The bombers had been radicalized by al-Qaeda propaganda on the internet.

The superb palm garden inside of Estación de Atocha *(inset)* ↑

In the Edificio Villanueva you'll find the library, with numerous antique books. There is also a collection of old instruments, including a meridian circle, precision clocks and even a polished bronze mirror for a telescope made by Sir Frederick William Herschel, the famous astronomer who discovered Uranus.

A Foucault's pendulum in the central rotunda displays the daily rotation of the earth. The building, crowned by a large equatorial telescope by Grubb (1912), also encloses the former living quarters of the astronomers.

 32 M

Palacio de Fernán Núñez

📍 G/H11 🏛 Calle de Santa Isabel 44 Ⓜ Estación del Arte ◷ Groups by appt 🌐 ffe.es/palacio

Also known as the Palacio de Cervellón, this building has a plain façade that gives scant indication of the riches within. Built for the Duke and Duchess of Fernán Núñez in 1847, the palace served as the family home until 1936. It was requisitioned by the Republican militia at the start of the Civil War; the lower part served as a bomb shelter while the upper floor was occupied by a Socialist Youth organization. Amazingly, when the palace was returned to the duke's family, they found that none of its treasures had been damaged or stolen.

In 1941, the palace was sold and became the headquarters of the spanish state railway. It now houses the Foundation of Spanish Railways, which organizes exhibitions here.

The palace was built in two phases and this is clear in its design; the large, restrained rooms in the first section contrast with the Rococo flourishes of the second. The older section has carpets from the Real Fábrica de Tapices *(p170)*, as well as antique furniture, clocks and copies of paintings by Goya. Attention, however, is inevitably drawn to the gold-plated ornamentation of the later section, especially the ballroom with its mirrors, chandeliers and cherubs playing musical instruments. Rooms in this part are often used for official receptions.

Near the palace is the cloistered Convento Santa Isabel, with its octagonal dome. It was founded in 1595 by Felipe II.

> 🔍 HIDDEN GEM
> ### La Neomudéjar
>
> In the Neo-Mudéjar-style former offices of the national railway company, adjacent to Estación de Atocha, this avant-garde art centre hosts international artists and presents video art festivals, exhibitions and talks.

A SHORT WALK
PASEO DEL PRADO

Distance 2.5 km (1.5 miles) **Time** 40 minutes **Nearest metro** Banco de España

In the late 18th century, before the museums and lavish hotels of East Madrid took shape, the Paseo del Prado was laid out and soon became a fashionable spot for strolling. Combine this original attraction with visits to the Paseo's museums and art galleries to make the most of the area. Take a detour to visit the Museo Nacional Thyssen-Bornemisza and the Museo del Prado (just south of the Plaza de Cánovas del Castillo). You'll pass grand monuments built under Carlos III along the route, including the Puerta de Alcalá, the Fuente de Neptuno and the Fuente de Cibeles. Surprisingly, they stand in the middle of busy roundabouts.

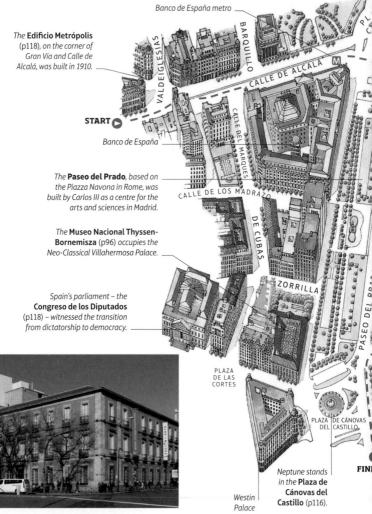

Banco de España metro

The **Edificio Metrópolis** (p118), *on the corner of Gran Vía and Calle de Alcalá, was built in 1910.*

VALDEIGLESIAS

BARQUILLO

CALLE DE ALCALÁ

CALLE DEL MARQUES

START ▶

Banco de España

The **Paseo del Prado**, *based on the Piazza Navona in Rome, was built by Carlos III as a centre for the arts and sciences in Madrid.*

CALLE DE LOS MADRAZO

DE CUBAS

The **Museo Nacional Thyssen-Bornemisza** (p96) *occupies the Neo-Classical Villahermosa Palace.*

ZORRILLA

PASEO DEL PRA

Spain's parliament – the **Congreso de los Diputados** (p118) – *witnessed the transition from dictatorship to democracy.*

PLAZA DE LAS CORTES

PLAZA DE CÁNOVAS DEL CASTILLO

FIN

*Neptune stands in the **Plaza de Cánovas del Castillo** (p116).*

Westin Palace

↑ The Neo-Classical exterior of the Museo Nacional Thyssen-Bornemisza

A fountain with a statue of the Roman goddess Cybele, stands in the **Plaza de Cibeles** (p110).

Sculpted from granite, the **Puerta de Alcalá** (p110) is especially beautiful when floodlit at night.

Palacio del Marques de Linares

Palacio de Comunicaciones and City Hall

PLAZA DE LA

INDEPENDENCIA

CALLE DE ALCALÁ

CALLE DE ALFONSO XI

CALLE DE MONTALBAN

CALLE DE ALFONSO XII

LA LEALTAD

CALLE ANTONIO MAURA

CALLE FELIPE IV

MORETO

Locator Map
For more detail see p94

↑ The statue of Cybele decorating the fountain in the Plaza de Cibeles

The **Museo Nacional de Artes Decorativas** (p111), *near the Retiro, was founded in 1912 as a showcase for the Spanish manufacturing industry.*

The former army museum of the Palacio del Buen Retiro, the **Salón de Reinos** (p114), *forms part of the Museo del Prado.*

The **Casón del Buen Retiro** (p120) *is an annex of the Museo del Prado.*

The **Monumento del Dos de Mayo** commemorates the War of Independence against the French.

With its belle époque interior, the **Hotel Ritz** (p110) is one of the most elegant hotels in Spain.

0 metres	100
0 yards	100

N ↑

A SHORT WALK
LAVAPIÉS AND LAS LETRAS DISTRICTS

Distance 3 km (2 miles) **Walking time** 45 minutes **Terrain** Easy
Nearest metro Estación del Arte **Stopping-off point** Pum Pum Café

Central Madrid is divided into *barrios* (districts) each with their own identity, and the contrasts you will encounter on this walk are fascinating. The cobbled streets of Lavapiés, the old Jewish Quarter, slope up towards the city centre, and the 19th-century *corralas* (tenements) here testify to the original working-class population. Today Arab tearooms, Indian restaurants and Chinese stores abound. In contrast Las Letras is so called because many giants of Spanish literature lived here, close to theatres and other cultural centres. Petty crime is rife in Lavapiés so it's wise to do this walk in daylight.

Carry on up Mesón de Paredes and turn right into Calle de Soler y González which becomes Calle de la Cabeza. Follow Cabeza to Calle de Rosa and ahead is the charming **Cine Doré** (p43) cinema building.

Walk up Mesón de Paredes, passing **Taberna Antonio Sánchez** at No. 13, which is named after a matador from 1870.

On the corner of Calle del Mesón de Paredes is **La Corrala** (p170), one half of a typical 19th-century tenement block.

The hipster **Pum Pum Café** is a great stop for a coffee.

Crossing the Plaza de Lavapiés to Calle del Ave María, you reach the **Barbieri Café**, an old haunt for artists and writers.

Tirso de Molina

PLAZA DE TIRSO DE MOLINA

CALLE DE LA MAGDALE

CALLE DE SOLER Y GONZÁLEZ

CALLE DE LA CABEZA

CALLE DE JUANELO

Taberna Antonio Sanchez

CALLE DE LAVAPIÉS

CALLE DEL OLIVAR

CALLE DEL AVE MAR

CALLE DE EMBAJADORES

CALLE DEL MESÓN DE PAREDES

CALLE DEL AMPARO

LAVAPIÉS

Barbieri Café

PLAZA DE LAVAPIÉS

La Alhambra

Lav

La Corrala

CALLE DE TRIBULETE

Pum Pum Café

0 metres   250
0 yards   250

N

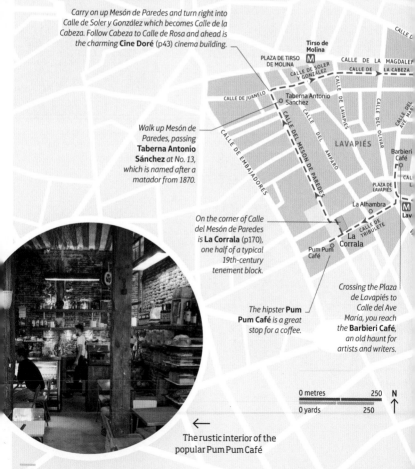

← The rustic interior of the popular Pum Pum Café

Turn right into Calle de los Madrazo, then left into Calle del Marqués de Casa Riera, and finish at the **Círculo de Bellas Artes** (p116) art complex.

Locator Map
For more detail see p94

Lavapiés and Las Letras Districts

EAST MADRID

FINISH

Take Calle Fernanflor to Calle de Jovellanos to view the **Teatro de la Zarzuela** (p47), where light opera is performed.

Círculo de Bellas Artes

CALLE DEL MARQUÉS DE CASA RIERA

C. DE LOS MADRAZO

Teatro de la Zarzuela

C. DE ZORRILLA

C. DE SAN JERONIMO

MARQUÉS DE CUBAS

PLAZA DE LAS CORTES

Walk up Duque de Medinaceli, pass the **Westin Palace** (p117) on your right and enter Plaza de las Cortes.

CALLE DEL PRADO

Westin Palace

CALLE DE LEÓN

Casa de Lope de Vega

CALLE DE

CERVANTES

Basilica of Jesus of Medinaceli

PASEO DEL PRADO

C. DE LOPE DE VEGA

Turn right into Calle de San Agustín to reach the burial place of Cervantes in the **Convento de las Trinitarias** (p114).

CALLE DE LAS HUERTAS

LETRAS

Convento de las Trinitarias

PLAZA DE SAN JUAN

PLAZA DE ANTÓN MARTÍN

CALLE DE MORATIN

M Antón Martín

Cine Doré

CALLE DE SANTA EUGENIO

CALLE DE

Head to **Plaza de Antón Martín** and cross Calle de Atocha to reach the start of Calle del León. You are now in Las Letras where the authors of the Spanish Golden Age lived (p40).

CALLE DE ZURITA

CALLE DE SANTA ISABEL

CALLE DE SANTA ISABEL

CALLE DE ATOCHA

C. DE DOCTOR PIGA

C. DR. MATA

PLAZA SANCHEZ BUSTILLO

C. DR. DRUMEN

Estación del Arte
M
PLAZA DEL EMPERADOR CARLOS V

LE DE JMOSA

DEL DOCTOR FOURQUET

CALLE DEL DOCTOR FOURQUET

CALLE DEL HOSPITAL

START

Museo Reina Sofía (MNCARS)

Start at the **Museo Reina Sofía** (p104) which displays Spanish art from 1900 to the present day.

RONDA DE ATOCHA

→ The modern Jean Nouvel-designed extension of the Museo Reina Sofía

MALASAÑA, CHUECA AND SALAMANCA

The area north of central Madrid marries commercial and artistic history. Affluent Salamanca is named after the 19th-century aristocrat, José de Salamanca y Mayol (1811–83), who built it. The neighbourhood was transformed by the Marqués in the 1860s and became instantly popular with the upper classes, who opted to live in the elegant mansions here over their houses in central Madrid, lacking as they were in hot water and flushing toilets. Conservative Salamanca's residents were later known for supporting the Franco regime. In stark contrast, Chueca, to the west of Salamanca, was originally the home of the city's talented tile-makers and blacksmiths. In the early 1980s, the street films of Pedro Almodóvar established Chueca as the city's premier gay district, which kickstarted a renaissance in the previously rundown area. LGBTQ+ culture became more mainstream in the 1990s, building to today's open and buzzing atmosphere. Neighbouring Malasaña was the principal character in the 1808 uprising against the French. It wasn't until the 1960s that it built an artsy name for itself, drawing in hipsters with its cheap rents.

MALASAÑA, CHUECA AND SALAMANCA

Must Sees

1. Museo Arqueológico Nacional
2. Museo Lázaro Galdiano

Experience More

3. Paseo de la Castellana
4. Plaza de Chueca
5. Calle del Almirante
6. Iglesia de Santa Bárbara
7. Biblioteca Nacional de España
8. Tribunal Supremo
9. Iglesia de San José
10. Palacio del Marqués de Linares
11. Salamanca
12. Museo de Cera
13. Palacio Longoria
14. Plaza de Colón
15. Calle de Zurbano
16. Fernán Gómez Centro Cultural de la Villa
17. Fundación Juan March
18. Calle de Serrano
19. Museo de Arte Público
20. Café Gijón
21. Museo Sorolla
22. Malasaña

23. Museo del Romanticismo
24. Museo de Historia de Madrid
25. Cuartel del Conde Duque
26. Palacio de Liria

Eat

1. La Tasquita de Enfrente
2. Naif Madrid
3. Foodtruck
4. Con 2 Fogones
5. La Musa

Drink

6. Santamaría
7. Los Grifos
8. 1862 Dry Bar

Stay

9. Hotel One Shot Luchana 22
10. Hotel Santo Mauro
11. Hotel Unico
12. 7 Islas

Shop

13. Agatha Ruiz de la Prada
14. Poncelet Cheese Bar

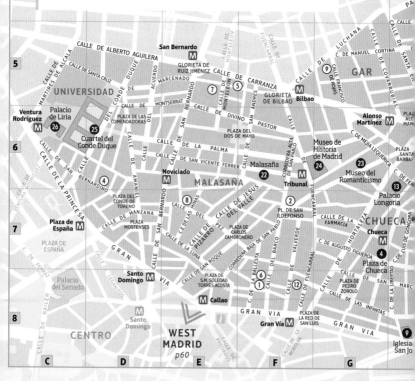

❶ ⬡ ⬡ ▢ ⬡

MUSEO ARQUEOLÓGICO NACIONAL

📍K7 🏠Calle de Serrano 13 🚌223, 223-A Ⓜ️Serrano, Retiro, Colón 🕐9:30am-8pm Tue-Sat, 9:30am-3pm Sun 🚫Some public hols 🌐man.mcu.es

With hundreds of impressive exhibits, ranging from prehistoric times to the 19th century, and more than 1,300,000 artworks and artifacts, this palatial archaeological museum in the smart district of Salamanca is one of Madrid's best.

Founded by Isabel II in 1867, Madrid's brilliant archaeological museum contains many items uncovered during excavations all over Spain, as well as pieces from Egypt, ancient Greece and the Etruscan civilization. Highlights of the earliest finds include an exhibition on the ancient civilization of El Argar in Andalucía, and a display of jewellery uncovered at the Roman settlement of Numantia, near Soria (northeast of Madrid). Other exhibited pieces include 7th-century AD gold votive crowns from Toledo province, Greek and Carthaginian coins, impressive Roman mosaics, including one from the 3rd century AD, and stunning Islamic pottery. The most outstanding treasure to look out for is the Romanesque *Madonna and Child* from Sahagún, considered to be a masterpiece of Spanish art.

Visigothic Crown

▽ A beautiful 7th-century AD gold crown with pearls, sapphires and garnets was found at Guarrazar, Toledo. Letters that spell out "RECCESVINTHVS REX OFFERET" hang from it, indicating it was a church offering from Visigoth King Recesvinto.

Ritual Sword

An exceptional laminated, gold-handled sword from the Bronze Age Argar culture (19th-14th centuries BC) was discovered in Guadalajara, Mexico.

Museum Highlights

Dama de Baza

△ This ancient Iberian statue from the 4th century BC represents a woman from Baza, Granada. It has a niche at the back for the ashes of the dead.

Mosaic of Gladiators

▷ This 3rd-century AD Roman mosaic depicts a combat between gladiators Simmachius and Maternus on the lower part while its upper register shows the victory of Simmachius.

GALLERY GUIDE

The museum's displays date from prehistory through to the 19th century and are in chronological order, starting with prehistory on the ground floor and finishing with the modern era on the top floor. You can find exciting temporary exhibitions, which are held regularly, in the basement.

← Photographing a variety of Roman antiquities in the grand Museo Arqueológico Nacional *(inset)*

MUSEO LÁZARO GALDIANO

📍L3 🏠Calle de Serrano 122 🚌 Ⓜ Rubén Darío, Gregorio Marañón 🕐9:30am-3pm Tue-Sun 🚫Public hols 🌐flg.es

Reflecting the broad and exquisite tastes of its founder, Lázaro Galdiano, this museum displays works by Europe's top names in the fields of fine and applied art. Take a stroll through the imposing Italianate mansion, marveling at the treasures.

This art museum is housed in the former mansion of the editor and financier José Lázaro Galdiano. In 1903, he married Argentine heiress Paula Florido and they built the home to celebrate – and to show off their growing art collection. By the time Lázaro Galdiano died, some 13,000 items were housed here. His private pieces were bequeathed to the nation in 1947.

The collection ranges from the 6th century BC to the 20th century and contains items of exceptional quality, from less familiar Goya portraits to a mass of fob watches, including one worn by Carlos I. Among the most beautiful objects are a series of Limoges enamels and *The Saviour*, a portrait attributed to a student of Leonardo da Vinci. The museum features paintings by English artists Constable, Gainsborough, Reynolds and Turner, as well as 17th-century works by the likes of Spanish painters Zurbarán, Ribera, Murillo and El Greco.

> **Did You Know?**
>
> Goya was rejected from Madrid's Real Academia de Bellas Artes de San Fernando in 1763 and 1766.

↑ Interior of the museum, adorned with paintings and sculptures

← Michelangelo Naccherino's *Christ at the Column* sculpture

↑ The pleasant red-brick exterior of the Museo Lázaro Galdiano

TOP 5 MUSEUM HIGHLIGHTS

The Witches' Sabbath
Goya's painting, dating from 1798, is based on a legend from Aragón and depicts a witches' Sabbath around the devil (represented by the scapegoat).

Christ at the Column
This life-size marble statue was sculpted by Michelangelo Naccherino in 1764.

St John the Baptist
Hieronymus Bosch's contemplative St John (painted c 1485–1510) reclines in an almost pastoral landscape punctuated by grotesque plants.

Crosier Head
This beautiful gilded object was made in Limoges in the 13th century for the top of a bishop's staff (crosier).

Tartessic Ewer
This Tartessic bronze jug, from the mid-6th century BC, is one of the museum's oldest items.

EXPERIENCE MORE

③

Paseo de la Castellana

📍K5 🅜Santiago Bernabéu, Cuzco, Plaza de Castilla, Gregorio Marañón, Colón

The axis of modern Madrid is a long, grand boulevard that cuts through the east of the city, starting in the south with the Paseo del Prado. A journey along it gives a glimpse of Madrid as Spain's commercial capital.

The Plaza de Colón marks the start of the Paseo de la Castellana. This northernmost section of the boulevard has several examples of modern architecture. Further north is the Estadio Santiago Bernabéu (p167), while at the far north end, in Plaza de Castilla, you can find the two Puerta de Europa buildings.

The boulevard's southern-most portion – the Paseo del Prado (p126) – starts north of the Estación de Atocha (p124). The oldest section, it dates from the reign of Carlos III, who built it as part of his embellishment of eastern Madrid. At the Plaza de Cibeles, the avenue becomes the Paseo de Recoletos (p154).

④

Plaza de Chueca

📍G7 🅜Chueca

The pedestrianized Plaza de Chueca sits between Calle de Augusto Figueroa and Calle de Gravina. It was originally called Plaza de San Gregorio after a statue of the saint that stood in Calle San Gregorio. In 1943 the square was renamed after Federico Chueca (1846–1908), a composer of *zarzuelas*.

On one side of the square is the Taberna de Ángel Sierra, a *taberna* full of character. Around the plaza is an intricate maze of little streets, one of which, Augusto Figueroa, is full of wonderful shoe shops. Drop into the Mercado de San Antón for tapas and drinks at the rooftop bar. The surrounding area makes up the Chueca neighbourhood, which is the main focus of Madrid's LGBTQ+ community, with a good selection of bars. A few blocks away is the Plaza de Pedro Zerolo, named after one of the most important LGBTQ+ activists in Spanish history who fought fiercely for homosexual couples to have the right to marry and adopt children.

⑤

Calle del Almirante

📍J7 🅜Banco de España, Colón, Chueca

Running between the Paseo de Recoletos and Calle de

LA MOVIDA

With Franco's death in 1975 came a new period of personal and artistic liberty. A momentous ideological shift occurred among the people, a phenomenon known as *la movida*, or "the action". At the time, it received the support of the mayor of Madrid, Tierno Galván, and saw flourishing creative expression in literature, photography, music, art, television and fashion. The movement also led to the rise and emergence of satirical film director Pedro Almodóvar (p42).

← The attractive Plaza de Chueca, enclosed by apartments and shops

6 Iglesia de Santa Bárbara

📍 J/H7 🏛 Calle General Castaños 2 Ⓜ Alonso Martínez, Colón 🕐 9am-1pm & 5-8pm Mon-Fri, 10am-1pm & 6-9pm Sat & Sun 🌐 parroquiadesanta barbara.es

No expense was spared on this fine Baroque church, which was built, along with an adjoining convent (now the Tribunal Supremo, p140), for Bárbara de Braganza, wife of Fernando VI. To run the convent, Bárbara chose Las Salesas Reales – an order of nuns founded in 1610. The church is sometimes called Las Salesas Reales.

François Carlier (1707–60) was appointed architect, and the first stone was laid in 1750. In 1757, the huge edifice was finished by builder Francisco de Moradillo.

The main door is reached through pleasant gardens, added in 1930. The central medallion on the façade, by Doménico Olivieri, shows *The Visitation* of the pregnant Virgin to her cousin Elizabeth. The angels on either side hold the Cross and the two tablets of the Ten Commandments.

The extravagant interior decoration was assigned to Doménico Olivieri. To the right of the entrance is a painting of St Francis de Sales and St Jane de Chantal by Corrado Giaquinto.

To the right of the central aisle is the tomb of Fernando VI, adorned with tiers of angels. The high altar is decorated with sculptures of San Fernando and Santa Bárbara.

Barquillo, this street is famous for its own-label fashion shops. For most of the 20th century it was known as "Calle de Cesterías" (basketwork street). In earlier days there were five cane shops where woven wares were sold, and several taverns where neighbours gathered.

During the transition to democracy following Franco's death in 1975, Calle del Almirante gained a certain notoriety. Fewer police patrolled the area, and street crime rose. During this time, Jesús del Pozo, a budding fashion designer, opened the first menswear boutique in the area. As his brand became popular, in 1980 he began focusing on high-end women's formal wear. Today his flagship store is on Calle de Lagasca, in the Salamanca area. As del Pozo's boutique flourished, along with the cultural movement of *la movida*, the area became fashionable and other clothes shops and decor outlets opened. Now Calle del Almirante is a favourite haunt of the wealthy and business people from neighbouring offices. Although few of the original shops remain, at No. 23 is the Regalos Originales, a must-see for browsers of antiques and old curiosity shops.

↑ The elaborate interior of the Iglesia de Santa Bárbara

TOP 4 SPANISH FEMALE WRITERS

Emilia Pardo Bazán
Countess (1851-1921) known for introducing feminist ideas to Spanish literature.

Corín Tellado
The author of over 5,000 books, Tellado (1927-2009) held the world record for the most books written in Spanish.

Rosa Montero
Well-known journalist and author (1951-) of contemporary fiction.

Elvira Navarro
Considered one of the best rising novelists (1978-) in Spain today.

❼ Biblioteca Nacional de España

📍K7 🏛Paseo de Recoletos 20-22 Ⓜ Colón, Serrano 🕐10am-8pm Mon-Fri, 9am-2pm Sat; Museum & exhibitions Sun only 🚫Public hols 🌐bne.es

This public library was founded in 1712 by King Philip V. Its many halls hold about 28 million publications, along with a large number of audio-visual records, maps and music scores. From the start, printers have had to submit a copy of every book printed in Spain. Among the library's prized possessions is the first edition of *Don Quixote*, and two handwritten codes by Leonardo da Vinci.

The museum traces the library's history, as well as the evolution of writing, reading and media

systems. There are regular exhibitions, talks and concerts, as well.

❽ Tribunal Supremo

📍J7 🏛Plaza Villa de Paris 📞913 97 12 00 Ⓜ Alonso Martínez, Colón 🕐To the public one week in Nov or by appt

Built by François Carlier in the 1750s as a convent and school for the adjoining Iglesia de Santa Bárbara (*p139*), this stately Baroque building was run by the Las Salesas Reales nuns. It was built on the orders of Bárbara de Braganza, wife of Fernando VI. After her death, the nuns were allowed to remain in the convent until 1870, when the building was expropriated by the secular government to become the Palace of Justice. The building fell into disrepair, which was made worse by fires in 1907 and 1915. Fortunately, the Iglesia de Santa Bárbara was unaffected. Restoration work was undertaken in 1991 to 1995. In the 1990s, the building became the country's supreme court. In front of the palace is the Plaza Villa de París, a large

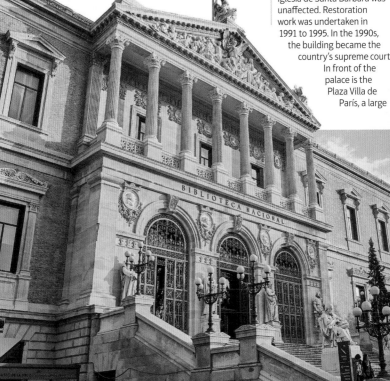

French-style square. In the middle of it are statues of Fernando VI and Bárbara de Braganza. Across the square is the Audiencia Nacional (National Court). Surrounding roads are often lined with official cars and reporters.

9

Iglesia de San José

📍 H8 🏠 Calle de Alcalá 43 📞 915 22 67 84 Ⓜ Banco de España 🕐 7am–12:30pm & 6–9pm daily 🔔 Daily Mass

This church was once part of a Carmelite convent founded in 1605. The convent was demolished in 1863 to build a theatre, and the church itself was rebuilt during the reign of Felipe V. The church was changed yet again in 1908. Adorning the façade, with its three arched entrances, is an attractive statue of the Virgen del Carmen. A number of the

church's treasures are housed in the Prado (p100), but a few interesting images remain on the Neo-Classical main altar and in the Baroque side chapels. Many are by French sculptor Robert Michel, who carved the Cibeles fountain's lions (p111). No 41, next door, is still referred to as the Casa del Párroco (parish priest's house). On 4 April 1910, Alfonso XIII symbolically struck the church with a pickaxe to signal the start of demolition work which would make way for the Gran Vía (p81).

Palacio del Marqués de Linares

📍 J8 🏠 Plaza de Cibeles 2 Ⓜ Banco de España 🕐 6pm & 7pm Fri; 11am, noon & 1pm Sat & Sun for guided tours only 🔒 Aug & some public hols 🌐 casamerica.es

In 1873 Amadeo I, the King of Spain from 1870 to 1873, rewarded the Madrid banker José de Murga for his financial support by granting him the title of Marqués de Linares. The newly designated aristocrat set about building himself the most luxurious, palatial residence Madrid had ever known. The rooms inside the palace are an extravaganza of ornate Rococo decor, resplendent with gold plate, inlaid wood and marble floors, glittering chandeliers and allegorical murals. The most striking rooms are on the first floor. They include the gala dining room, ballroom, Salón Chino (Oriental Room) and Byzantine-style chapel. In the garden is the Pabellón Romántico, a fairy-tale-style pavilion known as the Casa de Muñecas (Dolls' House).

← Steps leading up to the entrance of the Biblioteca Nacional de España

After the Marqués died, the family fortunes declined. Many furnishings and decorations were sold, and the rest disappeared during the Spanish Civil War. By 1977 the palace was almost derelict. However, it was saved by the Spanish government's decision to restore it for Madrid's year as European Capital of Culture in 1992. The main entrance to this French Baroque palace is on Plaza de Cibeles and access to the exhibition rooms is by a side entrance on Paseo de Recoletos. A theatrical tour guided by actors will take you back to the 19th century.

The building now houses the Casa de América, an organization promoting Latin American literature, art and cinema.

 11

Salamanca

L6 **M** Velázquez, Serrano, Núñez de Balboa, Lista, Príncipe de Vergara, Goya, Diego de León

Madrid's Salamanca district (Barrio de Salamanca) was developed in 1862–3 as an area for the bourgeoisie, and takes its name from its founder, José "Pepito" Salamanca, Marqués de Salamanca (1811–83). He was a lawyer who, by the age of 23, had already been elected as a deputy to the Cortes (Spanish parliament). The Marqués had a great flair for politics and business, and made his vast fortune from salt, railways and the building of Salamanca. He was also the founder of the Banco de Isabel II, created in 1844,

PICTURE PERFECT
Tile-Tastic

The beautiful Neo-Mudéjar façade of the ABC Serrano shopping centre in Salamanca *(Calle de Serrano 61)* presents one of the best examples of red brick and *azulejo* tiles in Madrid.

Platea market, offering an array of produce *(inset)*, housed in a former cinema ↑

which was the forerunner of the Banco de España *(p112)*.

The Marqués inaugurated his magnificent palace at Paseo de Recoletos 10 (now the BBVA Bank) in 1858, and by 1862 began developing his land behind it. The streets were planned to run north–south or east–west, and the area was to comprise apartment blocks, churches, schools, hospitals and theatres. He also built the first tramways in Madrid, connecting the Barrio de Salamanca with the centre of the city. A grand statue of the Marqués stands at the confluence of Ortega y Gasset and Príncipe de Vergara.

To this day the *barrio* consists mainly of six- to eight-floor apartment blocks, and is home to many well-to-do families. This is an area where just a hint of cool weather brings out the mink coats. Some of Madrid's best shops and markets can be found here, as well as a number of discreet restaurants. Many gather at the *cervecerías* and bars around Calle de Goya and Calle de Alcalá.

The oldest church of the *barrio*, San Andrés de los Flamencos *(Calle de Claudio Coello 99)*, built in 1884, now houses the Fundación Carlos de Amberes, a cultural centre maintaining links between Spain, Holland and Belgium. Behind the altar is a painting of *St Andrew* by Rubens. The unofficial parish church of Salamanca is the Iglesia de la Concepción *(Calle de Goya 26)*, built between 1902 and 1914, with a notable white iron spire topped by a statue of the Virgin. At Calle de Hermosilla 45 is the charming Protestant Church of St George (1926).

The best-preserved of the area's Neo-Classical palaces is Palacio de Amboage (1918) by Joaquín Roji on the corner of Velázquez and Juan Bravo. It is now the Italian Embassy, and features a lovely garden.

The architecture inside Platea, an avant-garde gourmet market in Plaza Colón, is modern and fascinating. Different food stalls, offering a variety of products, can be found here. On the first floor, visit the restaurant, Canalla Bistro Madrid, and the cocktail bar, El Palco, both arranged near the stage.

Museo de Cera

📍 J7 🏛 Paseo de Recoletos 41 📞 913 19 93 30 Ⓜ Colón
🕐 May–Sep: 11am–8:30pm; Oct–Apr: 11am–7pm
🌐 museoceramadrid.com

Madrid's Wax Museum, off Plaza de Colón, houses some 450 wax dummies of well-known Spanish as well as international figures, mostly set in scenes. A wax likeness of Miguel de Cervantes, author of *Don Quixote*, sits at his desk writing, with windmills behind him. Another scene imitates Goya's famous painting, *The 3rd of May*, depicting French reprisals for the rebellions of 2 May 1808 in Madrid. Also shown is Christopher Columbus's return from the Americas. Other scenes show navigators and scientists, the Last Supper and the history of the Spanish colonies. The museum also displays darker figures such as Freddy Krueger and scenes from the Spanish Inquisition.

More recent figures include cowboys from the Wild West, pop stars, Hollywood actors, sports people, including the newly added figure of famous footballer Cristiano Ronaldo, and the Pope. There is also a café scene where you are encouraged to try to identify Spanish intellectuals, past and present. Those with children should bear in mind that some of the scenes are quite ghoulish and gruesome; one scene

→
The ornamental exterior of the Palacio Longoria, topped by an impressive dome

includes a matador being blinded by a bull.

Upstairs is *Multivision*, a cinema where 27 projectors are used simultaneously to show a 30-minute history of Spain.

Palacio Longoria

📍 H6 🏛 Calle de Fernando VI 4 Ⓜ Alonso Martínez
🚫 To the public
🌐 monumentamadrid.es

Occupied since 1950 by the Sociedad General de Autores y Editores (Spanish Society of Authors and Publishers), the main copyright enforcer for songwriters, composers and music publishers in Spain, the highly ornamental exterior of this sumptuous building is the leading example of Modernista architecture (*p49*) in Madrid.

The palace, located in the Malasaña district, was originally constructed in 1912 for financier Javier González Longoria, who placed his banking offices on the ground floor and made the higher floors his private residence. The elaborate carved vegetal and organic forms on the artificial stone façade are typical of late Modernisme. The building also has a magnificent iron and glass dome. Inside, the main staircase is the most striking feature, with a circular outline that takes its inspiration from French Art Nouveau architecture – as do the rest of the decorations within the palace.

⓮ Plaza de Colón

📍 K6 Ⓜ Serrano, Colón

This large square, one of Madrid's undisputed focal points, is dedicated to 15th-century navigator and colonist Christopher Columbus (Colón in Spanish). It is overlooked by 1970s high-rise buildings, which replaced the 19th-

---

🗻 GREAT VIEW
Lounge Up High

Head to the Picos Pardos Sky Lounge of BLESS Hotel Madrid *(www.blesscollection hotels.com/es/madrid)* for sweeping views of the city accompanied by signature cocktails and an extraordinary menu. Visitors can enjoy the pool for a fee, too.

---

century mansions that once stood here. On the south side of the square is a palace housing the National Library and the Archaeological Museum *(p134)*. Standing on the north side, on the corner of La Castellana, the Postmodern skyscraper of the Heron Corporation towers over the square.

The real feature of the square, however, is the pair of monuments dedicated to Columbus and his journey to the Americas. The oldest, and prettiest, is a Neo-Gothic spire built in 1885, with Columbus at its top, pointing west. Carved reliefs on the plinth give highlights of his landings. Across the square is the more modern monument – a cluster of four large concrete shapes inscribed with quotations relating to Columbus's historic journey to America.

Although constantly busy with traffic, the plaza is a hotspot for cultural events.

⓯ Calle de Zurbano

📍 J4 Ⓜ Alonso Martínez, Rubén Darío

This bustling street connects the trendy neighbourhoods of Chueca and Salesas to the business hub further north. There is much to discover here – from early 20th-century Revivalist buildings, charming shops and art galleries to bakeries, restaurants, hotels and beautiful mansions with verdant gardens.

⓰

Fernán Gómez Centro Cultural de la Villa

📍 K7 🏛 Plaza de Colón 4 🌐 teatrofernangomez.es

Opposite the Museo de Cera *(p143)* and beneath the Plaza de Colón is an extensive

complex, the Fernán Gómez cultural centre. It includes the city's municipal art centre, exhibition halls, Sala Jardiel Poncela - an assembly hall and a theatre, known as Sala Guirau. Built as the Centro Cultural de la Villa, it was renamed in honour of Spanish actor, writer and director Fernando Fernán Gómez. The tourist information office is also housed here.

The complex is surrounded by fountains and gardens in the Colón roundabout's oasis of quiet. The main theatre, the

Sala Guirau, is devoted to contemporary Spanish drama productions, *zarzuela* (light opera) and flamenco, with occasional performances of ballet and Spanish folk music. The smaller Sala Jardiel Poncela venue is reserved for conferences and workshops for adults and children.

Fundación Juan March

M5 Calle de Castelló 77 Núñez de Balboa 11am-8pm Mon-Sat, 10am-2pm Sun march.es

Established in 1955 with an endowment from financier Juan March, this cultural and scientific foundation is best known for its art exhibitions and concerts. The marble-and-glass headquarters, in Barrio de Salamanca, opened in 1975. It owns the Museo de Arte Abstracto in Cuenca and an art gallery in Palma de Mallorca.

The ground floor houses a shop, as well as the main exhibition area. Works by Kandinsky, Picasso and Matisse have been shown here, alongside some of the collection of over 1,300 contemporary Spanish pieces. There is a 400-seat auditorium in the basement where free concerts are held. It is advisable to reserve seats online or at the ticket office. The second-floor library has a collection of contemporary Spanish music, with listening desks. There is also a library on contemporary theatre and entertainment.

Hidden away from the public are the Centre for Advanced Study in the Social Sciences and the Juan March Institute for Study and Investigation – one of the top forums in the field of biology.

←

Night lights enhance the statue of Columbus at the centre of the Plaza de Colón

EAT

La Tasquita de Enfrente

There's no menu here; you're offered a choice of Spanish recipes with a modern twist, based on fresh local produce.

F8 Calle de la Ballesta 6 latas quitadeenfrente.com

€€€

Naif Madrid

A boho-chic, loft-style restaurant with fancy burgers and sandwiches.

F7 Calle de San Joaquín 16 910 07 20 71

€€€

Foodtruck

Massive hamburgers, nachos and pulled pork sandwiches are served here. Make sure you try a "freakshake".

H7 Calle San Lucas 11 foodtruckburger.es

€€€

Con 2 Fogones

An attractive, warmly decorated restaurant with a weekly changing menu.

D6 Calle de San Bernardino 9 condosfogones.com

€€€

La Musa

A classic in Malasaña since the 1990s, this restaurant is always lively. A varied menu changes regularly.

E5 Calle de Manuela Malasaña 18 grupolamusa.com/ en/restaurante-lamusa

€€€

STAY

Hotel One Shot Luchana 22

Housed in a Neo-Classical building with sleek, minimalist rooms with splashes of colour.

 G5 🏠 Calle de Luchana 22 🌐 hoteloneshot luchana22.com

€€€

Hotel Santo Mauro

Luxurious hotel in an opulent private palace with rooms in calming tones of grey and taupe. Adjoining structures feature the famed La Biblioteca restaurant and the cool Gin Bar.

📍 J5 🏠 Calle de Zurbano 36 🌐 marriott.com

€€€

Hotel Unico

The lobby of this boutique hotel exudes self-confident high style with its swirling black-and-white marble mosaic floors and dramatic red sculpture. Chef Ramon Freixa holds two Michelin stars.

 L5 🏠 Calle de Claudio Coello 67 🌐 unicohotel madrid.com

€€€

---

7 Islas

This designer boutique hotel has an arty look with industrial details. The guest rooms have whimsical touches like bronze wall hooks that are sculptures of feet.

 F8 🏠 Calle de Valverde 14 🌐 7islas hotel.com

€€€

 Shoppers admiring a window display of high-end goods on Calle de Serrano

18
Calle de Serrano

📍 L4 Ⓜ Serrano

Named after a 19th-century politician, Madrid's smartest shopping street runs north from the triumphal Plaza de la Independencia to the Plaza del Ecuador, in the well-heeled district of El Viso.

The street is lined with shops – many specializing in luxury items – housed in old-fashioned mansion blocks. Several of Spain's top designers, including Adolfo Domínguez, Purificación García and Roberto Verino, have boutiques in the middle of the street. Towards the northern end are the ABC Serrano mall and the Museo Lázaro Galdiano (p136).

A wide selection of luxury goods shops can be found on Calle de José Ortega y Gasset, including branches of the Italian shops Valentino and Gucci, as well as Chanel, Hermès and Escada. Lower down Calle de Serrano, towards Serrano metro station, are two branches of El Corte Inglés and the stylish clothes and leather goods shop Loewe. On the Calle de Claudio Coello, which runs parallel with Serrano, there are several lavish antique shops, in keeping with the area's upmarket atmosphere.

19
Museo de Arte Público

 K4 🏠 Paseo de la Castellana Ⓜ Rubén Dario

In the early 1970s J Antonio Fernández Ordóñez and Julio Martínez Calzón, the architects of the Calle Juan Bravo bridge, filled the space underneath it with abstract sculptures by 20th-century Spanish artists. The space on the east side of Paseo de la Castellana is dominated by *Sirena Varada, or Stranded Mermaid* (1972–3), a concrete sculpture hanging from four rods by Eduardo Chillida, the noted Basque sculptor. Alberto Sánchez's *Toros Ibéricos* is another dramatic installation, plus a penguin by Miró. Some of the other sculptors represented here are Andreu Alfaro, Julio González, Rafael Leoz, Gustavo Torner and Francisco Sobrino. On the west side are two

---

 PICTURE PERFECT
Optical Illusion

The *Barandillas en "S"* fountain, designed by kinetic sculptor Eusebio Sempere, is the shot to get at the Museo de Arte Público. Its curvilinear forms connecting straight railings creates an optical illusion of alternating wave forms.

> **Many intellectuals' cafés once thrived, but the Gijón is one of the few that survives and it still attracts a lively crowd of *literati*.**

bronzes by Pablo Serrano. Take care when crossing the busy Paseo de la Castellana.

Café Gijón

📍 J7 🏠 Paseo de Recoletos 21 Ⓜ Banco de España
🕒 7am–2am daily
🌐 cafegijon.com

Madrid's café life was one of the most attractive features of the city from the 19th century right up to the outbreak of the Civil War. Many intellectuals' cafés once thrived, but the Gijón is one of the few that survives and it still attracts a lively crowd of *literati*. It was a popular meeting place for "Generation of '36", a group of Spanish artists and writers working during the Spanish Civil War (1936–9). The café

has a striking interior with cream-painted wrought-iron columns, black-and-white table tops and a lovely terrace.

Museo Sorolla

📍 J3 🏠 Paseo del General Martínez Campos 37
Ⓜ Rubén Darío, Iglesia, Gregorio Marañón
🕒 9:30am–8pm Tue–Sat, 10am–3pm Sun ⛔ Mon & some public hols
🌐 culturaydeporte.gob.es/msorolla/el-museo

The former studio-mansion of Valencian Impressionist

Museo Sorolla's impressive collection of art and its pretty garden *(inset)* ↓

painter Joaquín Sorolla is now a museum displaying his art, left virtually as it was when he died in 1923.

Although Sorolla is perhaps best known for his brilliantly lit Mediterranean beach scenes, the changing styles of his paintings are well represented in this museum, with examples of his gentle portraiture and a series of works depicting people from different parts of Spain.

Also on display are objects amassed during the artist's lifetime, including tiles and ceramics. The house, built in 1910, is surrounded by an Andalucían-style garden, designed by Sorolla himself.

 Malasaña

F6 **Tribunal, Bilbao**

A feeling of the authentic old Madrid pervades this district of narrow streets that slope down from Carranza and Fuencarral to its hub, the Plaza del Dos de Mayo. In 1808, *Madrileños* made a heroic last stand here against Napoleon's occupying troops at the gate of Monteleón barracks. The arch in the square is all that is left of the barracks. In front is a memorial by Antonio Solá to artillery officers Daoiz and Velarde, who defended the barracks.

In the 1940s and 1950s the area deteriorated, but residents fiercely fended off demolition threats. It acquired its artistic atmosphere in the 1960s, when hippies were lured into the district by cheap rents. Later it became the centre of *la movida* (p138), the creative scene that began after the death of Franco.

Today Malasaña's streets combine the best of both worlds. Artists and writers have once again moved into the area, along with antique-sellers and hipsters. The charming streets have been home to pretty fountains and plenty of trees. At night, however, the streets are still thronged with people looking for a wild time.

Malasaña is rich in sites of historical and cultural interest. Plaza de San Ildefonso, one of many squares remodelled by José I (Joseph Bonaparte), has an attractive central fountain with serpents entwined around conch shells. Near the Neo-Classical Iglesia de San Ildefonso, built in 1827, one can still see the façade of the Vaquería, a dairy shop that opened in 1911 and closed in 2007. Decorative cows frame the door in Art Deco style.

In Calle de la Puebla, the 17th-century Iglesia de San Antonio de los Alemanes is remarkable for its elliptical

↑ TupperWare, a popular nightspot in the Malasaña quarter

MANUELA MALASAÑA

The daughter of Juan Manuel Malasaña, a leader of the 1808 uprising, Manuela Malasaña died at the age of 16 in the struggle against Napoleon. She was a seamstress who, according to local legend, was caught carrying a pair of scissors by the French and was subsequently shot for possession of a weapon. In 1961, Calle de Manuela Malasaña, which lies between Fuencarral and San Bernardo where the Monteleón barracks had been, was named after this local icon.

interior, swathed in frescoes by Juan Carreño, Francisco de Ricci and Luca Giordano.

Close by is the 17th-century Iglesia de San Plácido with a cupola painted by Francisco Rizi and the work of Claudio Coello adorning the altars.

The Iglesia de San Martín, in Calle de San Roque, was built in 1648. The painting above the altar depicts St Martin of Tours giving half his cloak to a naked beggar.

Museo del Romanticismo

🗺 G6 🏛 Calle de San Mateo 13 Ⓜ Tribunal, Alonso Martínez 🕐 9:30am-8:30pm Tue-Sat (Nov-Apr: to 6:30pm), 10am-3pm Sun & hols 🚫 1 & 6 Jan, 1 & 15 May, 24, 25 & 31 Dec 🌐 museo romanticismo.mcu.es

This Neo-Classical mansion was designed by Manuel Martín in 1776 for the Marqués de Matallana. By 1924 it had been turned into a museum by the Marqués de la Vega-Inclán, the founder of Spain's fine network of state-owned parador hotels, who was an avid art collector. In 1921, the Marqués donated his 19th-century paintings, books and some furniture to form the nucleus of a museum. In 1927, the museum was acquired by the state, and reorganized to look like the home of a wealthy mid-19th century family, evoking the Romantic period.

The exhibits are housed in 26 rooms on the ground floor and first floor of the building. As well as a vast array of 19th-century objects, such as dolls, musical instruments and photographs, there are many portraits by leading artists. They include *General Prim* by Esquivel and *María Cristina* by Salvador Gutiérrez. Several works by Leonardo Alenza include the disturbing *Satire of a Romantic Suicide*.

In the ballroom is a Pleyel piano that belonged to Isabel II.

The ceiling is by Zacarías González Velázquez, and the carpet comes from the Real Fábrica de Tapices (*p170*).

Earlier works on display in the museum include a painting of *St Gregory the Great* by Goya above the altar in the chapel in room 13.

The Mariano José de Larra Room is dedicated to this great satirical journalist and writer, and holds a number of his personal items.

Museo de Historia de Madrid

🗺 G6 🏛 Calle de Fuencarral 78 Ⓜ Tribunal 🕐 10am-8pm Tue-Sun 🌐 esmadrid.com

The Museo de Historia de Madrid is worth visiting just for its majestic Baroque doorway by Pedro de Ribera, arguably the finest in Madrid. Housed in the former hospice of St Ferdinand, the museum was inaugurated in 1929. On the subterranean level, a series

of maps shows how radically Madrid has changed. Among them is Pedro Texeira's 1656 map, thought to be the oldest of the city, as well as Francisco de Goya's *Alegoría de la Villa de Madrid* (Allegory of the City of Madrid). There is also a meticulous model of the city, made in 1830 by León Gil de Palacio.

Modern exhibits include the reconstructed study of Ramón Gómez de la Serna, a key figure of the literary gatherings at the Café de Pombo, a famous café in Madrid where intellectuals would meet in the 20th century. In the garden is the *Fuente de la Fama* (Fountain of Fame), also by de Ribera.

↑ The impressive Baroque doorway leading into the Museo de Historia de Madrid

A pretty bookshop, Libros, in the Malasaña quarter

LIBROS

@ ESCRITURA
CREATIVA
disfruta
tu lengua

@ escribir para
estar bien
@ circulo de lectura

↑ One of the lavishly furnished rooms in the Palacio de Liria

DRINK

Los Grifos

Buy a membership card and serve yourself from the craft beer taps, or opt for a bottled beer.

📍 E5 🏠 Calle de Manuela Malasaña 33 🌐 losgrifos.es

1862 Dry Bar

Stylish, cosy bar serving a wide variety of fun cocktails.

📍 E7 🏠 Calle del Pez 27 📞 609 53 11 51

Santamaría

Formerly a brothel, this classic cocktail bar has a retro feel.

📍 F8 🏠 Calle de la Ballesta, 6 📞 911 66 05 11

㉕

Cuartel del Conde Duque

📍 D6 🏠 Calle del Conde Duque 9-11 Ⓜ Noviciado, San Bernardo ⊙ Cultural Centre: 10am-2pm, 5:30-9pm Tue-Sat, 10:30am-2pm Sun & public hols 🌐 conde duquemadrid.es

This huge rectangular complex is named after Gaspar de Guzmán (1587–1645), Conde Duque de Olivares. As a minister of Felipe IV, the count had a palace on this site. After his death, the palace was neglected. Subsequently, the plot was divided into two distinct sections. On one section, the Palacio de Liria was built for the Duke of Alba. On the other, the barracks for Los Guardias de Corps were constructed between 1720 and 1754 by Pedro de Ribera, who adorned them with a Baroque façade. The three-storey barracks were in use for over a century but, in 1869, they suffered a major fire and fell into a state of dilapidation. A hundred years later Madrid's city hall made the decision to restore the old army barracks.

The building now houses a cultural centre including the Museum of Contemporary Art and an auditorium within the 1718 chapel, built by Ribera. A theatre and rehearsal rooms were added to the complex after extensive renovation.

㉖

Palacio de Liria

📍 C6 🏠 Calle de la Princesa 20 Ⓜ Ventura Rodríguez ⊙ For tours only: times vary, check website 🌐 palaciodeliria.com

The lavish but much-restored Palacio de Liria was completed by Ventura Rodríguez in 1780. Once the home of the Alba family, and still owned by the duke, it can be visited by a maximum of 15 people at one time by appointment only.

The palace houses the Albas' collection of art and Flemish tapestries. There are paintings by Rembrandt, Rubens and Titian. Spanish art is well represented, with works by Goya, such as his 1795 portrait of the Duchess of Alba, as well as examples of works by El Greco, Zurbarán and Velázquez.

CASTIZOS OF MADRID

The true working-class *Madrileños* are known as *castizos*, their families having lived in the neighbourhoods of Old Madrid, Chamberí and Cuatro Caminos for many generations. In around 1850, *castizos* revolted against the bourgeoisie, who were basking in the Romantic and patriotic cultural revolution that followed the defeat of the French earlier in the 19th century. The *castizos* sought to reclaim their proud heritage. Madrid's equivalent of London's cockneys, *los castizos Madrileños* not only revived their district fiestas, one of the best neighbourhood-bonding traditions, but reinvented costumes to go with them and formed associations that still thrive today.

FUN FIESTAS

In May, the *castizos* are out in force during the Dos de Mayo fiesta. On 15 May is the Fiesta de San Isidro, with a *romería* from the Puerta de Toledo down to the Río Manzanares. The next major fiestas are on 13 June at San Antonio de la Florida; and 15 August, with the Fiesta de la Virgen de Paloma, a *castizo* favourite. *Castizo* processions include the Romería de San Blas on 3 February and the Romería de San Eugenio on 15 November.

TRADITIONAL ATTIRE

At the fiestas, or *romerías* (pilgrimage), you will see the *castizos*, or *majos* (dandies), with their *manolas*, or partners, in their traditional uniform. Typical *manola* costume consists of a flowery headscarf, an *alfombra* (an embroidered shawl) and a *falda vestida* (long dress). Men's clothes include a black-and-white *parpusa* (cap), a white *barbosa* (shirt), a black *chupín* (waistcoat), black *alares* (trousers) and shining *calcos* (shoes).

↑ Children dressed in typical *castizo* uniform

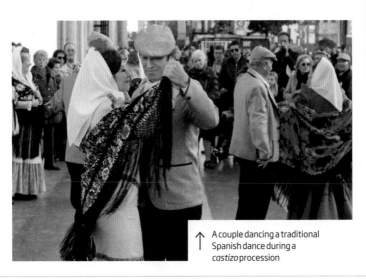

↑ A couple dancing a traditional Spanish dance during a *castizo* procession

A SHORT WALK
PASEO DE RECOLETOS

Distance 2 km (1 mile) **Time** 30 minutes
Nearest metro Chueca

Flanked by iconic buildings, the tree-lined walkway of Paseo de Recoletos stretches from Plaza de Colón to the Fuente de Cibeles. Step back in time in the Museo Arqueológico Nacional, or lose yourself among the well-heeled in the fashion boutiques along Calle del Almirante and Calle Piamonte as you walk through the area and its alluring side streets. Small museums, galleries and theatres add to the cultured feel of the area, and by night the bars are bustling in the neighbouring Chueca *barrio*.

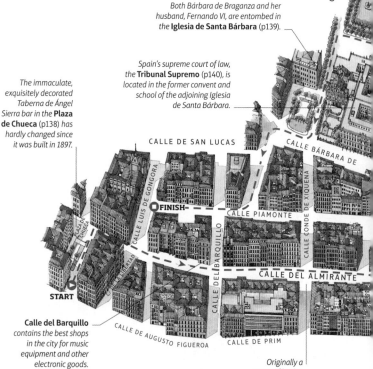

Both Bárbara de Braganza and her husband, Fernando VI, are entombed in the **Iglesia de Santa Bárbara** (p139).

Spain's supreme court of law, the **Tribunal Supremo** (p140), is located in the former convent and school of the adjoining Iglesia de Santa Bárbara.

The immaculate, exquisitely decorated Taberna de Ángel Sierra bar in the **Plaza de Chueca** (p138) has hardly changed since it was built in 1897.

CALLE GENERAL CASTAÑOS

CALLE DE SAN LUCAS

CALLE BÁRBARA DE

CALLE LUIS DE GÓNGORA

FINISH

CALLE PIAMONTE

CALLE CONDE DE XIQUENA

PLAZA DE CHUECA

CALLE DEL BARQUILLO

CALLE DEL ALMIRANTE

START

CALLE DE AUGUSTO FIGUEROA

CALLE DE PRIM

Calle del Barquillo contains the best shops in the city for music equipment and other electronic goods.

Originally a street of basket shops, **Calle del Almirante** (p138) is now home to several of Madrid's own-label fashion shops.

← A waiter cutting meat at the historic, *belle époque* El Espejo

El Espejo *is the most beautifully decorated belle époque bar and restaurant in the city.*

Madrid's wax museum, the **Museo de Cera** *(p143), has likenesses of historical figures.*

Locator Map
For more detail see p132

MALASAÑA, CHUECA AND SALAMANCA

Paseo de Recoletos

The large **Plaza de Colón** *(p144) is a monument to Christopher Columbus (Colón).*

The **Museo Arqueológico Nacional** *(p134) houses a collection of treasures from some of the world's ancient civilizations. The Biblioteca Nacional de España (p140) is located in the same building.*

CALLE DE GENOVA

PLAZA DE COLON

PASEO DE RECOLETOS

CALLE DE RECOLETOS

CALLE DE SERRANO

↑ The imposing façade of the Tribunal Supremo

For over a century, intellectuals have held discussion groups or tertulias (p115) in the wood-panelled **Café Gijón** *(p147).*

Calle de Serrano *(p146) is Madrid's smartest shopping street, home to top Spanish designers.*

0 metres 100
0 yards 100

N ↑

Arganzuela bridge at Madrid Río park, along the Río Manzanares

BEYOND
THE CENTRE

Several of Madrid's best sights lie just outside
the city centre. To the north lies Azca, an area of
skyscrapers, office blocks and upmarket shops,
developed in 1969 as a modern, commerical
district away from the busy city centre. To
the west is the impressive Templo de Debod,
constructed in Egypt in the 2nd century
BC and gifted to Spain in 1968. West of Old
Madrid, across the Río Manzanares, is the vast,
green recreation ground of the Casa de Campo –
a former royal hunting ground.

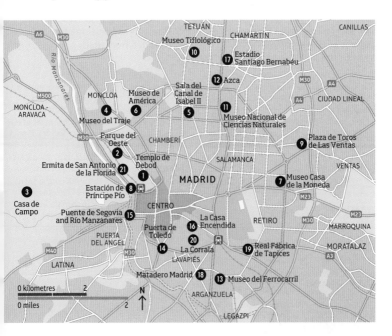

The gateways of the temple reflected in the water ↑

❶

TEMPLO DE DEBOD

🏠 Calle Ferraz 1 🚇 Plaza de España, Ventura Rodríguez ⏰ Summer: 10am-7pm Tue-Sun; winter: 10am-8pm Tue-Sun 🚫 Public hols & afternoons in Aug 🌐 madrid.es/templodebod

A somewhat incongruous sight in Madrid, the authentic temple of Debod, built in Egypt in the 2nd century BC, was gifted to Spain in 1968. Standing on high ground above the Río Manzanares, in the landscaped gardens of the Parque del Oeste, it's a peaceful location from which to watch the sun set over the Spanish capital.

The Templo de Debod was given to Spain in 1968 by the Egyptian government as a tribute to Spanish engineers involved in rescuing ancient monuments from the floodwaters of the Aswan Dam on the River Nile. The temple was packed and transported to Spain, where it was rebuilt, stone by stone, in its original East-West configuration. This careful process involved two phases: the first lasted from October to December 1970, and also involved the planting of the surrounding gardens; the second phase took place in 1972 and concerned reconstructing the lost parts of the temple, including the entrance hall. It officially opened to the public in 1972.

The Templo de Debod stands in a line with two of its original three gateways. From here there are sweeping views stretching as far as the Guadarrama mountains. The temple's carvings depict Amun, a Theban god with a ram's head, symbolizing life and fertility, to whom the temple is dedicated. Although the interior of the temple can no longer be visited, you can walk through the platforms.

←

Enjoying the sunset at the site of the Templo de Debod in the Parque del Oeste

EXPERIENCE MORE

↑ Ancient hieroglyphs that decorate the Egyptian temple

EGYPTIAN BEGINNINGS

Dating from the 2nd century BC, the shrine was originally erected south of Aswan in Egypt, near the River Nile. It was initially constructed by Adikhalamani, the Kushite king of Meroë, as a shrine in which to worship the god Amun. Later, various kings of the Ptolemaic dynasty extended it on all four sides and it became a temple. Decorations were completed by the Roman emperors Augustus and Tiberius.

②
Parque del Oeste

🏛 Paseo Moret 2 Ⓜ Moncloa, Plaza de España, Príncipe Pío 🅆 esmadrid.com

Winding paths and lovely landscaping give this vast park the feel of an English-style garden. It gains an even more international character from the fascinating Templo de Debod, which lies within the park. At the south end, 20,000 specimens of 600 rose varieties thrive in the Ramón Ortiz rose garden. Designed by the city's head gardener in 1955, the lovely garden is the site of an annual competition for new rose varieties.

③
Casa de Campo

🏛 Avenida de Portugal Ⓜ Batán, Príncipe Pío, Casa de Campo, Lago 🚗 To cars 🅆 esmadrid.com

This former royal hunting ground of pine forests and scrubland extends over 17.5 sq km (6.7 sq miles) of southwestern Madrid. Its range of amenities and proximity to the centre make it a popular recreation area for *Madrileños*. Among its many attractions are tennis courts, swimming pools, a boating lake, a zoo and a funfair – the **Parque de Atracciones** with over 50 rides. In summer the park also stages concerts and special events. One way to visit the park and take in the city's sights is to ride the **Teleférico** (cable car), which connects the Parque del Oeste with the Casa de Campo.

Parque de Atracciones
♿ Ⓜ Batán ⏰ Times vary, check website 🅆 parquede atracciones.es

Teleférico
♿ 🏛 Paseo del Pintor Rosales Ⓜ Argüelles ⏰ Mid-Mar–Sep: noon–dusk daily; Oct–mid-Mar: 11am–dusk Sat, Sun & public hols 🅆 teleferico.emtmadrid.es

11
The number of minutes it takes to ride between the two parks on the Teleférico.

↑ A wonderful vista of La Almudena Cathedral from the terrace at the Parque del Oeste

159

↑ Fashion display from contemporary designers at the Museo del Traje

Museo del Traje

🏠 Avenida Juan de Herrera 2 Ⓜ Moncloa, Ciudad Universitaria ⏰ 9:30am-7pm Tue-Sat (Jul & Aug: to 10:30pm Thu), 10am-3pm Sun & public hols 🚫 Mon & some public hols 🌐 es madrid.com

This fascinating museum is devoted to fashion, with outfits from the Middle Ages to those by contemporary designers. There are over 160,000 pieces in its collection, and since many of the items are fragile, the costumes are displayed on

🔍 HIDDEN GEM
Chamberí Ghost Station

Chamberí was one of the original stations of the 1919 Madrid metro. It's now a time capsule of mid-20th-century Madrid, complete with colourful tiles advertising products of the day.

rotation. The museum hosts special events, temporary exhibitions, courses and interesting workshops.

The current building, designed by Jaime López de Asiaín, won the National Prize for Architecture in 1969. The building was inaugurated in 1975, when it first housed the Spanish Museum of Contemporary Art. This later became the Museo Reina Sofía (p104), but once the museum relocated to central Madrid, the Museo del Traje was founded.

5

Sala del Canal de Isabel II

🏠 Calle de Santa Engracia 125 Ⓜ Rios Rosas, Canal ⏰ 11am-8:30pm Tue-Sat, 11am-2pm Sun & public hols 🚫 Some public hols 🌐 esmadrid.com

This renovated water tower is used to host photographic exhibitions but most visitors come to marvel at its complex construction. In the late 19th

century the water supply for Madrid was based on a project patronized by the queen in 1851 and known as the Canal de Isabel II, the name given to Madrid's water company. The first dam was built in the Lozoya valley, about 80 km (50 miles) north of Madrid in the Guadarrama mountains, and a duct carried the water south to a reservoir.

More reservoirs were built to cope with the capital's ever-increasing needs but, in 1903, the development of the high-lying suburbs of Chamberí and Cuatro Caminos dictated the need for a water tower to supply new pipes by gravity. Luis Moya Ydígoras and Ramón Aguinaga were enlisted and designed a polygonal tower of brick and iron, 36 m (118 ft) high, surmounted by a 1,500-sq-m (16,145-sq-ft) tank resting on an iron ring. Work started in 1908, and by 1911 the water tower was finished at a cost of nearly 350,000 pesetas. It was in service until 1952.

The regional government of Madrid restored the tower in

> **The highlight of the Museo de América is the rare Mayan *Códice Tro-cortesiano* (AD 1250-1500) from Mexico. This is a type of parchment illustrated with hieroglyphics.**

1985, taking out the water works but retaining the tank. The exhibition floors within the tower can be accessed by hydraulically driven lifts and steel staircases.

Bordering the tower are the busy Calle de Santa Engracia and the gardens and turf that form a roof over one of the major underground reservoirs of the Canal de Isabel II.

Museo de América

🏛 Avenida de los Reyes Católicos 6 Ⓜ Moncloa
🕐 9:30am-3pm Tue-Sat (to 7pm Thu), 10am-3pm Sun
🚫 Some public hols
🌐 esmadrid.com

This museum houses artifacts relating to Spain's colonization of parts of the Americas. Many of the exhibits, which range from prehistoric times to the present, were brought back to Europe by the early colonizers of the Americas.

The collection is arranged on the first and second floors, and individual rooms have

various themes such as society, religion and communication. Exhibits document the Atlantic voyages made by the first navigators.

For many visitors, the highlight of the Museo de América is the rare Mayan *Códice Tro-cortesiano* (AD 1250–1500) from Mexico. This is a type of parchment illustrated with hieroglyphics of scenes from everyday life.

Also worth seeing are the Treasure of the Quimbayas, a collection of pre-Columbian gold and silver objects from around AD 500–1000, and the collection of contemporary folk art from some of Spain's former American colonies.

Museo Casa de la Moneda

🏛 Calle del Doctor Esquerdo 36 Ⓜ O'Donell, Goya
🕐 10am-8pm Tue-Fri (to 2pm Sat & Sun) 🚫 Some public hols 🌐 museocasa delamoneda.es

The Spanish mint and stamp factory is located in a vast granite building. The museum, which is housed in the north side of the building, was founded in the 18th century by Carlos III's Director of the Mint. It traces the history of currency, from early trading in salt, shells and bracelets up to the euro. There are 17 rooms that hold around 200,000 pieces. The collection was first put on show to the public in 1867. Coins feature

← A Quimbaya civilization golden sculpture on show in the Museo de América

EAT

Bodegas Rosell
This traditional tavern opened in 1920 and serves a variety of classic tapas, along with some excellent wine from the barrel.

🏛 Calle del General Lacy 14 🌐 bodegas rosell.es

€€€

Los Caracoles
This old-fashioned 1940s tavern has a varied menu. Locals tend to drop in for tapas on Sunday afternoons.

🏛 Calle de Toledo 106
📞 913 66 42 46

€€€

Santceloni
The late great chef Santi Santamaria's legacy lives on in this Michelin-starred restaurant.

🏛 Paseo de la Castellana 57 🌐 restaurante-santceloni.com

€€€

prominently, with maps and photographs complementing displays of Greek and Roman coins. The earliest coins that can be seen have images of mythical gods; the picture of Cybele, mother of the gods, on a Roman coin from 78 BC is similar to the sculpture in the Plaza de Cibeles.

As well as later Roman coins endowed with more symbolic images, there are Visigothic and Moorish coins. Early Moorish coins are inscribed in Latin and later ones in Arabic.

There are also engravings for currency notes, stamps, medals and official documents.

EXPERIENCE **Beyond the Centre**

8

Estación de Príncipe Pío

🏠 Paseo de la Florida 2
Ⓜ Príncipe Pío ⏰ Shopping centre: 10am-10pm daily

Also known as Estación del Norte, this railway station was opened in 1880 to supply train services between Madrid and the north of Spain. Built by French engineers Biarez, Grasset and Mercier, iron from French and Belgian foundries was its main component. In 1915, the station's look was enhanced by Mudéjar-style pavilions designed by Demetrio Ribes. The entrance façade was added by architect Luis Martínez Ribes in 1926.

The interior of the main building of the former station has been transformed into a stunning modern space with a glass roof, but it still retains the character of the old station. There are some good bars, restaurants, a cinema complex and a shopping centre. Another part of the station is a major transport interchange. Above the platforms is a splendid latticework canopy. Looking out along the tracks, you can see the Sierra de Guadarrama.

BULLFIGHTING

While bullfighting is an integral part of southern Spanish life, it is highly controversial due to the prolonged nature of the kill purely for entertainment. Opinion is divided on this, with a growing number of Spaniards opposing the tradition, and Catalonia banned the sport on grounds of cruelty in 2010. If you do attend a *corrida*, try to see a prestigious event where chances are high that you'll see a "clean" kill.

9

Plaza de Toros de Las Ventas

🏠 Calle de Alcalá 237
Ⓜ Ventas ⏰ For bullfights & concerts, and tours by appt; Museo Taurino: 10am-6pm daily
🌐 lasventastour.com

Whatever your opinion of bullfighting, Las Ventas is undoubtedly one of the most beautiful bullrings in Spain. Built in 1929 in Neo-Mudéjar style, it replaced the city's original bullring, which stood near the Puerta de Alcalá *(p110)*. With its horseshoe arches around the outer galleries and elaborate tilework decoration, it's a dramatic venue for the *corridas* held during the bullfighting season, from May to October. The statues outside are of two renowned Spanish bullfighters: Antonio Bienvenida and José Cubero. Adjoining the

bullring is the Museo Taurino, which displays memorabilia such as portraits and sculptures of famous matadors, as well as their elaborate costumes. Look out for a costume that belonged to Juanita Cruz, a female bullfighter who rose to fame in the 1930s. The museum is a fascinating insight into the culture that surrounds this traditional part of Spanish life. Do keep in mind before visiting, though, that some of the exhibits are pretty gruesome, such as the heads of bulls killed

---

Did You Know?

Female bullfighter Juanita Cruz was forced, in the face of prejudice, to leave Spain.

uring fights at Las Ventas nd a bloody *traje de luces* raditional costume worn the bullring).

Museo Tiflológico

Calle La Coruña 18 Estrecho 10am-3pm, -7pm Tue-Fri; 10am-2pm at museo.once.es

his museum opened in 1992 a two-storey space designed facilitate easy navigation r people with visual impair- ents. Each room has a recor- ed voice telling you where to and what is before you.

Highlights of the tactile xhibits include models of gnificant buildings from round the world and art- orks made by people who re blind or visually impaired. xhibits about Braille, other rms of communication and ssistive devices offer insight to the daily life of people ith limited or no vision.

Museo Nacional de Ciencias Naturales

Calle José Gutierrez Abascal 2 Gregorio Marañón 10am-5pm Tue-Fri, 10am-8pm Sat, Sun & public hols (Aug: to 3pm) 1, 6 Jan, 1 May & 25 Dec mncn.csic.es

The National Museum of Natural Science,, built in 1887, contains more than 15,000 minerals, 237 meteorites, 30,000 birds, 27,000 mammals and many more items in its archives. The entrance leads to the Biodiversity section. This is an ecological display of nume- rous examples of wildlife, from exotic birds to rare animals, insects and butterflies. Lions, tigers and deer stare out from the walls, while the shelves are heavy with bottled lizards, fish and snakes. An interactive computer display room pro- vides insight into the sounds and habitats of animals.

↑ A life-size elephant exhibit at the National Museum of Natural Science

In another part of the exhibition is information on the Atapuerca site near Burgos, north of Madrid, where Europe's earliest human remains (some 780,000 years old) were discovered in 1997. There is also a huge African elephant, shot by the Duke of Alba in the Sudan in 1916. The elephant's skin was sent back to Spain and reassembled.

The museum also houses displays on the origins of the earth and of life. The star of the show is the 1.8-million-year-old skeleton of *Megatherium americanum*, a bear-like creature from the late Cenozoic period found in Argentina in 1788. Nearby is a Glyptodon (giant armadillo), also from Argentina, along with a life-size reproduction of a diplodocus dinosaur skeleton found in the United States. The exhibition concludes with a collection of minerals that includes metals and precious stones.

The Industrial Engineers' School is also housed in the museum building, and behind are the headquarters of Spain's state scientific institute, CSIC.

←
Plaza de Toros de Las Ventas, Madrid's beautiful Neo-Mudéjar bullring

↑ Aerial view of the Azca district, dotted with skyscrapers

STAY

Hotel Silken Puerta America

Staying northeast of the centre brings the cost of five-star rooms down to three-star prices. Norman Foster, Zaha Adid and Jean Nouvel all had a hand in the room designs here.

 Avenida de América 41 hotelpuert america.com

€€€

Hotel Exe Moncloa

Near the Parque del Oeste, this modern hotel is known for its views of the sun setting over the Guadarrama mountains.

Calle Arcipreste de Hita 10 exe hotels.com

€€€

Azca

Ⓜ Nuevos Ministerios, Santiago Bernabéu

In 1969, work began on the development of this "mini-Manhattan" along the west side of the Paseo de la Castellana. It stretches from the Nuevos Ministerios complex in the south to the Palacio de Congresos y Exposiciones in the north. The idea was to create a modern commercial area away from the congested city centre. Today, some 30,000 people work here.

By day Azca is a mecca for shoppers. The popular department store El Corte Inglés runs alongside Nuevos Ministerios station, and the Moda shopping mall is served by Santiago Bernabéu metro. Across from the Plaza de Lima is the Estadio Santiago Bernabéu (p167), home of Real Madrid Football Club, which was built in 1947.

Major companies operate in the tower blocks, alongside apartments, hotels, bingo halls, nightclubs, cinemas, and plenty of well-regarded restaurants and bars.

In the centre of Azca is the multilevel pedestrian Plaza Pablo Ruíz Picasso with trees, benches, fountains and walkways. Azca is dominated by the aluminium-clad Torre Picasso designed by Minoru Yamasaki, architect of the now destroyed twin towers of New York's World Trade Center. It has 46 floors and a heliport.

Further north on Paseo de Castellano is the stretch known as Cuatro Torres Business Area (CTBA), home of the four tallest skyscrapers in Spain. Of these the Torre de Cristal, designed by Cesar Peli, was finished in 2008 and stands at a height of 249 m (817 ft), while Torre Cespa, designed by Norman Foster, is 248 m (814 ft) tall.

The Torre Europa on Plaza de Lima is another notable building. Designed by Miguel de Oriol e Ybarra and completed in 1982, its exterior concrete supports incorporate a clock. It has 28 floors of offices and three commercial floors below street level.

HIDDEN GEM
La Tabacalera

An old tobacco-factory-turned-art centre (Calle Embajadores 51) is the pride of the up-and-coming Lavapiés neighbourhood, at 1.5 km (1 mile) north-west of the Museo del Ferrocarril. The site hosts exhibitions and performances but is best known for the dynamic murals on its walls.

the rust-coloured Banco Ilbao Vizcaya, on Azca's south corner, was designed by Francisco Javier Sáenz de Oiza. Built in 1980, it stands over the underground rail line between Chamartín and Atocha.

Museo del Ferrocarril

📍 Paseo de las Delicias 61
🚇 Delicias ⏰ Oct-May: 30am-3pm Mon-Fri, Jam-7pm Sat, Sun & public hols; Jun-Sep: 10am-3pm daily 🚫 1 & 6 Jan, 1 May, Aug & 25 Dec 🌐 museodel errocarril.org

though railways had existed Spain since 1848, it was only 1880 that Madrid's first oper railway terminus pened – the station of elicias. This was the main

station serving Portugal, and it remained in use until 1971.

In 1984 the station reopened as a railway museum. The majority of exhibits, in the form of trains, are located in the main terminus on tracks next to the original platforms. There are more than 30 loco-motives – steam, diesel and electric – as well as rolling stock. Explanatory plaques give details and describe the routes of the locomotives. You can explore some of the carriages, including a 1930s dining car that now serves as the site's cafeteria.

One of the most interesting engines is *La Pucheta*, a steam locomotive built in 1884 by Sharp Stewart in Britain. Its water supply was on top of the boiler, in a vessel that resembles a bowler hat.

A 1931 electric locomotive, built in Spain, earned itself

the nickname "The Lioness" because of its weight – more than 150 tonnes. This was the heaviest engine ever used by the Spanish state railway (RENFE), and the longest, measuring approximately 25 m (82 ft). Also of special interest is a 1950s Talgo. These Spanish-designed express trains revolutionized railway transport in the country, and this model was in service until 1971. The train was light, with a very low centre of gravity, reduced height and an articulated system, all of which enabled it to travel much faster than conventional carriages.

The 1928 wooden-sided carriage, the ZZ-307 Coche Salon, was the most luxurious the West Railway Company had to offer. Peering through the windows, you can still see an elegantly laid table in the dining room, the various sleeping compartments and a tiny galley.

One of the popular sights on show is the *Mikado*, a steam locomotive built in 1960, which has been cut away to reveal the mysteries of steam propulsion. This engine was in service until 1975, when the use of regular steam-hauled services came to an end in Spain. To one side of the station are four halls housing model train layouts and railway memorabilia, such as signals, lights, telegraphs and photographs.

Azca is dominated by the aluminium-clad Torre Picasso designed by Minoru Yamasaki, architect of the now destroyed twin towers of New York's World Trade Center.

SHOP

Generación X

One of many branches in Madrid, this store is a must for comic book fans. It stocks a range of comics and even holds events and games.

⌂ Calle de Santa Casilda 3 🌐 generacionx.es

Lavinia

A vast emporium, specializing in wine from the regions of Spain. Be sure to opt for a tasting.

⌂ Calle de José Ortega y Gasset 16 🌐 lavinia.es

La Duquesita

This pâtisserie opened over a century ago, stocking exquisite pastries, cupcakes and chocolates, all beautifully wrapped.

⌂ Calle de Fernando VI 2 🌐 laduquesita.es

---

⑭ Puerta de Toledo

⌂ Glorieta de Puerta de Toledo Ⓜ Puerta de Toledo

The construction of this triumphal arch began in 1813 on the orders of French-born Joseph Bonaparte, José I (p55). It was intended to commemorate his accession to the Spanish throne after the 1808 rout of Madrid. But in 1814, after a short-lived reign, José I fled Spain and was replaced by Fernando VII. By the time the arch was completed in 1827, by the architect Antonio López Aguado, it had to be dedicated to Fernando VII.

The Puerta de Toledo is one of Madrid's two remaining city gates, and is topped by a group of sculptures that represent a personification of Spain. On either side of these are the allegorical figures of Genius and the Arts. All were carved in their entirety from Colmenar stone by Ramón Barba and Valeriano Salvatierra, and are flanked by some military-themed sculptures.

---

⑮ Puente de Segovia and Río Manzanares

⌂ Calle de Segovia Ⓜ Puerta del Ángel

Puente de Segovia, a grand granite bridge over the Río Manzanares, was commission[ed] by Felipe II not long after he had decided to establish his court in Madrid. The bridge was to be a main entry point to Madrid and he chose Juan [de] Herrera, his favourite archite[ct] to build it. Construction bega[n] in 1582. The bridge, with nin[e] arches topped with decorati[ve] bosses, was rebuilt in 1682.

Downstream is the superb pedestrian bridge, Puente d[e] Toledo, built between 1718 and 1732 for Felipe V. The architect was Pedro de Riber[a]. A long stretch of the riversid[e] has been landscaped with cycling and walking paths an[d] is given the name Madrid Río.

The Manzanares, which is more of a stream than a rive[r,] never deserved such splend[id] bridges. It was the butt of ma[ny] jokes; a German ambassado[r]

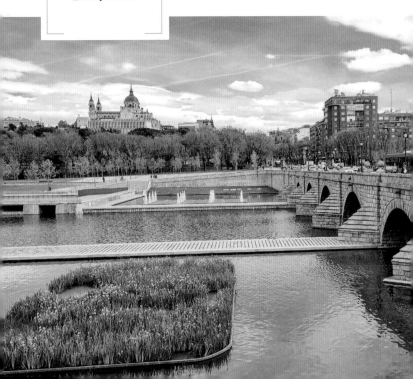

by the name of Rhebiner once said the river was the best in Europe because it had the advantage of being "navigable by horse and carriage". Author of *The Three Musketeers*, Alexandre Dumas (1802–70), wrote of the Manzanares during his visit to Madrid that "however hard I looked for it, I could not find it". Rising in the Sierra de Guadarrama and eventually joining the River Tagus, the river forms a link between Spain's capital and Lisbon, the capital of Portugal.

↑ Silverware at the Real Madrid museum based at the Estadio Santiago Bernabéu

16

La Casa Encendida

🏠 Ronda de Valencia, 2
Ⓜ Lavapiés ⏰ 10am-10pm Tue-Sun 📅 2 wks mid-Jan
🌐 lacasaencendida.es

Housed in a 1913 Moorish-style building, La Casa Encendida is one of the city's most avant-garde and socially conscious institutions. Its programme embraces new forms of expression in visual arts, film and literature, while

↑ The buttressed arches of Puente de Segovia over the Río Manzanares

lectures and workshops touch on environmental and social issues and encourage debate. The large building also houses a café, perfect for light meals and snacks made with chemical-free ingredients. There is also a rooftop terrace, which is a favourite for film screenings during the summer. Be sure to stop by the Ecoshop, which stocks locally made goods as well as other fair-trade merchandise.

17

Estadio Santiago Bernabéu

🏠 Avenida de Concha Espina 1 Ⓜ Santiago Bernabéu ⏰ Non-match days: 10am-7pm Mon-Sat, 10:30am-6:30pm Sun
🌐 realmadrid.com

Inaugurated in December 1947, the Estadio Santiago Bernabéu bears the name of a great football player for Real Madrid who was the 1943-78 club president. It hosted the finals of the European Cup/UEFA Champions League in 1957, 1969, 1980 and 2010, as well as the 1982 FIFA World Cup.

The stadium, which hosts both the Real Madrid football and basketball clubs, has been altered on many occasions, and currently seats just over 81,000. A further €575m

renovation, completed in 2022, has greatly modernized the stadium with a retractable roof, a new and larger museum with interactive, virtual reality displays and a greater selection of restaurants.

A GLORIOUS HISTORY

Football in Madrid dates from 1897, when English students at the Institución Libre de Enseñanza formed a club that played Sunday mornings in Moncloa. The Madrid Football Club arose from this casual organization in 1902, and won its first title in 1905 - the Spanish Cup. In 1920, King Alfonso XIII granted the title "royal" to the club, which has been known as Real Madrid ever since. One of the most widely supported and lucrative teams in the world, Real Madrid was recognized as the FIFA "Club of the 20th Century". Its players are sometimes nicknamed "*los blancos*" in reference to their white kits.

Lush foliage lining the Río Manzanares

18

Matadero Madrid

📍 Plaza de Legazpi 8
Ⓜ Legazpi ⏰ 9am-10pm daily 🌐 mataderomadrid.org

From its inauspicious beginnings as a slaughterhouse (*matadero*) sat on the side of the Manzanares river, this complex of hangars has been part of a stunning transformation of the area south of the centre. A lively, creative space, the Matadero Madrid is a cultural centre that promotes artistic experimentation.

The buildings bear grisly reminders of their original function in the shape of tiled signs indicating "poultry slaughter", "throat-cutting" and so on, but the architecture – Madrid's characteristic Neo-Mudéjar style of elaborate brickwork – is far from gloomy. From the performing arts, theatre and music, to design, architecture and literature, the centre is dedicated to design in all forms. There are regular exhibitions, performances and workshops, but it is also worth a visit just to stroll around, soaking up the lively atmosphere and making the most of its three eateries: La Cantina, the Café Teatro and, in summer, the Terraza Matadero.

19

Real Fábrica de Tapices

📍 Calle Fuenterrabía 2
Ⓜ Menéndez Pelayo ⏰ For tours: 10am-2pm Mon-Fri 🚫 Public hols & Aug
🌐 realfabricadetapices.com

Founded by Felipe V in 1721, the Royal Tapestry Factory is the only surviving factory opened by the Bourbons in the 18th century. In 1889 the factory was moved to this building, just south of the Parque del Retiro (*p108*).

You can see the carpets and tapestries being made by hand, a process which has changed little since the factory was built. Goya and his brother-in-law Francisco Bayeu drew cartoons on which the tapestries for the royal family were based. Some of the cartoons are on display here, in the museum; others are in the Museo del Prado (*p100*). Several tapestries can be seen at the Palacio Real de El Pardo (*p194*) and at El Escorial (*p174*). Today the factory makes and repairs the beautiful carpets decorating the Hotel Ritz (*p110*).

 GREAT VIEW
Magnificent Madrid

The 90-m (295-ft) elevator ride to the observation deck of the Faro de Moncloa (*Avenida de la Memoria*) only takes 50 seconds. Once you reach the spire towering over Madrid's University City, you can see for miles on a clear day.

20

La Corrala

📍 Calle del Mesón de Paredes, between Calle Tribulete & Calle del Sombrerete Ⓜ Lavapiés
🚫 To the public

Corralas are timber-framed apartment blocks, or tenements, built during the 19th century mainly in humbler parts of the city, especially in the neighbourhood of Lavapiés

↑ The beautiful ceiling painted by Goya inside the Ermita de San Antonio de la Florida

The buildings were arranged around an interior courtyard; balconies overlooked the courtyard and provided access to individual apartments. La Corrala exemplifies this type of housing. Construction began in 1872, but as some of the building permits were not in order, only half of the building seems to exist. The courtyard, rather than being completely surrounded by the building, opens out on to a plaza. Its exposure means that there are good views of the building, and of all the laundry hanging from the balconies.

In 1977, La Corrala became a monument of historic interest, and later underwent complete restoration. In the past, zarzuela (light opera) performances have been staged at the site, a fitting backdrop since *La Revoltosa*, the best-known zarzuela, is set in a *corrala*.

Nearby are several other *corralas* – one on the corner of Calle de Miguel Servet with Calle del Espino, one at Calle de Provisiones 12 and another at Calle de la Esperanza 11.

Ermita de San Antonio de la Florida

🏛 Glorieta San Antonio de la Florida 5 🚇 Príncipe Pío 🕘 9:30am–8pm Tue–Sun 🔒 Public hols 🌐 esmadrid.com

Goya enthusiasts should not miss a visit to this remarkable Neo-Classical church, built during the reign of Carlos IV. Standing on the site of two previous churches, the present building is dedicated to St Anthony and is named after the pastureland of La Florida, on which the original churches were built. It took Goya just four months in 1798 to paint the cupola's immense fresco. It depicts St Anthony raising a murdered man from the dead so that he can prove innocent the saint's falsely accused father. Ordinary characters from late 18th-century Madrid are also featured in the painting. The fresco is considered one of Goya's finest works. The artist lies buried under the dome of this church.

DRINK

Bar Casa Paco
Friendly tapas bar worth a visit to sample from more than 20 varieties of tortilla and traditional Spanish meat dishes.

🏛 Calle de Altamirano 38 🔒 Sat & Sun 🌐 barcasapaco.es

Verguenza Ajena
This bookstore and bar in the heart of Chamberí champions good literature with a healthy side of beer. It also hosts readings.

🏛 Calle de Galileo 56 🌐 verguenzajena.es

Jarritus Madrid Cervecería
Sit outside on the terrace to take in the adjacent Las Ventas bullring. As well as a wide range of beers, Jarritus carries a vermouth crafted just for the tavern and uses a distinct house gin in its cocktails.

🏛 Calle de Alcalá 233 🌐 jarritus.com

The stunningly transformed slaughterhouse, now home to the Matadero Madrid complex

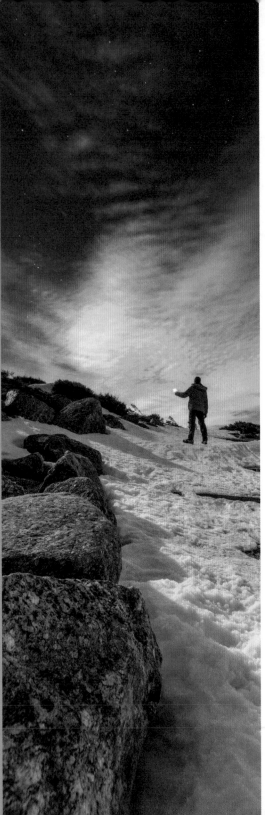

Beautiful snowy mountains at the Guadarrama National Park

Must Sees

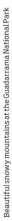

1 El Escorial
2 Segovia
3 Toledo
4 Cuenca

Experience More

5 Santa Cruz del Valle de los Caídos
6 Museo del Aire
7 Palacio Real de El Pardo
8 Manzanares el Real
9 Sierra Norte
10 Monasterio de Santa María de El Paular
11 Sierra Centro de Guadarrama
12 Buitrago del Lozoya
13 Palacio Real de Aranjuez
14 Alcalá de Henares
15 Chinchón
16 Parque de El Capricho
17 La Granja de San Ildefonso
18 Guadalajara
19 Illescas
20 Sigüenza
21 Palacio de Riofrío

DAYS OUT FROM MADRID

Just outside of Madrid's dormitory towns and industrial estates lies the real countryside. At the foothills of the Sierra de Guadarrama mountains stands El Escorial, the royal monastery-palace built by Felipe II, from which he ruled his empire. Felipe II's predecessors ruled Castile in Segovia, while Toledo, which was the capital of Visigothic Spain, has a rich architectural and artistic heritage derived from a coalescence of Muslim, Christian and Jewish cultures. Historic towns outside of Madrid include Alcalá de Henares – the birthplace of renowned writer Cervantes – and Sigüenza, with its impressive castle parador.

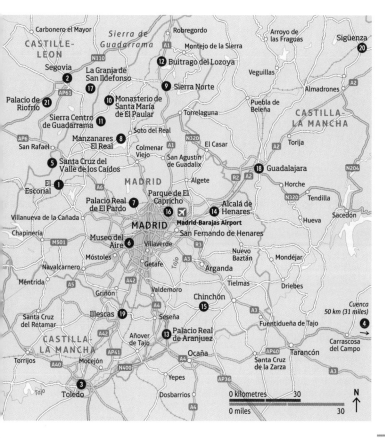

❶ ⊘ ⊘ ⊡ ⊡

EL ESCORIAL

⌂ Avenida de Juan de Borbón y Battemberg, San Lorenzo de Escorial 🚇 From Estación del Arte, Sol or Chamartín 🚌 661, 664 from Moncloa ⏰ Apr-Sep: 10am-8pm Tue-Sun; Oct-Mar: 10am-6pm Tue-Sun 🚫 1 May, 8 Sep, 24, 25 & 31 Dec 🌐 patrimonionacional.es

Felipe II's imposing grey palace stands out against the foothills of the Sierra de Guadarrama. Built between 1563 and 1584, its unornamented severity sparked an influential architectural style in Spain.

El Escorial was conceived as a mausoleum and retreat rather than a splendid residence. When architect Juan Bautista de Toledo died in 1567, he was replaced by Juan de Herrera, royal inspector of monuments. His former role explains the plain architectural style of El Escorial – called *desornamentado*, literally, "unadorned". Despite its sober appearance the palace is home to some of the most important works of art of the royal Habsburg collections.

↑ The breathtaking ceiling of the main staircase in El Escorial

Architectural Museum

Sala de Batallas

Bourbon Palace

The Alfonso XII College was founded by monks in 1875 as a boarding school.

Did You Know?

El Escorial is laid out to a gridiron shape in honour of St Lawrence, who burned to death on a grill.

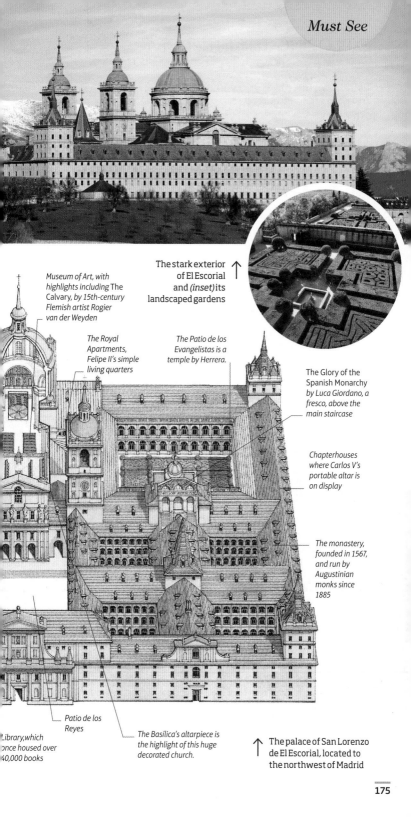

The stark exterior of El Escorial and *(inset)* its landscaped gardens ↑

Museum of Art, with highlights including The Calvary, by 15th-century Flemish artist Rogier van der Weyden

The Royal Apartments, Felipe II's simple living quarters

The Patio de los Evangelistas is a temple by Herrera.

The Glory of the Spanish Monarchy by Luca Giordano, a fresco, above the main staircase

Chapterhouses where Carlos V's portable altar is on display

The monastery, founded in 1567, and run by Augustinian monks since 1885

Patio de los Reyes

Library, which once housed over 40,000 books

The Basílica's altarpiece is the highlight of this huge decorated church.

↑ The palace of San Lorenzo de El Escorial, located to the northwest of Madrid

EXPLORING THE INTERIOR

Royal Apartments

The Palacio de los Austrias, or Royal Apartments, are built around and adjoining the Basílica. From her bed, the Infanta Isabel Clara (Felipe II's daughter) could see the high altar and the officiating priest. On the right wall are paintings of her and her sister Catalina by Bartolomé González (1564–1627).

The Sala de Retratos is full of portraits, beginning above the fireplace with Carlos I by Juan Pantoja de la Cruz (1553–1608) – a copy of the original painting by Titian lost in a fire in 1604. Moving anticlockwise, the next portrait is of Felipe II by Antonio Moro (1519–76).

At both ends of the Salas de los Paseos are magnificent German marquetry doors. Blue Talavera tiles cover the lower part of the walls, while the upper parts are decorated with 16th-century maps and paintings of famous Spanish military victories.

In the king's chamber, the bed stands where Felipe II died in 1598, with a view of the Basílica's high altar. In his study is the last portrait of the king from Pantoja's studio.

The Basílica

Historically, only the aristocracy were permitted to enter the Basílica, while the townspeople were confined to the vestibule at the entrance. The Monks' Choir above is still closed to the public.

The Basílica contains 45 altars. Among its highlights is the exquisite marble statue of *Christ Crucified* (1562) by Benvenuto Cellini, in the chapel to the left of the entrance.

The enormous altarpiece was designed by Juan de Herrera with coloured marble, gilt-bronze sculptures and paintings. The central tabernacle took Italian silversmith Jacoppo da Trezzo (1515–89) seven years. The paintings are by Federico Zuccaro (1542–1609) and Pellegrino Tibaldi.

Pantheons

Directly beneath the high altar of the Basílica is the Royal Pantheon, where almost all Spanish monarchs since Carlos I are laid to rest. This pantheon, with Spanish black marble, was finished in 1654. Kings lie on the left and queens on the right.

Of the other pantheons, the most notable is that of Juan de Austria, Felipe II's half-brother, who defeated the Turks at the Battle of Lepanto. Also worth seeing is La Tarta, a white marble polygonal tomb that resembles a cake.

The Museums

Within El Escorial are several small museums. The north façade entrance leads to St Maurice's Hall, home of *The Martyrdom of St Maurice* by El Greco. Nearby stairs lead to the Architectural Museum, with models of the palace. Upstairs, the Museum of Art covers mostly 16th- and 17th-century works. The first room is dedicated to Italian masters, the next two, to Flemish art. *The Calvary* by Rogier van der Weyden (c 1400–64) dominates the fourth room. In the fifth room is *St Jerome Doing Penance* by José de Ribera (1591–1652), while the last room holds 16th- and 17th-century Spanish and Italian art.

Palace of the Bourbons

The Bourbon apartments are sumptuously furnished. They were created by Carlos IV, and are hung with tapestries, some by Goya, from the Real Fábrica de Tapices (*p172*).

A china cabinet displays the dinner service which was part of the trousseau of Victoria Eugenia (Queen Victoria's granddaughter) when she married Alfonso XIII in 1906.

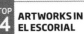

TOP 4 ARTWORKS IN EL ESCORIAL

The Martyrdom of St Maurice (1580–82)
El Greco's masterpiece contrasts the peril surrounding St Maurice with angels welcoming the martyrs to heaven.

Joseph's Tunic (1630)
Diego Velázquez depicts the deceitful brothers as they present the tunic dipped in blood to their father Jacob.

The Washing of the Feet (1548–49)
Jacopo Robusti Tintoretto references the Last Supper.

The Martyrdom of St Lawrence (1567)
Felipe II was so struck by the 1558 original that he commissioned this version.

↑ Antonio Moro's portrait of Felipe II, hanging in the Sala de Retratos

↑ The library, with a vaulted ceiling and marble floor

Chapterhouses

The four Salas Capitulares, or Chapterhouses, in the monastery's southeast corner, contain wooden benches for the monastery's 100 monks. These rooms have fine vaulted ceilings and some paintings by Titian (1490–1576), including *The Last Supper*, which was unfortunately trimmed to fit its place. A collection of paintings by Hieronymus Bosch (1450–1516), known as "El Bosco", is found here. A triptych version of *The Haywain* – the original of which hangs in the Prado (*p100*) – was kept in Felipe II's bedroom.

Nearby is the beautiful enamelled and gold-plated wooden retable of Carlos I.

The king took this portable altar with him on his various military campaigns.

The Library

In 1619 the king issued a decree that a copy of each new publication in his empire should be sent to him. At its zenith, this library contained some 40,000 books and manuscripts, mainly from the 15th and 16th centuries. The long Print Room has glorious frescoes on its vaulted ceiling by Pellegrino Tibaldi (1527–96), which depict Philosophy, Grammar, Rhetoric, Dialectics, Music, Geometry, Astrology and Theology. The Doric wooden shelving was designed by Juan de Herrera (1530–97).

On each of the four main pillars hang portraits of the members of the royal House of Austria – Carlos I, Felipe II, Felipe III and Carlos II.

↑ The impressive exterior of the Royal Monastery of El Escorial

 2

SEGOVIA

🏠 86 km (53 miles) NW of Madrid centre 🚉🚌 🛈 Plaza del Azoguejo, 1; www.turismodesegovia.com

Segovia is the most spectacularly sited city in Spain, set high on a rocky spur and surrounded by the Río Eresma and Río Clamores. It is often compared to a ship – the Alcázar on its sharp crag forming the prow, the pinnacles of the cathedral rising like masts, and the aqueduct trailing behind like a rudder. The view of it from the valley below at sunset is magical.

① Museo de Segovia

🏠 Casa del Sol, Calle Socorro 11 📞 921 46 06 15 🕐 Jul-Sep: 10am-2pm & 4-7pm Tue-Sat, 10am-2pm Sun; Oct-Jun: 10am-2pm & 4-7pm Tue-Sat, 10am-2pm Sun

This archaeological museum contains 15,000-year-old Stone Age engravings, as well as historic tools, arms, pottery and metalwork. There are Roman coins, wall fragments from Arab houses and a collection of belt buckles. Also worth seeing are two huge Celtic stone bulls that were excavated in the Calle Mayor. It is thought they may have been divine protectors of people or livestock. In the nearby province of Ávila, such icons are linked with burials.

② Convento de los Carmelitas

🏠 Paseo del Segundo Rincón, 2 📞 921 43 13 49 🕐 4-7pm Mon, 10am-1:30pm & 4-8:30pm Tue-Sun

In a secluded Eresma valley, St John of the Cross founded this convent in the 16th century and was Prior from 1588–91. The mystical poet was also co-founder, along with Santa Teresa, of a bare-footed (*descalzos*) order of Carmelites that ran to the strictest of disciplines.

③ Casa de los Picos

Just inside the city walls is the Casa de los Picos, a mansion whose 15th-century façade is adorned with diamond-shaped stones. The building houses an art gallery and school.

④ Palacio Quintanar

🏠 Calle San Esteban 🕐 11am-2pm & 5-9pm Wed-Sat, 11am-3pm Sun 🌐 palacioquintanar.com

This 16th-century Renaissance palace, built around a central courtyard, has been converted into an exhibition hall where art, workshops and cultural events coexist.

⑤ Monasterio de Santa María del Parral

🏠 Subida al Parral 📞 921 43 12 98 🕐 11am & 5pm Wed-Sun (booking is advised)

Just north of the city walls is Segovia's largest monastery, which has four cloisters and a Plateresque altarpiece. The tombs of its benefactor, the Marqués de Villena,

Segovia's two-tiered Roman aqueduct, built in the 1st century AD

and his wife, María, can be found here.

 6

Cathedral

🕓 Plaza Mayor ⏰ 9:30am-6:30pm Mon-Sat, 1:30-6:30pm Sun 🌐 catedral segovia.es

Dating from 1525, this massive Gothic structure replaced the old cathedral, which was destroyed in 1520 during the revolt of the Castilian towns. The old cloister, however, survived and was rebuilt alongside architect Juan Gil de Hontañón's austere but elegant design. The flying buttresses, pinnacles, tower and dome form an impressive silhouette, while the interior is light and elegantly vaulted, with stained-glass windows.

Inside there is a high altar designed by Sabatini in 1768. Lining the nave and apse are 18 beautiful chapels, most enclosed by graceful ironwork grilles. The most interesting is the Chapel of the Pietà, which

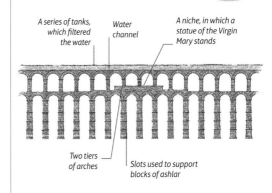

A series of tanks, which filtered the water

Water channel

A niche, in which a statue of the Virgin Mary stands

Two tiers of arches

Slots used to support blocks of ashlar

↑ An illustration showing Segovia's Roman aqueduct in detail

took its name from the beautiful sculpture by Juan de Juni. The cloister, filled with pointed arches, is accessed through an outstanding Gothic arch by Juan Guas in the Chapel of Christ's Solace. The cloister leads to the chapterhouse museum, which houses 17th-century Brussels tapestries, paintings, sculptures, silver, furniture, books and coins.

7

Aqueduct

📍 Plaza del Azoguejo 1

In use until the late 19th century, this aqueduct was

built at the end of the 1st century AD by the Romans, who turned ancient Segovia into an important military base. Two tiers of arches, which reached a total of 728 m (2,400 ft) in length, were needed to cope with the ground's gradient. In terms of height, the arches stretched to a maximum of 29 m (95 ft). With this elaborate feat of engineering, water from the Río Frío flowed into the city, filtered through a series of tanks along the way.

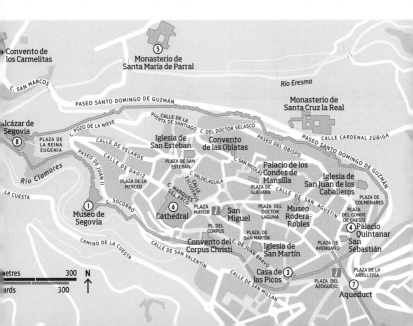

(8)

ALCÁZAR DE SEGOVIA

🏛 Plaza de la Reina Victoria Eugenia 🕐 Apr-Oct: 10am-8pm daily; Nov-Mar: 10am-6pm daily 🚫 1 & 6 Jan, 24 & 25 Dec 🌐 alcazardesegovia.com

Rising sheer above crags with a multitude of gabled roofs, turrets and crenellations, the Alcázar de Segovia appears like the archetypal fairy-tale castle. It contains a museum of weaponry and a series of elaborately decorated rooms.

The layout of Segovia's royal castle is determined by the contours of the rocky outcrop on which it stands. Although first records date from the 12th century, it was mostly built between 1410 and 1455, and had to be largely rebuilt following a fire in 1862. Its rooms are decorated with armour, paintings and furniture that enhance its medieval atmosphere. In 1764 Carlos III founded the Royal School of Artillery here. Two of the school's pupils, Daoíz and Velarde, became key figures in the 1808 uprising of *Madrileños* against the French.

Did You Know?

The castle served as Joyous Gard - Sir Lancelot du Lac's home - in the 1967 musical film *Camelot*.

GREAT VIEW
Juan's Tower

Torre de Juan II tower was completed during the 15th-century reign of Enrique IV and named after his father. It is worth climbing to the top for breathtaking views of Segovia and the Guadarrama mountains.

→

The sprawling layout of the Alcázar de Segovia

Bartizan turrets

Torre de Juan II, which contained the dungeons

The barbican, which contains the portcullis and guards' watchrooms

↑ The imposing exterior of the castle, nestled in the hills above Segovia

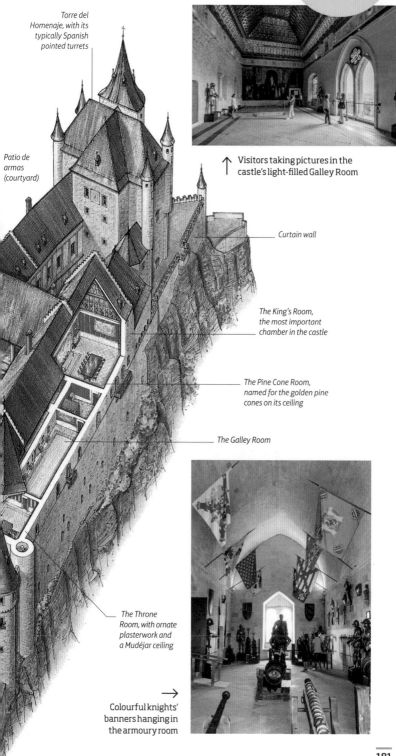

Torre del Homenaje, with its typically Spanish pointed turrets

Patio de armas (courtyard)

↑ Visitors taking pictures in the castle's light-filled Galley Room

Curtain wall

The King's Room, the most important chamber in the castle

The Pine Cone Room, named for the golden pine cones on its ceiling

The Galley Room

The Throne Room, with ornate plasterwork and a Mudéjar ceiling

→ Colourful knights' banners hanging in the armoury room

The Alcázar seen from the charming Plaza Mayor in Segovia

3

TOLEDO

🏠 75 km (46 miles) SW of Madrid centre 🚆🚌 🛈 Plaza del Consistorio 1; www.toledo-turismo.com

Picturesquely sited on a hill above the River Tagus is the richly historic centre of Toledo. Home to reminders of its Roman, Visigothic and Moorish past, as well as its time as a melting pot of Christian, Muslim and Jewish cultures, it's an atmospheric area to explore. Nowadays, these monument are floodlit after dark, causing the city to resemble one of the moon-lit landscapes painted by Toledo's most famous inhabitant – El Greco, who came to live here in the 16th century.

Did You Know?

Toledo was known as the "city of three cultures" because of its Christian, Muslim and Jewish citizens.

① ⊘ ⊗

Alcázar

🏠 Calle de la Paz s/n 📞 925 23 88 00 🕙 10am-5pm Tue-Sun

Carlos V's fortified palace stands on the site of former Roman, Visigothic and Moorish fortresses. Its severe, square profile suffered damage by fire three times before being almost completely destroyed in 1936, when the Nationalists survived a 70-day siege by the Republicans. Restoration followed the original plans, and the siege headquarters have been preserved as a monument to Nationalist heroism. The former National Museo del Ejército was transferred from Madrid to this building, making the Alcázar the main army museum in Spain.

The Alcázar is also home to the Borbón-Lorenzana Library, which contains 100,000 books and manuscripts from the 16th to 19th centuries.

The Iglesia de San Román houses a museum dedicated to the Visigoths.

To Monasterio de San Juan de los Reyes (600 m/ 655 yd) and Sinagoga de Santa María la Blanca (450 m/490 yd)

⑨
⑤
②
④
⑧

To Sinagoga del Tránsito (250 m/275 yd) and Museo del Greco (200 m/220 yd)

Must See

💬 **INSIDER TIP**
Overnight Stay

To visit all of Toledo's main sights you will need at least two days, but it is possible to walk around the medieval and Jewish quarters in a long morning. To avoid heavy crowds, go mid-week and stay for a night, when the historic city is at its most atmospheric.

← The rambling city of Toledo as night falls

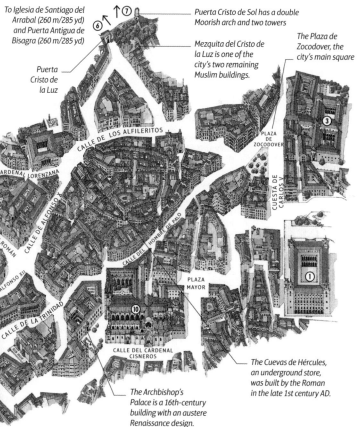

To Iglesia de Santiago del Arrabal (260 m/285 yd) and Puerta Antigua de Bisagra (260 m/285 yd)

Puerta Cristo de la Luz

Puerta Cristo de Sol has a double Moorish arch and two towers

Mezquita del Cristo de la Luz is one of the city's two remaining Muslim buildings.

The Plaza de Zocodover, the city's main square

CALLE DE LOS ALFILERITOS

CARDENAL LORENZANA

CALLE DE ALFONSO

N ROMÁN

ALFONSO XII

CALLE DE LA TRINIDAD

CALLE DEL HOMBRE DE PALO

PLAZA MAYOR

PLAZA DE ZOCODOVER

CUESTA DE CARLOS V

CALLE DEL CARDENAL CISNEROS

The Cuevas de Hércules, an underground store, was built by the Roman in the late 1st century AD.

The Archbishop's Palace is a 16th-century building with an austere Renaissance design.

↑ The gilded interior of Toledo's Iglesia de Santo Tomé, a church thought to date from the 11th century

②

Iglesia de Santo Tomé

🅐 Plaza del Conde 4
🕒 Mar-mid-Oct: 10am-6:45pm daily; mid-Oct-Feb: 10am-5:45pm daily
🌐 santotome.org

The main attraction of this church is El Greco's masterpiece, *The Burial of the Count of Orgaz*. This count paid for much of the restored 14th-century building that stands today. The painting, commissioned in his memory by a parish priest, depicts the miraculous appearance of St Augustine and St Stephen at his burial, to raise his body to heaven. It is remarkable for its contrast of glowing and sombre colours. In the foreground, allegedly, are the artist and his son (both looking out), as well as Cervantes. The church is thought to date back to the 11th century, and its tower is a fine example of Mudéjar architecture. Nearby is the Pastelería Santo Tomé, a good place to buy locally made marzipan.

---

③

Museo de Santa Cruz

🅐 Calle Miguel de Cervantes 3
🕒 9:30am-6:30pm Mon-Sat, 10am-2pm Sun
🌐 cultura.castillalamancha.es

This museum is housed in a 16th-century hospital, which has some Renaissance features, including the main doorway, staircase and cloister. The four main wings, laid out in the shape of a cross, are dedicated to the fine arts. The collection holds medieval and Renaissance tapestries, paintings and sculptures. There are also works by El Greco, including one of his last paintings, *The Virgin of the Immaculate Conception* (1613). Decorative arts on display include two typically Toledan crafts: armour and damascened swords, made by inlaying steel with gold wire.

④

Sinagoga del Tránsito, Museo Sefardí

🅐 Calle Samuel Leví
🕒 Mar-Oct: 9:30am-7:30pm Tue-Sat, 10am-3pm Sun; (Nov-Feb: 9:30am-6pm Tue-Sat, 10am-3pm Sun)
🚫 Public hols
🌐 museosefardi.mcu.es

The most elaborate Mudéjar interior in the city is hidden behind the humble façade of this former synagogue, built in the 14th century by Samuel Ha-Leví, the Jewish treasurer to Pedro the Cruel. The interlaced frieze of the lofty prayer hall fuses Islamic, Gothic and Hebrew geometric motifs below a wonderful coffered ceiling. The synagogue houses a museum of Sephardi (Spanish Jewish) culture, with items on display from both before and after the Jews' expulsion from Spain in the late 15th century.

---

⑤

Monasterio de San Juan de los Reyes

🅐 Calle de los Reyes Católicos 17
🕒 Mar-mid-Oct: 10am-6:45pm daily; mid-Oct-Feb: 10am-5:45pm daily
🚫 1 Jan, 25 Dec
🌐 sanjuandelosreyes.org

A brilliant mix of architectural styles, this monastery was commissioned by the Catholic Monarchs in honour of their victory at the battle of Toro in 1476. It was originally intended to be their burial place, but they were actually laid to rest in Granada. Largely designed by Juan Guas, the church's main Isabelline structure was completed in 1496. Although badly damaged by Napoleon's troops in 1808,

Horseshoe-shaped arches within the Sinagoga de Santa María la Blanca

has been restored to its
original splendour with
features such as a Gothic
cloister (1510) with a multicoloured Mudéjar ceiling.

Iglesia de Santiago del Arrabal

📍 **Calle Real del Arrabal**
📞 **925 22 06 36** ⏰ **For Mass**

This is one of Toledo's most
beautiful Mudéjar monuments.
It can be easily identified by
its tower, which dates from
the 12th-century *reconquista*.
The church, which was built
slightly later, has a beautiful
woodwork ceiling and an
ornate Mudéjar pulpit, but
only the exterior of the
building can be visited.

Puerta Antigua de Bisagra

When Alfonso VI took control
of Toledo in 1085, he entered
it through this gateway,
alongside El Cid. It is the only
gateway in the city to have
kept its original 10th-century
military architecture. The
huge towers are topped by a
12th-century Arab gatehouse.

EL GRECO

Born in Crete in 1541, El
Greco ("the Greek") came
to Toledo in 1577 to
paint the altarpiece in
the convent of Santo
Domingo el Antiguo.
Enchanted by the city,
he remained, painting
other religious works,
and came to be closely
identified with Toledo.
He died in the city
in 1614.

⑧

Museo del Greco

📍 **Paseo del Tránsito**
⏰ **9:30am-7:30pm Tue-Sat
(Nov-Feb: to 6pm), 10am-
3pm Sun** 🌐 **museodel
greco.com**

Located in a house near to the
one in which El Greco lived, this
museum has a wide collection
of his works. Canvases on
display include *View of Toledo*,
a detailed depiction of the
city at the time, and the
superb series *Christ and the
Apostles*. On the ground floor
is a domestic chapel with a
fine Mudéjar ceiling and an
excellent collection of art
by other painters associated
with Toledo.

⑨

Sinagoga de Santa María la Blanca

📍 **Calle de los Reyes
Católicos 4** 📞 **925 22 72 57**
⏰ **10am-6:45pm daily (mid-
Oct-Feb: to 5:45pm)**
🚫 **1 Jan, 25 Dec**

The oldest and largest of the
city's original synagogues, this
monument dates back to the
12th century. In 1391 a massa-
cre of Jews took place on this
site. In 1405 it was taken over
as a church by San Vincente
Ferrer after the expulsion of
the Jews, but restoration has
returned it to its original state –
carved stone capitals stand
out against white horseshoe
arches and plasterwork.

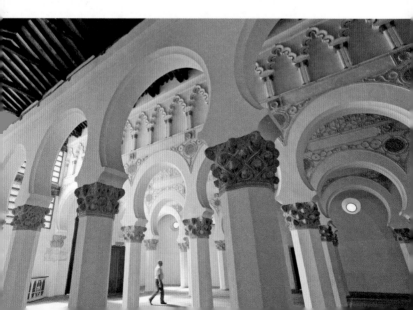

⑩ 🖉

TOLEDO CATHEDRAL

📍 **Calle Cardenal Cisneros 1** 🕐 **10am-6pm Mon-Sat, 2-6:30pm Sun**
🌐 **catedralprimada.es**

The splendour of Toledo's massive cathedral reflects its history as the spiritual heart of the Church in Spain and the seat of the Primate Archdiocese over all of Spain's Catholic churches. This illustrious past is particularly apparent during the saying of Mozarabic Mass, which dates back to Visigothic times.

The Catedral Primada Santa María de Toledo is interesting from an architectural point of view. It was built on the site of a 7th-century church. Work began in 1226 and spanned three centuries, until the completion of the last vaults in 1493. This long period of construction explains the cathedral's mixture of styles: pure French Gothic – complete with flying buttresses – on the exterior; with Spanish decorative styles, such as Mudéjar and Plateresque work, used in the interior.

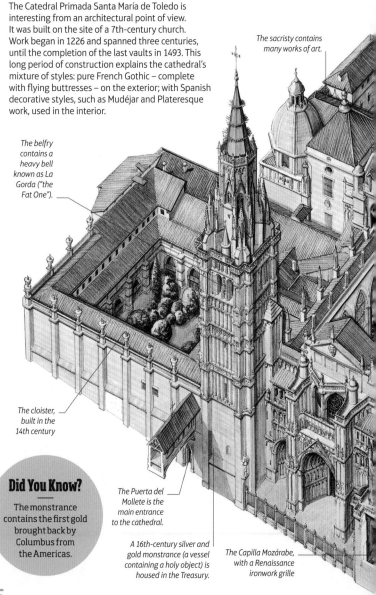

The sacristy contains many works of art.

The belfry contains a heavy bell known as La Gorda ("the Fat One").

The cloister, built in the 14th century

Did You Know?

The monstrance contains the first gold brought back by Columbus from the Americas.

The Puerta del Mollete is the main entrance to the cathedral.

A 16th-century silver and gold monstrance (a vessel containing a holy object) is housed in the Treasury.

The Capilla Mozárabe, with a Renaissance ironwork grille

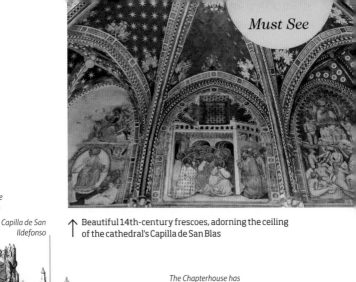

↑ Beautiful 14th-century frescoes, adorning the ceiling of the cathedral's Capilla de San Blas

Capilla de Santiago

Capilla de San Ildefonso

The Chapterhouse has a unique multicoloured Mudéjar ceiling.

←
Toledo Cathedral, with its French Gothic exterior

The Mozarbic Mass is held in this chapel. Said in Latin, this Mass developed among Spain's Christian community while it was under Moorish rule. It has its own sacraments and hymnal.

Puerta de los Leones

Entrance via Puerta Llana

High altar reredos, one of the most beautiful in Spain

↑ Toledo Cathedral, the city's most famous landmark, on the Plaza del Ayuntamiento

→ Hanging Houses in Cuenca, perched dramatically at the edge of a ravine

4

CUENCA

163 km (101 miles) SE of Madrid centre Calle Alfonso VIII 2; www.visitacuenca.es

Sitting on a rocky outcrop, Cuenca's enchanting old town seems like something out of a stage set, with its *Casas Colgadas* (Hanging Houses) perched over the gorge below. Wander through the city's atmospheric streets and you'll be transported back to times gone by.

Cuenca's picturesque old town is built astride a steeply sided spur, which drops precipitously on either side to the deep gorges of the Júcar and Huécar rivers. At its heart is the Plaza Mayor, a café-lined, arcaded square that still hums with activity. Around the Moorish town's narrow, winding streets grew the Gothic and Renaissance city, its monuments built with the profits of the wool and textile trade.

Perhaps the biggest draw for visitors is the cathedral, which is one of the most original works of Spanish Gothic, with Anglo-Norman influences. One of the charming *Casas Colgadas*, which jut out over the Huécar ravine, has been converted into the excellent Museo de Arte Abstracto Español *(www.march.es)*. Here, you'll find works by the movement's leading artists, including Tàpies and Chillida.

↑ The imposing Gothic cathedral on the Plaza Mayor

HIDDEN GEM

Museo Tesoro

The Museo Tesoro (Treasure Museum) is a collection of valuable pieces - mostly ecclesi-astical, although there is also some glinting jewellery and small artworks - found in a set of rooms adjoining the cathedral.

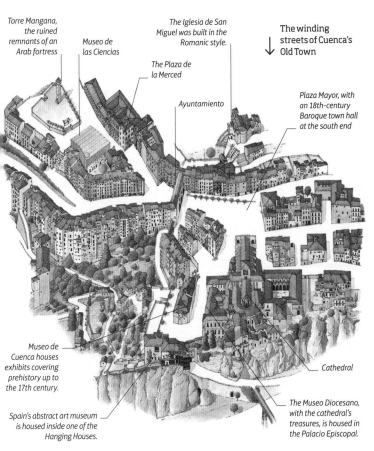

Torre Mangana, the ruined remnants of an Arab fortress

Museo de las Ciencias

The Iglesia de San Miguel was built in the Romanic style.

The winding streets of Cuenca's Old Town
↓

The Plaza de la Merced

Ayuntamiento

Plaza Mayor, with an 18th-century Baroque town hall at the south end

Museo de Cuenca houses exhibits covering prehistory up to the 17th century.

Cathedral

Spain's abstract art museum is housed inside one of the Hanging Houses.

The Museo Diocesano, with the cathedral's treasures, is housed in the Palacio Episcopal.

Colourful medieval houses within Cuenca's old town

EXPERIENCE MORE

5

Santa Cruz del Valle de los Caídos

⬛ North of El Escorial on M600 🚌 From El Escorial ⏰ Crypt: 10am-6pm Tue-Sun (Oct-Mar: to 7pm) 🔒 Some public hols 🌐 patrimonionacional.es

General Franco had the Holy Cross of the Valley of the Fallen built as a memorial to those who died in the Civil War. The vast cross is located some 13 km (8 miles) north of El Escorial (p174), and dominates the countryside. Some Spanish people find it too chilling a symbol of the dictatorship to be enjoyable, while for others its sheer size is rewarding.

The cross is 150m (490 ft) high and rises above a basilica carved 250 m (820 ft) deep into the rock by prisoners. A number of them died during the 20-year project. Access to the cross is currently closed to visitors for safety reasons.

Next to the basilica's high altar is the plain white tomb-stone of Franco and, opposite, that of José Antonio Primo de Rivera, founder of the Falange Española party. Another 40,000 coffins of soldiers from both sides in the Civil War lie here out of sight, including those of two unidentified victims.

6

Museo del Aire

⬛ A5, km 10.5 🚌 518, 521, 522, 523 from Estación de Príncipe Pío ⏰ 10am-2pm Tue-Sun 🔒 1 & 6 Jan, Easter, Aug, 12 Oct, 10, 24, 25 & 31 Dec 🌐 museodelaire.com

Among the many magnificent flying machines on display at the museum of Spanish aviation, the star exhibit is the Breguet-XIX *Jesús del Gran Poder*, which made the first Spanish transatlantic flight in 1929. Others include the Henkel 111 German warplane, the only one ever made, as well as *La Cierva* – half-plane, half-helicopter.

Some of the planes are linked with famous people: in 1936 General Franco flew from the Canary Islands to Tetuán to start the Spanish Civil War in the *De Havilland Dragon Rapide*; and in the Trener Master, Tomás Castaños won the 1964 World Aerobatic Championships. The museum covers the lives of famous aviators,

Did You Know?

The Museo del Aire houses the 1911 Vilanova-Acedo, one of the first planes made in Spain.

and features Air Force regalia, flight plans and models. There are also films and art.

7

Palacio Real de El Pardo

⬛ El Pardo, northwest of Madrid on A6 🚌 601 from Moncloa ⏰ 10am-6pm daily (Apr-Sep: to 8pm daily) 🔒 For royal visits & public hols 🌐 patrimonio nacional.es

This royal hunting lodge and palace, set in parkland, lists General Franco among its former resi-dents. A tour takes in the moated palace's original Habsburg wing and identic-

A herd of Iberian wild goats grazing at La Pedriza del Manzanares

...8th-century extension by Francesco Sabatini. The Bourbon interior is decorated with frescoes, gilt mouldings and tapestries. Today the palace hosts heads of state and royalty. Surrounding the palace is an enormous oak forest, popular for picnicking.

8
Manzanares el Real

⌂ 50 km NW of Madrid centre 🚌 ℹ Plaza del Pueblo 1; www.manzana reselreal.es

The skyline of Manzanares el Real is dominated by its restored 15th-century castle. Although the castle has some traditional military features, such as turrets, it was used mainly as a residential palace by the Dukes of Infantado. Below the castle is a 16th-century church, a Renaissance portico and fine capitals.

Behind the town, bordering the foothills of the Sierra de Guadarrama, is the geological feature La Pedriza, a mass of granite screes and ravines, popular with climbers, and part of a nature reserve.

Colmenar Viejo, 12 km (7.5 miles) to the southeast of Manzanares, has a superb church called Basílica de la Asunción de Nuestra Señora.

←

Gigantic cross at Valle de los Caídos, a memorial to those who died in the Civil War

Autumn colours on display in a beech forest at Montejo, Sierra Norte

The monastery is an excellent starting point for exploring the towns of Rascafría and Lozoya. To the southwest is the nature reserve Lagunas de Peñalara.

Sierra Centro de Guadarrama

🏠 75km (46 miles) NW of Madrid centre 🚉 Puerto de Navacerrada, Cercedilla 🚌 Navacerrada, Cercedilla 🛈 Paseo de los Españoles, 10, Navacerrada; www. sierraguadarrama.info

The pine-covered granite slopes of the Sierra de Guadarrama are dotted with holiday chalets. Villages such as Navacerrada and Cercedilla have grown into popular resorts for skiing, mountain biking, rock climbing, horse

9

Sierra Norte

🏠 50 km (30 miles) N of Madrid centre 🚌 Montejo de la Sierra 🛈 Calle Real 39, Montejo; www.sierra norte.com

The black slate hamlets of the Sierra Norte, which was once known as the Sierra Pobre ("Poor Sierra"), are located in the most attractively rural part of the Comunidad de Madrid (Madrid province).

At Montejo de la Sierra, the largest village in the area, an information centre organizes riding, rental of traditional houses and visits to the nature reserve of the Hayedo de Montejo de la Sierra. Made a World Heritage Site in 2017, this is one of the most southern beech woods in Europe and a relic of an era when climatic conditions here were more suitable for the beech.

From Montejo, you can drive on to picturesque hamlets such as La Hiruela or Puebla de la Sierra, both of which are in lovely walking country.

The drier southern hills slope down to the Embalse de Puentes Viejas, a reservoir where summer chalets cluster around artificial beaches. On the eastern edge of the Sierra Norte is the village of Patones, which supposedly escaped invasion by the Moors and Napoleon due to its isolated location.

10

Monasterio de Santa María de El Paular

🏠 SW of Rascafría on M604 🚌 Rascafría 🕐 11am–2pm, 4–7pm daily (Nov–mid-Apr: to 6pm) 🚫 Some public hols 🌐 monasterio paular.com

Castile's first Carthusian monastery was founded in 1390 on the site of a medieval royal hunting lodge. Although it was built in the Gothic style, Plateresque and Renaissance features were added later.

In 1836, the monastery was abandoned and fell into disrepair. In the 1950s the state decided to restore it. Today the complex houses a private hotel, a working Benedictine monastery and a church.

The church's delicate alabaster altarpiece dates from the 15th century and is thought to be the work of Flemish craftsmen. Its panels depict scenes from the life of Jesus Christ. The sumptuous Baroque camarín (chamber), behind the altar, dates from 1718 and was designed by Francisco de Hurtado.

Every Sunday, the monks sing an hour-long Gregorian chant. It is worth asking them to show you the cloister's Mudéjar brick vaulting and double sundial, or Vicente Carducho's restored paintings. They are happy to do this if they are not busy.

Man in the Miradores

Buitrago del Lozoya is surrounded by *miradores*, but the most jaw-dropping is the Mirador Butre de Lozoya, over the Río Lozoya, north of town. From here, you can admire the fortified town below.

riding and walking. The Valle de Fuenfría, a nature reserve of wild forests, is best reached via Cercedilla. It has a well-preserved stretch of Roman road, as well as marked walks.

12

Buitrago del Lozoya

🚗 78km (48 miles) N of Madrid centre 🚌 ℹ️ Calle Tahona 19; www.turismo.buitrago.org

Picturesquely sited above a meander in the Río Lozoya is the walled town of Buitrago del Lozoya. Founded by the Romans, it was fortified by the Arabs, and became a market town in medieval times. The 14th-century Castillo de Buitrago del Lozoya is in ruins, but the gatehouse and parts of the original wall survive. Today, the castle is used as a venue for summer festivals.

The old quarter, within the town's walls, retains its charming atmosphere. The 14th-century church of Santa María del Castillo has a Mudéjar tower and ceilings moved here from the old hospital. In the newer part of Buitrago, the town hall houses the **Museo Picasso**. The prints, drawings and ceramics on display were collected by the artist's friend and barber, Eugenio Arias, an inhabitant of the town.

Museo Picasso
📍 Plaza de Picasso 1
🕐 Times vary, check website
🌐 madrid.org/museopicasso

EAT

Casa José
Set in a mansion, serving refined dishes such as leek with broccoli foam and sea anemone.

📍 Calle de los Abastos 32, Aranjuez
🌐 casajose.es

€€€

El Doncel
A beautiful 18th-century mansion provides a sublime setting for exciting Spanish and contemporary cuisine at this fine restaurant.

📍 Paseo de la Alameda 3, Sigüenza
🌐 eldoncel.com

€€€

↑ The walled town of Buitrago del Lozoya, set beside the Río Lozoya

Palacio Real de Aranjuez

🏛 Plaza de Parejas, Aranjuez 🚍🚌 🕐 10am-6pm Tue-Sun (Apr-Sep: to 8pm) 🚫 Some public hols 🌐 patrimonionacional.es

The Royal Summer Palace and gardens of Aranjuez grew up around a medieval hunting lodge standing beside a natural weir, the meeting point of the Tagus and Jarama rivers.

Today's palace was built in the 18th century and later redecorated by the Bourbons.

A guided tour takes you through numerous Baroque rooms, including the Chinese Porcelain Room, the Hall of Mirrors and the Smoking Room, modelled on the Alhambra in Granada. Walk in the shady gardens that inspired Joaquín Rodrigo's *Concierto de Aranjuez*. The Parterre Garden and Island Garden survive from the original 16th-century palace.

The 18th-century Prince's Garden is decorated with fountains and lofty trees from the Americas. The Casa de Marinos (Sailors' House) is a museum housing boats once used by the royal family. At the far end of the garden stands the Casa del Labrador (Labourer's Cottage), a richly decorated royal pavilion by Carlos IV.

→
Plaza de Cervantes at Alcalá, bordered by historic buildings and plane trees

14 Alcalá de Henares

🏛 35km (21 miles) NE of Madrid centre 🚍🚌 ℹ Plaza de los Santos Niños s/n; www.turismoalcala.es

Founded by Cardinal Cisneros in 1499, Alcalá's university became one of the foremost places of learning in 16th-century Europe. Most of the original colleges have since been destroyed, but the most historic, San Ildefonso, with its Plateresque façade (1543) by Rodrigo Gil de Hontañón, survives. Former students include playwright Lope de Vega. The university produced Europe's first polyglot bible in 1517, which had text in Latin, Greek, Hebrew and Chaldean.

Alcalá's other sights are the cathedral, the **Museo Casa Natal de Cervantes**, birthplace of the author and now a museum, and the 19th-century Neo-Moorish Palacio de Laredo.

Museo Casa Natal de Cervantes

🏛 Calle Mayor 48 🕐 10am-6pm Tue-Sun (to 7pm Sat, Sun & hols) 🚫 Some public hols 🌐 museocasanataldecervantes.org

15 Chinchón

🏛 50km (31 miles) SE of Madrid 🚌 ℹ Plaza Mayor 6; www.ciudad-chinchon.com

Chinchón is arguably Madrid province's most picturesque town. The typically Castilian,

---

MIGUEL DE CERVANTES

Miguel de Cervantes Saavedra, Spain's greatest literary figure, was born in Alcalá de Henares in 1547. After fighting in the naval Battle of Lepanto (1571), he was held captive by the Turks for more than five years. In 1605, when he was almost 60 years old, the first of two parts of his comic masterpiece *Don Quixote* was published to popular acclaim. He continued writing novels and plays until his death in Madrid on 23 April 1616, the same day that Shakespeare died.

5th- to 16th-century, orticoed Plaza Mayor has a plendidly theatrical air. It omes alive for the Easter assion Play. The 16th-century hurch, above the square, has n altar painting by Goya, vhose brother was a priest ere. Just off the square an 8th-century Augustinian nonastery has been converted into a *parador* (hotel) vith a peaceful patio garden. ruined 15th-century castle tands on a hill to the west of own. It is closed to the public ut, from the outside, there are ood views of Chinchón and he surrounding countryside.

Madrileños often come o the town at weekends to ample the superb chorizo.

Parque de El Capricho

🅐 Paseo de la Alameda de Osuna s/n, Madrid Ⓜ El Capricho 🕒 9am–6:30pm Sat, Sun & public hols (Apr–Sep: to 9pm) 🌐 esmadrid.com

Created in the late 18th century, this lesser-known, remote park, just outside of Madrid and a delightful day out from the busy centre, is one of the most unique and charming examples of a landscape garden in Spain. Built in the Romantic style on the whim of a duchess in the late 18th century, it displays both Italian and French influences. The plant life is abundant, particularly in spring, when the garden comes to life with lilacs and roses.

Other interesting places include an artificial canal that leads to a lake with ducks and swans, the reed-covered boathouse known as the Casa de Cañas, the Casino del Baile (Dance Casino), a small temple, and underground bunkers from the Spanish Civil War.

DRINK

Terraza Los Huertos
Named for the kitchen garden of the convent that formerly stood here, Los Huertos is a sunny spot – perfect for an afternoon *caña* – with tables outside.

🅐 Calle de los Huertos 3, Chinchón
📞 918 94 00 02

Habana Café
On warm summer nights, the place to be seen sipping a cocktail is the terrace of elegantly kitsch Habana Café, a stone's throw from the royal palace.

🅐 Carretera de Andalucía 11, Aranjuez
📞 678 50 95 96

La Granja de San Ildefonso

📍 Plaza de España 15, Segovia 🚌 From Madrid or Segovia 🕐 10am–6pm Tue–Sun (Apr–Sep: to 8pm) 🔒 Some public hols 🌐 turismorealsitiodesan ildefonso.com

This royal pleasure palace stands on the site of a hunting lodge built by Enrique IV in the 15th century. In 1720, Felipe V embarked on a project to build the palace and numerous artists and architects contributed to the rich furnishings and the splendid gardens. Some rooms were damaged by fire in 1918, but have been respectfully restored. There are many salons decorated with *objets d'art* and Classical frescoes. From the ceilings hang huge chandeliers. The church is adorned in high Baroque style.

Out in the picturesque gardens, stately chestnut trees, manicured hedges and statues frame a complex series of pools that are enhanced with fountains.

18

Guadalajara

📍 60 km (37 miles) NE of Madrid centre 🚍🚌 ℹ Plaza Aviación Militar Española; www.guadalajara.es

Although Guadalajara's history is largely lost in the modern industrial city, traces of its past splendour survive. It was founded as the Roman settlement of Arriaca, and then replaced by the Moorish settlement of Wad-al-

The stunning façade and interior *(inset)* of La Granja de San Ildefonso

> **Did You Know?**
>
> The Royal Mausoleum at La Granja de San Ildefonso contains the tomb of Felipe V and his queen, Isabel.

Hajarah. In 1085 it was taken by Alfonso VI in the Christian Reconquest, and rose to prominence in the 14th century.

The **Palacio de los Duques del Infantado**, built from the 14th to the 17th century by the powerful Mendoza dynasty, is an outstanding example of Gothic-Mudéjar architecture. The main façade and the two-storey patio are adorned with delicate carvings. Following Civil War bombing, the palace was restored. It now houses the Museo Provincial – the local art museum.

Among the churches in the town is the Iglesia de Santiago, with a Gothic-Plateresque chapel designed by Alonso de Covarrubias. The cathedral is built on the site of a mosque. The 13th-century Iglesia de

↑ Renaissance architecture on display in Sigüenza's Plaza Mayor

ta María has typical
...éjar horseshoe arches
...a bell tower.

**...acio de los Duques
...Infantado**

...laza de los Caidos en
...erra 13 **☎**949 21 33 01
...0am–2pm & 4–7pm
...–Sun

...scas

...B km (23 miles) SW of
...rid centre **☐☐**
...laza Mercado 14;
...w.illescas.es

...town of Illescas was
...summer venue for the
...t of Felipe II. While there
...le to see of the old town,
...es have two interesting
...ches. The Parroquial de la
...nción, built between the
...and 16th centuries, is
...y identified by its Mudé-
...ower, one of the best
...mples of its kind in the
...on. Nearby is the 16th-
...ury church of the **Museo
...Greco del Santauario de
...aridad**, which houses an
...ortant art collection.

The church owns five works
by El Greco, the most famous
of which is *The Virgin Dictating
to Saint Ildefonso*. In its Chapel
of Relics there is a portrait of
Francisco Pacheco de Toledo
by Pantoja de la Cruz and,
in the sacristy, there is an
original *Ecce Homo* by Luis
de Morales.

**Museo del Greco del
Santauario de la Caridad**

🅰 ☐ Calle Cardenal Cisneros
2 ☐ Times vary, check website
W elgrecoillescas.com

---

⑳

Sigüenza

☐ 136 km (84 miles) NE
of Madrid centre ☐☐
🅳 Calle Serrano Sanz 9;
www.siguenza.es

Dominating the hillside town
of Sigüenza is its impressive
castle-parador. The cathedral,
in the old town, was begun
in the 12th century. It is
Romanesque in style, with
later additions, such as the
Gothic-Plateresque cloisters.
In one of the chapels is the
Tomb of *El Doncel* (the young

nobleman). It was built for
Martín Vázquez de Arce, Isabel
of Castile's pageboy, who was
killed in a battle against the
Moors in Granada in 1486.
The sacristy has a beautifully
carved ceiling with flowers
and cherubs, created by
Alonso de Covarrubias.

㉑

Palacio de Riofrío

☐ Bosque de Riofrió, Navas
de Riofrió ☐ From Madrid
☐ 10am–6pm Tue–Sun (Apr–
Sep: to 8pm) W patrimonio
nacional.es

Set in a wooded deer park
near the city of Segovia (p180),
the Italian-style Palacio de
Riofrío, built around a central
courtyard, hints at royal
intrigue. When Felipe V died
in 1746, his widow Elisabeth
Farnese, strong-willed and an
avid huntswoman, was not
well-received in the court of
her stepson Ferdinand VI. In
1751, she began construction
of this beautiful palace, but
never lived in it. Over the
years, the three-storey
palace – with more
than 3,000 rooms – was
used as a hunting lodge by
the royal family. The rich
furnishings and artworks
indicate the lavish royal
lifestyle even while on
retreat from the capital.

**Set in a wooded deer park near the city
of Segovia, the Italian-style Palacio de
Riofrío, built around a central courtyard,
hints at royal intrigue.**

NEED TO KNOW

Moving through Atocha train station

BEFORE
YOU GO

Things change, so plan ahead to make the most of your trip. Be prepared for all eventualities by considering the following points before you travel.

AT A GLANCE

CURRENCY
Euro (EUR)

AVERAGE DAILY SPEND

SAVE	SPEND	SPLURGE
€70	€100	€200+

BOTTLED WATER	COFFEE	BEER	DINNER FOR TWO
€0.80	€1.50	€3.00	€60

ESSENTIAL PHRASES

Hello	Hola
Thank you	Gracias
Please	Por favor
Goodbye	Adiós
Do you speak English?	¿Hablas inglés?
I don't understand	No comprendo

ELECTRICITY SUPPLY
Power sockets are type F, fitting a two-prong, round-pin plug. Standard voltage is 230 volts.

Passports and Visas

For entry requirements, including visas, consult your nearest Spanish embassy or check the **Exteriores** website. EU nationals may visit for an unlimited period, registering with local authorities after three months. Citizens of the UK, the US, Canada, Australia and New Zealand can reside without a visa for up to 90 days.
Exteriores
w exteriores.gob.es

Government Advice

Now more than ever, it is important to consult both your and the Spanish government's advice before travelling. The **UK Foreign and Commonwealth Office**, the **US Department of State**, the **Australian Department of Foreign Affairs and Trade** and the Spanish Exteriores website offer the latest information on security, health and local regulations.
Australian Department of Foreign Affairs and Trade
w smartraveller.gov.au
UK Foreign and Commonwealth Office
w gov.uk/foreign-travel-advice
US Department of State
w travel.state.gov

Customs Information

You can find information on the laws relating to goods and currency taken in or out of Spain on the **Turespaña** website.
Turespaña
w spain.info

Insurance

We recommend taking out a comprehensive insurance policy covering theft, loss of belongings, medical problems, cancellations and delays, and read the small print carefully.
   UK citizens are eligible for free emergency medical care in Spain provided they have a valid European Health Insurance Card (EHIC) or UK Global Health Insurance Card (**GHIC**).

GHIC
W ghic.org.uk

Vaccinations

For information regarding COVID-19 vaccination requirements, consult government advice.

Booking Accommodation

Madrid offers a huge range of accommodation to suit any budget, varying from modern luxury hotels to hostels. A useful list of accommodation can be found on the Turespaña website.

Book your accommodation well in advance if you plan to visit in the peak season (July and August). Rates are also higher during major fiestas in the city. Also bear in mind that most hotels quote their prices without including tax (IVA), which is 10 per cent.

Money

Most urban establishments accept major credit, debit and prepaid currency cards. Contactless payments are common in the city, but it's a good idea to carry cash for smaller items. ATMs are widely available throughout the city, although many do apply a charge for cash withdrawals.

Spain does not have a big tipping culture, but it is appreciated and it's common to round-up the bill.

Travellers with Specific Requirements

The city's facilities have improved consistently during the last decade. The Confederación Española de Personas con Discapacidad Física y Orgánica (**COCEMFE**) and **Accessible Spain** provide useful information, and companies, such as **Tourism For All**, offer specialist tours for those with reduced mobility, sight and hearing.

Madrid's public transport system generally caters for all passengers, providing wheelchairs, adapted toilets, ramps and reserved car parking at airports and stations. Metro maps in Braille are available from the Organización Nacional de Ciegos (**ONCE**).
Accessible Spain
W accessiblespaintravel.com
COCEMFE
W cocemfe.es

ONCE
W once.es
Tourism For All
W tourismforall.org.uk

Language

Castellano (Castilian) is Spain's primary language, and is the language you will hear most frequently in Madrid. As an international city, English is also widely spoken, particularly in business and tourism.

Opening Hours

> **COVID-19** Increased rates of infection may result in temporary opening hours and/or closures. Always check ahead before visiting museums, attractions and hospitality venues.

Lunchtime Many places close for the siesta between 1 and 5pm.
Monday Many museums, public buildings and monuments are closed all day.
Sunday Churches and cathedrals are closed to the public during Mass.
Public holidays Most museums and many shops either close early or do not open at all.

PUBLIC HOLIDAYS

1 Jan	New Year's Day
6 Jan	Los Reyes Magos
Mar/Apr	Maundy Thursday
Mar/Apr	Good Friday
1 May	Labour Day
2 May	Madrid Province Day
15 May	St Isidore the Labourer Day
15 Aug	Assumption Day
12 Oct	Spain's National Day
1 Nov	All Saints' Day
9 Nov	Virgin of Almudena Day
6 Dec	Spanish Constitution Day
8 Dec	Feast of the Immaculate Conception
25 Dec	Christmas Day

GETTING
AROUND

Despite its apparent size, Madrid is surprisingly easy to get around on foot, but the bus and metro systems are also reliable and cheap.

AT A GLANCE

PUBLIC TRANSPORT COSTS

METRO

€1.50

(one way)

BUS

€1.50

(one way, bought on board)

DAY TICKET

€8.40

(zone A)

TOP TIP
Some multi-tickets available in Madrid can be shared between people.

SPEED LIMIT

MOTORWAY

120 km/h (75mph)

MAIN/SECONDARY ROAD

90 km/h (55mph)

URBAN AREAS

30 km/h (30mph)

Arriving by Air

Madrid's international airport, the **Madrid-Barajas Adolfo Suárez**, is 12 km (7 miles) east of the city. There are four terminals: T4 is the newest and furthest-flung, but all four are linked via free shuttle buses. If your departure gate is in T4S, check in at T4 and take the automatic train to the T4S building.

For more information on getting to and from Madrid's airport and different terminals, see the table opposite.

Madrid-Barajas Adolfo Suárez
 aeropuertomadrid-barajas.com

Train Travel

International Train Travel

Spain's international rail services are operated by the state-run Red Nacional de Ferrocarriles Españoles (**RENFE**). Safety and hygiene measures, timetables, ticket information, transport maps, and more can be obtained from the Renfe website. Services include direct TALGO (long-distance express) trains to Madrid from Paris, and a sleeper train from Lisbon. For international train trips, it is advisable to purchase your ticket well in advance. **Eurail** and **Interrail** sell passes (to European non-residents and residents respectively) for international journeys lasting from five days up to three months. Both passes are valid on RENFE trains.

Eurail
 eurail.com
Interrail
 interrail.eu
RENFE
 renfe.com

Domestic Train Travel

RENFE also runs suburban rail services *(cercanías)* to towns around the city, which are connected at several points with Madrid's metro. They are useful for crossing longer distances within the city, particularly between the two main train stations: Atocha in the south and Chamartín in the north. There are eight colour-coded *cercanía* lines, each with a number and the prefix "C".

GETTING TO AND FROM THE AIRPORT

Terminal	Transport to centre	Price	Journey Time
All terminals	Taxi	€30	25 mins
1, 2 & 4	Airport Express (bus)	€5	35 mins
2 & 4	Metro	€4.50–€6	35 mins
4	Local train	€2.60	25 mins

Maps are displayed at stations. Trains run 5:30am–11:30pm daily, but hours vary from line to line. Madrid is also served by four other types of train: regional, *largo recorrido* (long-distance), TALGO and AVE (high-speed link to various regions in Spain, operated by RENFE).

You can purchase tickets online with RENFE or at the station. The fastest intercity services are the TALGO and AVE, which link Madrid with Seville in two and a half hours, and with Barcelona in three hours. The *largo recorrido* (long-distance) trains are much cheaper than the high-speed trains, but they are so slow that you usually need to travel overnight. Book at least a month in advance. *Regionales y cercanías* (the regional and local services) are frequent.

Long-Distance Bus Travel

Travelling by coach in Spain can quite often be a quicker – and cheaper – way to get around than trains. There are three main long-distance bus stations in Madrid. The Estación Sur de Autobuses serves the whole of Spain, Estación Auto-Res operates services to Valencia, eastern Spain, Lisbon and northwest Spain, and Estación de Avenida de América serves towns in northern Spain. The transport interchange at Calle de Méndez Álvaro also offers convenient access to buses and trains, linking three local railways, the Estación Sur de Autobuses and metro line 6.

Spain has no national coach company, but private regional companies operate routes around the country. The largest of these is **Alsa**, which runs in all regions. Tickets and information for long-distance travel are available at all main coach stations as well as on company websites, but note that it is not always possible to book tickets in advance.

Alsa
w alsa.es

Public Transport

Most attractions in Madrid are within a 20-minute walk of the Puerta del Sol, at the centre of the city, but those further away are generally easy to reach by metro or bus. Madrid suffers from traffic congestion, and you can help to reduce this by strolling around on foot, and by using the excellent public transport network. The metro is efficient, and the buses, though slower, are good for short hops.

Planning Your Journey
Metro maps are available at stations. Bus maps for tourists, listing the best routes for seeing the sights, are available on the **EMT** website.
EMT
w emtmadrid.es

Tickets
While the public transport system itself is easy to use, the ticketing is somewhat complicated, particularly since the introduction of the Tarjeta Multi, a contactless card onto which you load virtual passes and tickets. The simplest solution is to buy the Tourist Travel Pass on arrival at the airport, which allows you to take unlimited trips on selected public transport for a set number of days. Passes are valid for two zones – Zone A is catered for those who plan on travelling within the city, while Zone T is best for also visiting the surrounding area. The cost varies depending on the number of days and zone you choose.

The Tarjeta Multi costs €2.50 and can be shared between people. You'll need to load any single metro tickets and all multiple tickets onto it (unless buying the Tourist Travel Pass). Metro tickets cost €1.50 for five stops and increase thereafter. The Metrobús is a useful multi-ticket – valid for 10 journeys on the bus or metro, it costs €12.20 and can be shared.

Metro

The **Metro de Madrid** has 13 lines that serve the whole city and are divided into various zones depending on different areas of the city. Work out the direction for the train's final destination; a full list of stops is posted at the entrance to each platform. Operating hours are 6am–1:30am daily and trains run every 2–5 mins during peak hours, and every 7–15 mins from 11pm–1:30am. Note that there is a €3 supplement for travel to/from the airport.

Metro de Madrid
w metromadrid.es

Buses

Buses are a good way to see the city but can be slow and crowded, particularly at peak times. Timetables for each line and a plan of the bus network are posted at bus stops. Each bus has the route number on the front. Operating hours are usually 6am–11:30pm, every 5–7 mins at peak times and 16–24 mins from 9–11pm, but it depends on the route. Night buses operate from 11pm–6am, and leave from the Plaza de Cibeles.

Trams

Madrid also offers a tram network. This is often a cheap way to travel, and can be more accessible than other modes of public transport for those with limited mobility or with pushchairs.

Taxis

Official taxis are ubiquitous, and prices are moderate by European standards, making them a good way to get around if public transport isn't an option. Taxis are white with a red stripe across the door. A green light on the roof is illuminated when the taxis are available, and look for a green sign saying *libre* in the front window. There are taxi ranks at train stations, near the Plaza Mayor, on the Plaza del Sol, along Gran Vía and near the Prado. Taxis can be hailed on the street, or you can call a **Radio Taxi** or **Tele Taxi** in advance. Fares start at €2.50, plus €1.10 per kilometre, with supplements for travel at weekends, evenings, and for journeys to or from train stations. Taxis to and from the airport have a flat rate of €30. Be aware that if you call for a taxi, you also have to pay for the journey to the pick-up point. **Uber** and **Cabify** apps also operate in Madrid and are a popular way to get around.

Cabify
w cabify.com
Radio Taxi
w radio-taxi.madrid
Tele Taxi
w tele-taxi.es
Uber
w uber.com

Trips and Tours

The sightseeing service offered by **Madrid City Tour** allows you to hop on or off at major sights multiple times in one day. It operates from 10am to 6pm between November and February, and from 9am to 10pm from March to October. There are two routes: both cover the Paseo del Prado, then the blue route heads west around the Palacio Real, and the green route goes north to Salamanca and the Estadio Santiago Bernabéu. Tickets are available for one or two days, and cost €22 for adults, or €10 for those under 16, for one day.

There are also plenty of greener tours to take advantage of in the city. The **Madrid Tourist Office** organizes a wide range of walking tours, including some geared towards travellers with specific requirements. Themes include art and literary tours, haunted Madrid, food and wine tasting, and even crime and mystery tours. Tickets can be purchased at the tourist office, via their website or in some cases at the start of the tour. **Bravo Bike** runs city tours with a choice of standard or electric bikes (some streets in the old centre are very steep). It also offers tours of towns outside Madrid, including bike tours of El Escorial, Aranjuez and Toledo.

More unique tours operate across the city, too. You could take a tour of Madrid on a Segway: tours of the essential sights, restaurant tours and flamenco tours are just some of the options available from **Segway Tours**, and all include a useful initial training session. Another fun alternative is to scoot around the city in a vintage **Seat 600**. There is a choice of three routes, and prices can include lunch or a pit stop for *chocolate con churros* (hot chocolate with fried dough strips). Alternatively, thrill-seekers can take a helicopter tour with **Heliflight Spain** and marvel at Madrid, Toledo or Aranjuez from the skies. Tours can be booked with the listed companies on their respective websites.

Bravo Bike
w bravobike.com
Heliflight Spain
w heliflightspain.com
Madrid City Tour
w madridcitytour.es
Madrid Tourist Office
w esmadrid.com
Seat 600
w 600tourmadrid.com
Segway Tours
w madrid-segway.com

Driving

Driving and parking in central Madrid are difficult thanks to a project known as "Madrid Central", which has seen whole swathes of the entre pedestrianized or open to residents only. In some cases your hotel may be part of a scheme that offers one-day passes to visitors, but it's best to check ahead. Otherwise, you're better off paying for an underground car park on the outskirts or avoiding car hire altogether.

Driving to Madrid

If you drive to Spain in your own car, you must carry the vehicle's registration document, a valid insurance certificate, a passport or a national identity card and your driving licence at all times. You must also display a sticker on the back of the car showing its country of registration and you risk on-the-spot fines if you do not carry a red warning triangle and a reflective jacket with you at all times.

Many people drive to Spain via the French motorways. From the UK there are also car ferries from Plymouth to Santander and from Portsmouth to Bilbao. From whichever direction you approach Madrid, make sure you are able to identify your motorway turn-off by its street name. Madrid has two major ring roads, the outer M40 and the inner M30. If you need to cross the city, it is advisable to take one of the two and get as close as possible to your destination before turning off. Highways lead to the M30 but most do not continue into the city.

Spain has two types of motorway: *autopistas*, which are toll roads, and *autovías*, which are toll-free. You can establish whether a motorway is toll-free by the letters that prefix the number of the road: A = free motorway, AP = toll motorway.

Carreteras nacionales, Spain's main roads, have black-and-white signs and are designated by the letter N (Nacional) plus a number. Those with Roman numerals start at the Puerta del Sol in Madrid, and those with ordinary numbers have kilometre markers giving the distance from the provincial capital.

Carreteras comarcales, secondary roads, have a number preceded by the letter C. Other minor roads have numbers preceded by letters representing the name of the province, such as the LE1313 in Lleida.

Car Hire

The most popular car-hire companies in Spain are **Europcar**, **Avis** and **Hertz**. All have offices at airports and major train stations. Fly-drive, an option for two or more travellers where car hire is included in the cost of your airfare, can be arranged by travel agents and tour operators. If you wish to hire a car locally for a week or less, you can arrange it with a local travel agent. A car for hire is called a *coche de alquiler*. You will need to provide an international driver's licence (if you are an EU citizen your ordinary licence is sufficient) and be over 21 years of age. You are also strongly advised to take out full insurance.

Avis
W avis.com
Europcar
W europcar.com
Hertz
W hertz-europe.com

Rules of the Road

Most traffic regulations and warnings to motorists are represented on signs by easily recognized symbols. However, a few road rules and signs may be unfamiliar to some drivers from other countries.

In Spain you drive on the right side of the road. If you have accidentally taken the wrong road and it has a solid white line, you can turn round as indicated by a *cambio de sentido* sign. At crossings, give way to all oncoming traffic unless a sign indicates otherwise.

The blood-alcohol concentration (BAC) limit is 0.5 mg/ml and is very strictly enforced.

Cycling

Madrid is gradually becoming more cycling-friendly, with an increasing number of bike lanes. **BiciMad** is a public bicycle hire service, with stations every 0.3 km (0.2 miles) across the city. Fares start at €2 per hour. Cycling around parks like the Retiro or Casa de Campo tends to be a lot safer than on the roads.

Centrally located private firms that offer bike tours and rentals include **Trixi** and **Bike Spain**. Experienced cyclists should try the Anillo Verde Ciclista (Green Cycling Ring), a 60-km- (37-mile-) long bike path surrounded by lush trees that rings the city.

Electric scooters have become a popular way to get around, with rates from €0.15 per minute through companies such as **Lime** and **Voi**.

BiciMad
W bicimad.com
Bike Spain
W bikespain.com
Lime
W li.me
Trixi
W trixi.com
Voi
W voiscooters.com

Walking

Paseo, a leisurely stroll, is a way of life in Madrid, and walking is arguably the best way to soak in the essence of the city. By walking, you can take in the architectural details, absorb street life and peek into any church, shop or bar that catches your interest. Many plazas and streets in the centre have been pedestrianized, making it even easier to get around on foot.

PRACTICAL
INFORMATION

A little local know-how goes a long way in Madrid. Here you will find all the essential advice and information you will need during your stay.

AT A GLANCE

EMERGENCY NUMBER

GENERAL EMERGENCY

112

TIME ZONE
CET/CEST: Central European Summer time runs from the last Sunday in March to the last Sunday in October.

TAP WATER
Tap water in Spain is safe to drink but bottled water is preferred for the taste.

WEBSITES AND APPS
España
Spain's official tourism website (*www.spain.info*).
Moovit
A route-planning app.
Visit Madrid
The city's tourism information website (*www.esmadrid.com*).
WiFi Map
Finds free Wi-Fi hotspots near you (*www.wifimap.io*).

Personal Security

Spain is a relatively safe country to visit, but petty crime does take place. Pickpockets work known tourist areas, stations and busy streets. Use your common sense and be alert to your surroundings and you should enjoy a stress-free trip.

If you do have anything stolen, report the crime within 24 hours to the nearest police station and take ID with you. Get a copy of the crime report (*denuncia*) to make an insurance claim. Contact your embassy if your passport is stolen, or in the event of a serious crime.

As a rule, Spaniards are very accepting of all people, regardless of their race, gender or sexuality. Homosexuality was legalized in Spain in 1979 and in 2007, the government recognized same-sex marriage and adoption rights for same-sex couples. Madrid is one of the most LGBTQ+-friendly cities in Europe and has an iconic nightlife scene. That being said, the Catholic church still holds a lot of sway in Spain in general, and some conservative attitudes prevail, especially outside of urban areas. If you do feel unsafe, head for the nearest police station.

Health

Spain has a world-class healthcare system. Emergency medical care in Spain is free for all UK and EU citizens. If you have an EHIC or GHIC (*p204*), present it right away. You may have to pay after treatment and reclaim the money later.

For visitors coming from outside the UK or EU, payment of medical expenses is the patient's responsibility, so it is important to arrange comprehensive insurance before travelling.

Seek medicinal supplies and advice for minor ailments from a pharmacy (*farmacia*), identifiable by a green or red cross. Each pharmacy displays a card in the window showing the address of the nearest all-night pharmacy.

Smoking, Alcohol and Drugs

Smoking is banned in enclosed public spaces and is a fineable offence, although you can still smoke on the terraces of bars and restaurants.

ain has a relaxed attitude towards alcohol nsumption, but it is frowned upon to be enly drunk. In Madrid it is common to drink the street outside the bar of purchase. Recreational drugs are illegal, and possession even a very small quantity can lead to an tremely hefty fine. Amounts that suggest an tent to supply drugs to other people can lead custodial sentences.

)

law you must carry identification with you at times in Spain. A photocopy of your passport ould suffice, but you may be asked to report a police station with the original document.

ocal Customs

famous Spanish tradition is the siesta, which es many shops closing between 1 and 5pm. Most churches and cathedrals will not permit sitors during Sunday Mass. Generally, entrance churches is free; however, a fee may apply to nter special areas, like cloisters. Spain retains a rong Catholic identity. When visiting religious uildings ensure that you are dressed modestly, nd mobile phones are on silent.

ullfighting

orridas (bullfights) are widely held in Madrid nd the south. Supporters argue that the bulls re bred for the industry and would be killed as alves were it not for bullfighting, while rganizations such as Asociación Defensa erechos Animal (**ADDA**) arrange protests hroughout Spain.

If you do decide to attend a corrida, bear in nind that it's better to see a big-name matador ecause they are more likely to make a clean nd quick kill. The audience will make their isapproval evident if they don't.

DDA

addaong.org

Mobile Phones and Wi-Fi

ree Wi-Fi is reasonably common in Madrid, articularly in libraries, large public spaces, estaurants and bars. Some hotels may charge or you to use their Wi-Fi.

Visitors with EU tariffs are able to use their devices abroad without being affected by roaming charges. Users will be charged the same rates for data, calls and texts as at home.

Since the UK exited the EU, some UK networks have reintroduced roaming charges for their customers. Check with your provider before travelling.

Post

Correos is Spain's postal service. Postal rates fall into three price bands: Spain; Europe and North Africa; and the rest of the world. Parcels must be weighed and stamped at Correos offices, which are open 8:30am–9:30pm Monday to Friday and 9:30am–1pm on Saturday.

Letters sent from a post office usually arrive more quickly than if posted in a *buzón* (postbox). Urgent or important post can be sent by *urgente* (express) or *certificado* (registered) mail.

Correos

🔲 correos.es

Taxes and Refunds

IVA (VAT) is normally 21 per cent, but with lower rates for certain goods and services. Under certain conditions, non-EU citizens can claim a rebate of these taxes. Retailers can give you a form to fill out, which you can then present to a customs officer with your receipts as you leave. If the shop offers DIVA (digital stamping technology), you can fill that form out instead and validate it automatically at self-service machines found in the airport.

Discount Cards

Madrid offers a few discount cards for museum entry and exhibitions. These are not free, so consider how many of the offers you are likely to take advantage of before purchasing a card.

Paseo del Arte Entry to the Golden Triangle art museums at a 20 per cent discount. The card costs €30.40. Available from the websites or ticket offices of the individual museums.

Tarjeta Anual de Museos Estatales Entry to the Prado, Reina Sofía and other government-run museums with the Annual State Museums Pass. It costs €36.06 and is available from participating museums.

INDEX

Page numbers in **bold** refer to main entries

PHRASE BOOK

IN AN EMERGENCY

Help!	¡Socorro!	soh-**koh**-roh
Stop!	¡Pare!	**pah**-reh
Call a doctor!	¡Llame a un médico!	yah-meh ah oon meh-dee-koh
Call an ambulance!	¡Llame a una ambulancia!	yah-meh ah oonah ahm-boo-**lahn**-a thee-ah
Call the police!	¡Llame a la policía!	yah-meh ah lah poh-lee-**thee**-ah
Call the fire brigade!	¡Llame a los bomberos!	yah-meh ah lohs bohm-**beh**-rohs
Where is the nearest telephone?	¿Dónde está el teléfono más próximo?	dohn-deh ehs-**tah** ehl teh-**leh**-foh-noh **mahs** prohx-ee-moh
Where is the nearest hospital?	¿Dónde está el hospital más próximo?	dohn-deh ehs-**tah** ehl ohs-pee-**tahl** **mahs** prohx-ee-moh

COMMUNICATION ESSENTIALS

English	Spanish	Pronunciation
Yes	Sí	see
No	No	noh
Please	Por favor	pohr fah-**vohr**
Thank you	Gracias	**grah**-thee-ahs
Excuse me	Perdone	pehr-**doh**-neh
Hello	Hola	**oh**-lah
Goodbye	Adiós	ah-dee-**ohs**
Goodnight	Buenas noches	**bweh**-nahs noh chehs
Morning	La mañana	lah mah-**nyah**-nah
Afternoon	La tarde	lah **tahr**-deh
Evening	La tarde	lah **tahr**-deh
Yesterday	Ayer	ah-**yehr**
Today	Hoy	oy
Tomorrow	Mañana	mah-**nyah**-nah
Here	Aquí	ah-**kee**
There	Allí	ah-**yee**
What?	¿Qué?	keh
When?	¿Cuándo?	**kwahn**-doh
Why?	¿Por qué?	pohr-**keh**
Where?	¿Dónde?	**dohn**-deh

USEFUL PHRASES

How are you?	¿Cómo está usted?	**koh**-moh ehs-**tah** oos-**tehd**
Very well, thank you.	Muy bien, gracias.	mwee bee-**ehn** **grah**-thee-ahs
Pleased to meet you.	Encantado de conocerle.	ehn-kahn-**tah**-doh deh koh-noh-**thehr**-leh
See you soon.	Hasta pronto.	ahs-tah **prohn**-toh
That's fine.	Está bien.	ehs-**tah** bee-**ehn**
Where is/are ...?	¿Dónde está/están ...?	**dohn**-deh ehs-**tah**/ehs-**tahn** ...?
How far is it to ...?	¿Cuántos metros/kilómetros hay de aquí a ...?	**kwahn**-tohs meh-trohs/kee-loh-meh-trohs **eye** deh ah-**kee** ah
Which way to ...?	¿Por dónde se va a ...?	pohr dohn-deh seh bah ah
Do you speak English?	¿Habla inglés?	ah-blah een-**glehs**
I don't understand	No comprendo	noh kohm-**prehn**-doh
Could you speak more slowly, please?	¿Puede hablar más despacio, por favor?	pweh-deh ah-**blahr mahs** dehs-pah-thee-oh pohr fah-**vohr**
I'm sorry.	Lo siento.	loh see-**ehn**-toh

USEFUL WORDS

big	grande	**grahn**-deh
small	pequeño	peh-**keh**-nyoh
hot	caliente	kah-lee-**ehn**-teh
cold	frío	**free**-oh
good	bueno	**bweh**-noh
bad	malo	**mah**-loh
enough	bastante	bahs-**tahn**-the
well	bien	bee-**ehn**
open	abierto	ah-bee-**ehr**-toh
closed	cerrado	thehr-**rah**-doh
left	izquierda	eeth-key-**ehr**-dah
right	derecha	deh-**reh**-chah
straight on	todo recto	toh-doh **rehk**-toh
near	cerca	**thehr**-kah
far	lejos	**leh**-hohs
up	arriba	ah-**ree**-bah
down	abajo	ah-**bah**-hoh

English	Spanish	Pronunciation
early	temprano	tehm-**prah**-noh
late	tarde	**tahr**-deh
entrance	entrada	ehn-**trah**-dah
exit	salida	sah-**lee**-dah
toilet	lavabos, servicios	lah-**vah**-bohs, sehr-**bee**-thee-oh
more	más	mahs
less	menos	**meh**-nohs

SHOPPING

How much does this cost?	¿Cuánto cuesta esto?	**kwahn**-toh **kwehs**-tah ehs-to
I would like ...	Me gustaría ...	meh goos-ta-**ree**-a
Do you have...?	¿Tienen...?	tee-**yeh**-nehn
I'm just looking, thank you.	Sólo estoy mirando, gracias.	**soh**-loh ehs-**toy** mee-**rahn**-doh **grah**-thee-ahs
Do you take credit cards?	¿Aceptan tarjetas de crédito?	ah-**thehp**-tahn tahr-**heh**-tahs deh **kreh**-dee-toh
What time do you open?	¿A qué hora abren?	ah keh oh-rah **ah**-brehn
What time do you close?	¿A qué hora cierran?	ah keh oh-rah thee-**ehr**-rahn
This one.	Este.	**ehs**-the
That one.	Ese.	**eh**-she
expensive	caro	**kahr**-oh
cheap	barato	bah-**rah**-toh
size, clothes	talla	**tah**-yah
size, shoes	número	**noø**-mehr-oh
white	blanco	**blahn**-koh
black	negro	**neh**-groh
red	rojo	**roh**-hoh
yellow	amarillo	ah-mah-**ree**-yoh
green	verde	**behr**-deh
blue	azul	ah-**thool**
antiques shop	la tienda de antigüedades	lah tee-**ehn**-dah deh ahn-tee-gweh-**dah**-dehs
bakery	la panadería	lah pah-nah-deh-**ree**-ah
bank	el banco	ehl **bahn**-koh
book shop	la librería	lah lee-breh-**ree**-ah
butcher's	la carnicería	lah kahr-nee-theh-**ree**-ah
cake shop	la pastelería	lah pahs-teh-leh-**ree**-ah
chemist's	la farmacia	lah fahr-**mah**-thee-a
fishmonger's	la pescadería	lah pehs-kah-deh-**ree**-ah
greengrocer's	la frutería	lah froo-teh-**ree**-ah
grocer's	la tienda de comestibles	lah tee-**yehn**-dah deh koh-mehs-**tee**-blehs
hairdresser's	la peluquería	lah peh-loo-keh-**ree**-ah
market	el mercado	ehl mehr-**kah**-doh
newsagent's	el kiosko de prensa	ehl kee-**ohs**-koh deh **prehn**-sah
post office	la oficina de correos	lah oh-fee-**thee**-na deh kohr-**reh**-ohs
shoe shop	la zapatería	lah thah-pah-teh-**ree**-ah
supermarket	el supermercado	ehl soo-pehr-mehr-**kah**-doh
tobacconist	el estanco	ehl ehs-**tahn**-koh
travel agency	la agencia de viajes	lah ah-**hehn**-thee-a deh bee-**ah**-hehs

SIGHTSEEING

English	Spanish	Pronunciation
art gallery	el museo de arte	ehl moo-**seh**-oh deh **ahr**-the
cathedral	la catedral	lah kah-teh-**drahl**
church	la iglesia	lah ee-**gleh**-see-a
	la basílica	lah bah-**see**-lee-k
garden	el jardín	ehl hahr-**deen**
library	la biblioteca	lah bee-blee-oh-**teh**-kah
museum	el museo	ehl moo-**seh**-oh
tourist information office	la oficina de turismo	lah oh-fee-**thee**-na deh too-**rees**-mo
town hall	el ayuntamiento	ehl ah-yoon-tah-mee-**ehn**-toh
closed for holiday	cerrado por vacaciones	thehr-**rah**-doh por bah-kah-cee-oh-ne
bus station	la estación de autobuses	lah ehs-tah-thee-**oh** deh owtoh-**boo**-se
railway station	la estación de trenes	lah ehs-tah-**thee**-ohn deh treh-ne

...AYING IN A HOTEL

...you have ...vacant room?	¿Tienen una habitación libre?	tee-eh-nehn oo-nah ah-bee-tah-thee-ohn lee-breh
...uble room	habitación doble	ah-bee-tah-thee-ohn doh-bleh
...h double bed	con cama de matrimonio	kohn kah-mah deh mah-tree-moh-nee-oh
...n room	habitación con dos camas	ah-bee-tah-thee-ohn kohn dohs kah-mahs
...gle room	habitación individual	ah-bee-tah-thee-ohn een-dee-vee-doo-ahl
...m with ...bath	habitación con baño	ah-bee-tah-thee-ohn kohn bah-nyoh
...ower	ducha	doo-chah
...ter	el botones	ehl boh-toh-nehs
...	la llave	lah yah-veh
...ave a ...servation.	Tengo una habitación reservada.	tehn-goh oo-na ah-bee-tah-thee-ohn reh-sehr-bah-dah

...TING OUT

...ve you got a ...ble for ...?	¿Tienen mesa para ...?	tee-eh-nehn meh-sah pah-rah
...ant to ...serve ...table.	Quiero reservar una mesa.	kee-eh-roh reh-sehr-bahr oo-nah meh-sah
...e bill, ...ease.	La cuenta, por favor.	lah kwehn-tah pohr fah-vohr
...'m a ...getarian	Soy vegetariano/a	soy beh-heh-tah-ree-ah-no/na
...itress/ ...aiter	camarera/ camarero	kah-mah-reh-rah/ kah-mah-reh-roh
...nu	la carta	lah kahr-tah
...ed-price ...enu	menú del día	meh-noo dehl dee-ah
...he list	la carta de vinos	lah kahr-tah deh bee-nohs
...ass	un vaso	oon bah-soh
...ttle	una botella	oo-nah boh-teh-yah
...fe	un cuchillo	oon koo-chee-yoh
...k	un tenedor	oon teh-neh-dohr
...on	una cuchara	oo-nah koo-chah-rah
...akfast	el desayuno	ehl deh-sah-yoo-noh
...ch	la comida/ el almuerzo	lah koh-mee-dah/ ehl ahl-mwehr-thoh
...ner	la cena	lah theh-nah
...in course	el primer plato	ehl pree-mehr plah-toh
...rters	los entrantes	lohs ehn-tran tehs
...h of the day	el plato del día	ehl plah-toh dehl dee-ah
...fee	el café	ehl kah-feh
...e (meat)	poco hecho	poh-koh eh-choh
...dium	medio hecho	meh-dee-oh eh-choh
...ll done	muy hecho	mwee eh-choh

...ENU DECODER

...ado	ah-sah-doh	roast
...aceite	ah-thee-eh-teh	oil
...aceitunas	ah-theh-toon-ahs	olives
...agua mineral	ah-gwa mee-neh-rahl	mineral water
...gas/con gas	seen gas/kohn gas	still/sparkling
...ajo	ah-hoh	garlic
...arroz	ahr-rohth	rice
...azúcar	ah-thoo-kahr	sugar
...carne	kahr-neh	meat
...cebolla	theh-boh-yah	onion
...cerveza	thehr-beh-thah	beer
...cerdo	therh-doh	pork
...chocolate	choh-koh-lah-teh	chocolate
...chorizo	choh-ree-thoh	chorizo
...cordero	kohr-deh-roh	lamb
...fiambre	fee-ahm-breh	cold meat
...to	free-toh	fried
...fruta	froo-tah	fruit
...s frutos secos	froo-tohs seh-kohs	nuts
...s gambas	gahm-bahs	prawns
...helado	eh-lah-doh	ice cream
...horno	ahl ohr-noh	baked
...huevo	oo-eh-voh	egg
...amón serrano	hah-mohn sehr-rah-noh	cured ham

el jerez	heh-rehz	sherry
la langosta	lahn-gohs-tah	lobster
la leche	leh-cheh	milk
el limón	lee-mohn	lemon
la limonada	lee-moh-nah-dah	lemonade
la mantequilla	mahn-teh-kee-yah	butter
la manzana	mahn-thah-nah	apple
los mariscos	mah-rees-kohs	seafood
la menestra	meh-nehs-trah	vegetable stew
la naranja	nah-rahn-hah	orange
el pan	pahn	bread
el pastel	pahs-tehl	cake
las patatas	pah-tah-tahs	potatoes
el pescado	pehs-kah-doh	fish
la pimienta	pee-mee-yehn-tah	pepper
el plátano	plah-tah-noh	banana
el pollo	poh-yoh	chicken
el postre	pohs-treh	dessert
el queso	keh-soh	cheese
la sal	sahl	salt
las salchichas	sahl-chee-chahs	sausages
la salsa	sahl-sah	sauce
seco	seh-koh	dry
el solomillo	soh-loh-mee-yoh	sirloin
la sopa	soh-pah	soup
la tarta	tahr-tah	pie/cake
el té	teh	tea
la ternera	tehr-neh-rah	beef
las tostadas	tohs-tah-dahs	toast
el vinagre	bee-nah-greh	vinegar
el vino blanco	bee-noh blahn-koh	white wine
el vino rosado	bee-noh roh-sah-doh	rosé wine
el vino tinto	bee-noh teen-toh	red wine

NUMBERS

0	cero	theh-roh
1	uno	oo-noh
2	dos	dohs
3	tres	trehs
4	cuatro	kwa-troh
5	cinco	theen-koh
6	seis	says
7	siete	see-eh-the
8	ocho	oh-choh
9	nueve	nweh-veh
10	diez	dee-ehth
11	once	ohn-theh
12	doce	doh-theh
13	trece	treh-theh
14	catorce	kah-tohr-theh
15	quince	keen-theh
16	dieciséis	dee-eh-thee-seh-ees
17	diecisiete	dee-eh-thee-see eh-the
18	dieciocho	dee-eh-thee-oh-choh
19	diecinueve	dee-eh-thee-nweh-veh
20	veinte	beh-een-the
21	veintiuno	beh-een-tee-oo-noh
22	veintidós	beh-een-tee-dohs
30	treinta	treh-een-tah
31	treinta y uno	treh-een-tah ee oo-noh
40	cuarenta	kwah-rehn-tah
50	cincuenta	theen-kwehn-tah
60	sesenta	seh-sehn-tah
70	setenta	seh-tehn-tah
80	ochenta	oh-chehn-tah
90	noventa	noh-vehn-tah
100	cien	thee-ehn
101	ciento uno	thee-ehn-toh oo-noh
102	ciento dos	thee-ehn-toh dohs
200	doscientos	dohs-thee-ehn-tohs
500	quinientos	khee-nee-ehn-tohs
700	setecientos	seh-teh-thee-ehn-tohs
900	novecientos	noh-veh-thee-ehn-tohs
1,000	mil	meel
1,001	mil uno	meel oo-noh

TIME

one minute	un minuto	oon mee-noo-toh
one hour	una hora	oo-na oh-rah
half an hour	media hora	meh-dee-a oh-rah
Monday	lunes	loo-nehs
Tuesday	martes	mahr-tehs
Wednesday	miércoles	mee-ehr-koh-lehs
Thursday	jueves	hoo-weh-vehs
Friday	viernes	bee-ehr-nehs
Saturday	sábado	sah-bah-doh
Sunday	domingo	doh-meen-goh

ACKNOWLEDGMENTS

DK would like to thank the following for their contribution to the previous edition: David Lyon and Patricia Harris, Ben Ffrancon Davies, Sally Davies, Adam Hopkins, Mark Little, Edward Owen

The publisher would like to thank the following for their kind permission to reproduce their photographs:

Key: a-above; b-below/bottom; c-centre; f-far; l-left; r-right; t-top

123RF.com: Ekaterina Belova 22cl; Pavel Dudek 40tl; Juan Jimenez Fernandez 20t; icekill 159cl; kasto 194-5b; Ivan Soto 51crb.

4Corners: Francesco Carovillano 180bl; Paolo Giocoso 88bl.

akg-images: Album / Oronoz 52t, 107clb; 148br.

Alamy Stock Photo: A.F. ARCHIVE 42clb; Mauricio Abreu 26-7t, 104cra; age fotostock / César Lucas Abreu 153cra, Agefotostock / Felix González 110-11t, / David Miranda 12cl, 138-9t, / FSG 90bl, / Javier Larrea 107cra, / María Del Valle Martín Morales 39crb, / Museo Nacional Centro de Arte Reina Sofia / Guernica (1937) by Pablo Picasso © Succession Picasso/DACS, London 2019 106t, / María Galán 11br, 28tl, / Paco Gómez García 102t. / Toño Labra 155crb; Akademie 80tl; Jerónimo Alba 187b; Art Kowalsky / Museo Nacional Centro de Arte Reina Sofia / Brushstroke (1996) by Roy Lichtenstein © Estate of Roy Lichtenstein/DACS 2019 104-5, / Museo Nacional Centro de Arte Reina Sofia designed by Jean Nouvel © Jean Nouvel / ADAGP, Paris and DACS, London 2019 104-5; The Artchives 99br, 103bl; Artexplorer 70cb; Alessandro Avondo 37cl; Azoor Photo 135ca; Lawrence JC Baron 50cra; Bildarchiv Monheim GmbH / Gerhard Hagen 97tr, 115br, 152t; Artur Bogacki 139br; Michael Brooks 108bc; Classic Image 174clb; Collection Christophel / Paola Ardizzoni / Emilio Pereda / Pathe films 42-3b; Phil Crean A 147cr; Marco Cristofori 32bl; Luis Dafos 125cra; Ian Dagnall 48-9b; DCarreño 32-3t, 35tr, 41br, 74tl; 149br, 198-9t, / Murals painted by Animalitoland, Gola Hundun, JM Yes, Rubén Sánchez and Doa Oa in 2016 for the 2nd edition of the Muros Tabacalera project, curated by Madrid Street Art Project on behalf of the Spanish Ministry of Culture. 26b; dleiva 109, 112-3b, 116br; dpa picture alliance 50cr; Adam Eastland 20cl, 24cl, 98-9t, 134-5b, 135tl, 135cra, 136-7b; Peter Eastland 82b, 143br; Education & Exploration 4 108crb; EFE News Agency 33br, / Javier Lopez 57br; EnriquePSans 16, 60-1, 137tl; Eduardo Estellez 52bl; Etabeta 67bc; Factofoto 18, 58-9, 83tl, 117t, 142t, 156l, 184-5t; Alexei Fateev 64, 97cla; FineArt 55cra; FLHC 1G 54tl; Maria Galan 38tl, 121tl; Ainara Garcia 36tl; GL Archive 65bc; Granger Historical Picture Archive / NYC 55br, 56tl, 56crb, 56bl, 65crb; hemis.fr / Bertrand Gardel 20cr, / Carmen (1974) by Alexander Calder © 2019 Calder Foundation, New York/DACS London 22bl, 30cb, 65cr, 99cra,114-5t, / Hervé Hughes 171tl,/ Ludovic, Maisant 34-5b, 112cb, /

Alessio Mamo 66-7b; Heritage Image Partnership L / Historica Graphica Collection 55cb, / Index 53bl, 53cla, / Mithra / Index 54-5t; Jeremy Sutton-Hibber / Museo Thyssen-Bornemisza, Madrid/ Woman in Bath (1963) by Roy Lichtenstein © Estate of Roy Lichtenstein/DACS 2019 98bl; The History Collectic 119cra; Horizon Images / Motion 186tl; Peter Horre 53tr, 99cb,154bl / Museo Nacional Centro de Arte Reina Sofia/ Untitled (Model for Trench Shaft and Tunnel) (1978) by Bruce Nauman © Bruce Nauman Artists Rights Society (ARS), New York and DACS, London 2019 106-7b; IanDagnall Computing 54cr, 54br, 65bl, 176bl; imageBROKER / Barbara Boensch 198bl, / Franz Walter 158bl, / Michael Fischer 195t; incamerastock / ICP 55tr, 103cra; Pressinphoto 47bl; Ingolf Pompe 85 167tr, / Museo Nacional Centro de Arte Reina Sofia / Guernica by Pablo Picasso © Succession Picasso/DACS, London 2019 27cla, Pete Jackson 77tl; Eric James 67cra; John Kellerman 96-7 Joana Kruse 80-1b; Lanmas 53cb; Lebrecht Music & Arts 70bc; Look / Ingolf Pompe 30-1t; Elijah Lovko 11t; De Luan 65clb; LucVi 72b; MARKA / Dario Fusa 175cra; Martin Thomas Photography 177t; Masterpics 70clb; Mehdi33300 192-3; MiraMira 46tr Dmitriy Moroz 161bl; North Wind Picture Archives 54clb; B.O'Kane / Museo Nacional Centro de Arte Reina Sofía / Wheat & Steak by Miralda © DACS 20 104bl; Pacific Press Agency / Jesús Calonge 35cl; Efrain Padro 68-9; Sean Pavone 100-1b; David Pearson 101tr; Jeremy Pembrey 10ca; Photo Art Lucas 153b; Prisma Archivo 52crb; 103cr; Alberto Sibaja Ramírez 17bl, 51cr, 130-1; M Ramírez 13t; RosaIreneBetancourt 6 142cra; Enrico Rossi 31cla; Sagaphoto.com / Patrick Forget 33cl; Alex Segre 13cr, 17t, 29tr, 86t, 92-3, 146tr; StockFood GmbH / Inga Wandinger 170b; Lucas Vallecillos 8-9, 10-1b, 22cr, 70cr, 76b, 124bl, 148t, 150-1; WENN Rights Lt / Oscar Gonzalez 46cla, 47crb; 119cr; World History Archive 56-7t, 187tr; ZUMA Press; Inc. 57clb, / Celestino Arce 57cr.

Apertura Madrid Gallery Weekend -Mahala: orlandogutierrez.es 50clb.

AWL Images: Matteo Colombo 181br; Hemis 101cl Karol Kozlowski 13br; Stefano Politi Markovina 117br; Travel Pix Collection 36-7b.

Bridgeman Images: Index Fototeca / Museo Municipal, Madrid / View of the Alcazar of Madrid, 1650 (oil on canvas) by Felix Castello (1602-1656) 53tl.

CaixaForum: Ruben Perez Bescos 27br, 122-3.

Cardamomo Flamenco Madrid: 45cl.

Casa Museo Sorolla: 24clb; Javier Rodriguez Barre 147b.

Cooking Point: Javier Jiménez 28-9b.

Depositphotos Inc: bloodua 168-9.

Desperate Literature: Andrea Dorantes Otero 40-